THE MELODY BOOK
300 Selections from the World of Music for Autoharp, Guitar, Piano, Recorder, and Voice

SECOND EDITION

PATRICIA HACKETT
San Francisco State University

Cover and interior
illustrations by **Florence Holub**

PRENTICE HALL, *Englewood Cliffs, New Jersey 07632*

Library of Congress Cataloging-in-Publication Data

The Melody book : 300 selections from the world of music for autoharp,
  guitar, piano, recorder, and voice / [compiled by] Patricia Hackett
  ; cover and interior illustrations by Florence Holub. -- 2nd ed.
    1 score.
    Principally songs.
    Words in English and other languages.
    Melodies with chord symbols.
    Includes indexes.
    Summary: Includes folk music from around the world, jazz, popular
  tunes, children's songs, and symphonic themes, with chord charts and
  strumming patterns.
    ISBN 0-13-574427-X
    1. Songs. 2. Children's songs. 3. Folk-songs. 4. Singing games.
  [1. Songs. 2. Folk songs.]   I. Hackett, Patricia,
  II. Holub, Florence, ill.
  M1627.M473 1991   90-753543
                                                         CIP
                                                         M AC

Editorial/production supervision and
  interior design: Margaret Lepera and Jordan Ochs
Prepress buyer: Herb Klein
Manufacturing buyer: Patrice Fraccio
Acquisitions editor: Bud Therien

Acknowledgements can be found on p. vi which constitutes a continuation of the copyright page.

Printed in the United States of America
10 9 8 7 6 5 4 3 2

ISBN 0-13-574427-X

Prentice-Hall International (UK) Limited, *London*
Prentice-Hall of Australia Pty. Limited, *Sydney*
Prentice-Hall Canada Inc., *Toronto*
Prentice-Hall Hispanoamericana, S.A., *Mexico*
Prentice-Hall of India Private Limited, *New Delhi*
Prentice-Hall of Japan, Inc., *Tokyo*
Simon & Schuster Asia Pte. Ltd., *Singapore*
Editora Prentice-Hall do Brasil, Ltda., *Rio de Janeiro*

CONTENTS

PREFACE

THE MELODY BOOK, Second Edition, is designed to serve a variety of needs and to provide a source of music for many occasions. It can be used as a source of music in beginning music, class piano, and music teaching curricula; it can supplement an instructor's primary text or personally developed materials.

THE MELODY BOOK, Second Edition, retains many of the songs and features of the earlier edition, but also has many new aspects.

The 300 selections in the *Anthology of Songs and Melodies* represent a wide variety of styles, as before, including folk music of the world, children's game songs, and themes from symphonic literature, jazz, and contemporary music. Several previously unpublished melodies are presented. Most of these are from the current repertoire of the ethnic groups they represent. Brief historical, stylistic, and biographical descriptions accompany some of the music.

New in this Second Edition are 45 different selections, including many from Mexico, Polynesia, and India, as well as recorder music from the Renaissance. The numerous foreign language songs now have an English text. The songs are notated in ranges suitable for a number of needs. Limited-range songs (middle C to A) have texts suitable for young children; songs for adult singers are notated in a wider (and often lower) range. Many rounds, quodlibets, and responsorial songs are appropriate for young choirs, as are the 20 two-part arrangements new in this edition. Game and dance directions accompany many songs.

Nearly every song has suggestions to help choose a suitable instrument or accompaniment. Use these to create your own accompaniment whenever possible.

The *Musical Instruments and Voice* section is revised, and material on the 21-bar Autoharp and the baritone ukulele has been added. This Autoharp, guitar, piano, recorder, and voice section has information for review, or to study a new instrument. Melodies in the anthology are in keys suitable for the instruments mentioned.

The revised *Appendix* presents reference material in these categories: music notation, scales, sol fa syllables, key signatures, meter signatures, rhythm syllables, musical terms and signs, lead sheet, and transposition.

A comprehensive *Classified Index* lists music by suitable instrument (Autoharp, guitar, piano, recorder), voice, modal and pentatonic scale, limited rhythm durations, rhythm and meter, dances/games/percussion accompaniments/dramatizations, holidays and special occasions, Western music by style period, and concludes with biographical and historical information.

The national origin and keys of 300 musical selections are indicated in the *Alphabetical Index of Songs and Melodies* that concludes *The Melody Book, Second Edition.*

PATRICIA HACKETT

ACKNOWLEDGMENTS

Every effort has been made to locate owners of music included in this book. Omission of any copyright acknowledgment will be corrected if brought to our attention. Credit and appreciation are due to many individuals for their contributions and assistance, and to many copyright owners for their permission to use the following:

"Buffalo Dance," "Handgame Song," Pipe Dance Song," "Prayer Song of the Peyote Religion," "Round Dance" and "War Dance" learned from Don Patterson, Sauk-Fox/Tonkawa tribal singer, Tonkawa, Oklahoma.

"Christmas is Here!" Swedish text and pronunciation guide by Jeannie Nolting, San Francisco.

"Circle 'Round the Zero" used by permission of Maureen Kenney. St. Louis: Magnamusic Baton, Inc., 1975.

"Clapping Land" from *Exploring Music,* book one, by Eunice Boardman and Beth Landis, ©1966 by Holt, Rinehart and Winston, Publishers.

"The Condor" Spanish text by Dolores Villagomez, San Francisco.

"De Colores, "Don Gato,"

"Hawaiian Rainbows," "La Raspa," "Laredo," Las Mañanitas," "Mister Sun," "Peace Like a River," "Ritsch Ratsch," and "Thanks for the Food" used by permission of Silver Burdett & Ginn Inc., from *World of Music,* ©1988.

"Dry Bones" from *Growing with Music,* book six, by Harry Wilson, et al. ©1966 by Prentice-Hall, Inc.

"Flower Drum Song" and "Song of Ali Mountains" pronunciation and standardization of Chinese texts into Yale Romanization by Lynn Tsai, San Francisco.

"Grinding Song" used by permission of the Lowie Museum of Anthropology, University of California, Berkeley, Tapes 115, 116.

"Heng Chwun Folk Song" and "Little Donkey" transcriptions and Chinese texts by D. J. Sun, San Francisco.

"It's a Small World" by Richard M. Sherman and Robert B. Sherman. ©1963 Wonderland Music Co., Inc. Reprinted by permission.

Ka Mate (Te Rauparaha)— arr. Freedman. Copyright Sevenseas Publishing Pty, Ltd; Box 152, Paraparaumu, New Zealand.

"Kang Ding City" Chinese text by Muriel Chan, San Francisco.

"Little Bird" translation and pronunciation by Col. David P. Smith, Santa Rosa, California, with additional help from David Lindeman, Washington, D.C., and Professor Ron Levaco, San Francisco.

"Lost My Gold Ring" and "Thank You for the Chris'mus" collected by Olive Lewin. Used by permission of the Organization of American States, Washington, D.C.

"Mayo Nafwa" used by permission of Barbara Reeder-Lundquist of Seattle Washington, and Grace Chiwama.

"Misty" by Erroll Garner and Johnny Burke ©1954, 1955 by Vernon Music Corp. (by arrangement with Octave Music Publishing Corp.). All rights reserved. Used by permission.

"Royal Garden Blues" by Clarence Williams and Spencer Williams. ©1919, renewed by Shapiro, Bernstein & Co. Inc. Used by permission.

"Shoes for Baby Jesus" melody and Spanish text courtesy of Gabriel Daneri, San Francisco.

"Song of Kuroda" Japanese text and pronunciation courtesy of Steven Haruta, San Francisco.

"Song for the Sabbath" courtesy of Ann Brostoff, San Diego, California.

"The Sound of Silence," ©1964, 1965, Paul Simon. Used by permission.

"Take the "A" Train" ©1941 Tempo Music, Inc. Used by permission of Ruth Ellington, New York City.

"This Beautiful World" used by permission of Patience Bacon, Honolulu, Hawaii.

"Winds of Morning" words and music by Tommy Makem ©Tin Whistle Music, BMI. 2 Longmeadow Road, Dover, NY 03820.

"Windy Weather" courtesy of Mary Helen Richards, Portola Valley, California.

"Yesterday" by Paul McCartney and John Lennon. ©1965 Northern Songs Limited, 24 Bruton Street, Mayfair, London WIX 7DA, England. All rights for the United States of America, Canada, Mexico and the Philippines controlled by Maclen Music, Inc., c/o ATV Music Corp, 6255 Sunset Blvd, Los Angeles, Calif. 90028. International copyright secured. Made in USA. All rights reserved.

How to Use On-page Suggestions and Symbols
Chromatic bells or soprano recorder are listed following melodies suitable for these instruments.
Autoharp or guitar strums, or piano accompaniments are suggested following suitable melodies. Each strum or accompaniment is identified with a letter or number. These letters and numbers correspond to accompaniment patterns on charts in the *Musical Instruments and Voice* section. Charts are found on these pages: Autoharp Strums, p. 329 Guitar Strums, p. 337 Piano Accompaniment Patterns, p. 345
When a two-part melody is notated, the melody is in large notes, the harmony in small notes.
Words in italics under a foreign language text are a pronunciation guide.
When verses follow a song, underlined words indicate a change of chord. A slur under a word means to sing more than one syllable to a single pitch.
An English version of a foreign language song retains the same slurs and phrasing as in the original.

ANTHOLOGY OF SONGS AND MELODIES

AIN'T GONNA STUDY WAR

Black American Spiritual

Vigorously (♩ = 84)

1. Gon - na   lay down   my   bur - den,
2. Gon - na   lay down   my   sword and shield,
3. Gon - na   put on   my   long white robe,   Down by   the
4. Gon - na   walk with   the   Prince of Peace,
5. Gon - na   join hands   a - round the world,

riv - er - side,   down by   the   riv - er - side,   down by   the

lay down   my   bur - den
lay down   my   sword and shield,
riv - er - side. Gon - na   put on   my   long white robe,   Down by   the
walk with   the   Prince of Peace,
join hands   a - round the world,

riv - er - side, Gon - na   stud - y_____ war   no   more.

Refrain:

I   ain't gon - na   stud - y   war   no   more, I ain't gon - na   stud - y   war   no

more,   I   ain't gon - na   stud - y_____ war   no   more.

I ain't gon-na stud-y war no more, I ain't gon-na stud-y war no

more, I ain't gon-na stud-y_____ war no more.

Guitar, strum 6
Piano, accompaniment pattern III

ALL AROUND THE KITCHEN

Black American Play Song

Designate one person to sing the calls, and all others to sing the response. The caller should perform different motions as suggested by each call. Responders can create one movement for "Cock-a-doodle, doodle, doo," and repeat it for every response.

ALLELUIA

Wolfgang Amadeus Mozart
(Austria, 1756—1791)

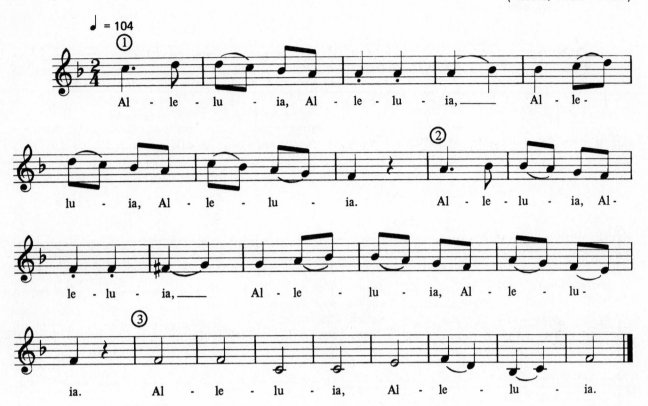

Al - le - lu - ia, Al - le - lu - ia, _____ Al - le -
lu - ia, Al - le - lu - ia. Al - le - lu - ia, Al -
le - lu - ia, _____ Al - le - lu - ia, Al - le - lu -
ia. Al - le - lu - ia, Al - le - lu - ia.

ALL MY TRIALS

Black American Spiritual

Freely, with intensity

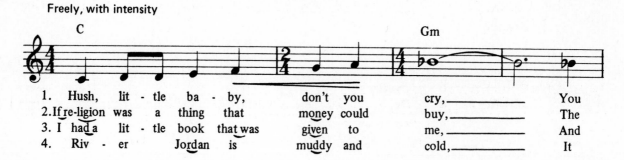

1. Hush, lit - tle ba - by, don't you cry,_____ You
2. If re-ligion was a thing that money could buy,_____ The
3. I had a lit - tle book that was given to me,_____ And
4. Riv - er Jordan is muddy and cold,_____ It

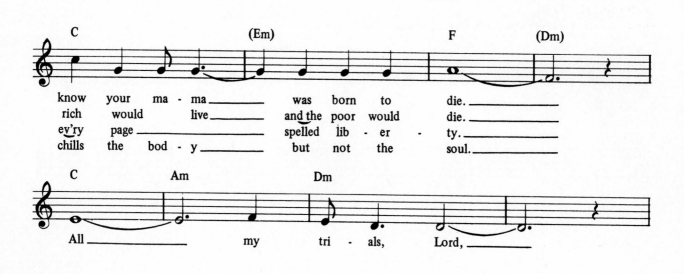

know your ma - ma _____ was born to die. _____
rich would live _____ and the poor would die. _____
ev'ry page _____ spelled lib - er - ty. _____
chills the bod - y _____ but not the soul. _____

All _____ my tri - als, Lord, _____

Soon _____ be o - ver. _____

Refrain:

Too late, my broth - ers, _____ Too late, _____ but nev - er

6

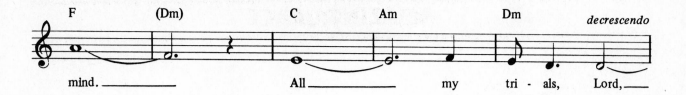

mind. _____   All _____   my   tri - als,   Lord, ___

___   Soon _____   be   o - ver. ___

Autoharp, measures 1-16 use strum M with the pad of the thumb;
        measures 17-31 use strum A with a soft pick.
Guitar, strum 2 or 6
Piano, accompaniment pattern XVII on each chord change.

AMAZING GRACE

John Newell
(1779)

Early American Melody

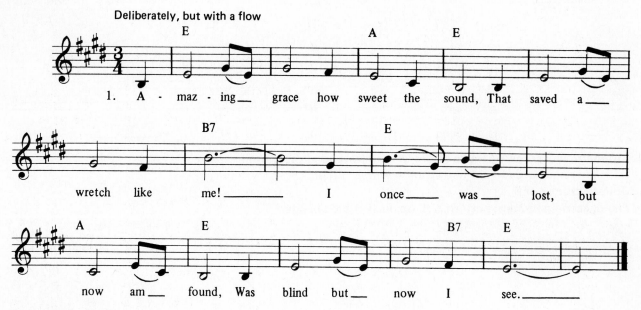

Deliberately, but with a flow

1. A - maz - ing___ grace how sweet the sound, That saved a___ wretch like me!_____ I once___ was___ lost, but now am___ found, Was blind but___ now I see._____

Guitar, strum 16 or 18
Piano, accompaniment pattern X

2. 'Twas grace that taught my heart to fear,
   And grace my fears relieved;
   How precious did that grace appear,
   The hour I first believed.

3. Through many dangers, toils and snares,
   I have already come;
   'Tis grace has brought me safe thus far,
   And grace will lead me home.

4. The Lord has promised good to me,
   His word my hope secures;
   He will my shield and portion be,
   As long as life endures.

AMERICA

Samuel F. Smith
(United States, 1808—1895)

Arr. Henry Carey
(England, c. 1690—1743)

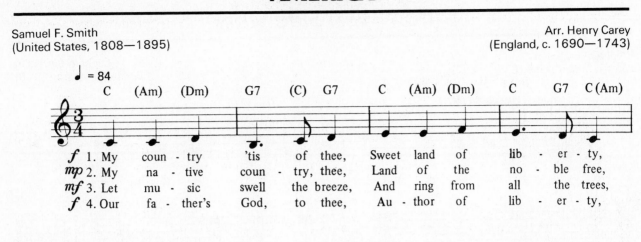

C (Am) (Dm)	G7 (C) G7	C (Am) (Dm)	C G7 C (Am)				

f 1. My coun - try 'tis of thee, Sweet land of lib - er - ty,
mp 2. My na - tive coun - try, thee, Land of the no - ble free,
mf 3. Let mu - sic swell the breeze, And ring from all the trees,
f 4. Our fa - ther's God, to thee, Au - thor of lib - er - ty,

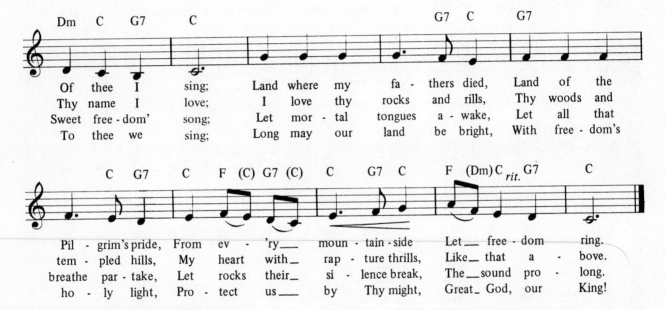

Of thee I sing; Land where my fa - thers died, Land of the
Thy name I love; I love thy rocks and rills, Thy woods and
Sweet free - dom' song; Let mor - tal tongues a - wake, Let all that
To thee we sing; Long may our land be bright, With free - dom's

Pil - grim's pride, From ev - 'ry moun - tain - side Let free - dom ring.
tem - pled hills, My heart with rap - ture thrills, Like that a - bove.
breathe par - take, Let rocks their si - lence break, The sound pro - long.
ho - ly light, Pro - tect us by Thy might, Great God, our King!

Autoharp, play melody rhythm
Piano, accompaniment pattern VI

On July 4, 1832, a choir trained by Lowell Mason gave the first public performance of what was then called "My Country 'Tis of Thee." Mason, who successfully introduced music into public school education, had loaned a German songbook to Samuel Smith. This young divinity student wrote a new patriotic American text for one of the hymns, apparantly unaware of "God Save the Queen," its British counterpart.

AMERICA
(from *West Side Story*)

Stephen Sondheim
(United States, b. 1930)

Leonard Bernstein
(United States, b. 1918)

Tempo di Huapango *(fast)*

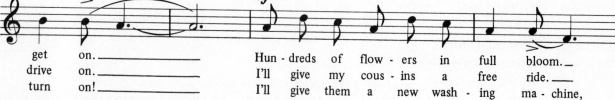

I like to be in A - mer - i - ca! O. K. by me in A-

mer - i - ca! Ev - 'ry - thing free in A - mer - i - ca

For a small fee in A - mer - i - ca! ____

1. I like the cit - y of San Juan.__ I know a boat you can
2. I'll drive a Bu - ick through San Juan,__ If there's a road you can
3. I'll bring a T. V. to San Juan,__ If there's a cur - rent to

mf

get on._____ Hun - dreds of flow - ers in full bloom._
drive on._____ I'll give my cous - ins a free ride.__
turn on!_____ I'll give them a new wash - ing ma - chine,

ff (nearly spoken)   *f*

Hun-dreds of peo - ple in each room._ Au - to - mo - bile in A-
How do you get all of them in - side? Im - mi - grant goes to A -
What have they got there to keep clean?_ I like the shores of A-

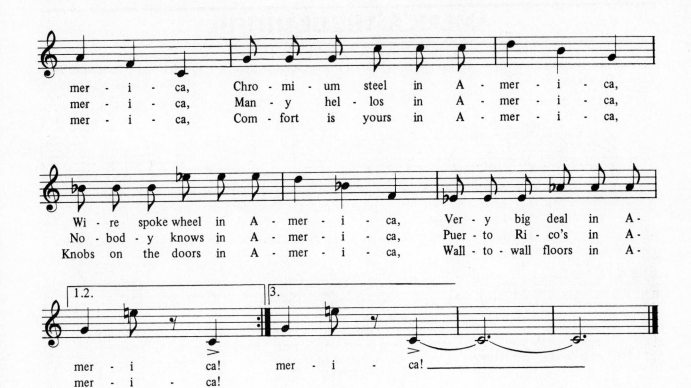

mer - i - ca,   Chro - mi - um steel in A - mer - i - ca,
mer - i - ca,   Man - y hel - los in A - mer - i - ca,
mer - i - ca,   Com - fort is yours in A - mer - i - ca,

Wi - re spoke wheel in A - mer - i - ca,   Ver - y big deal in A -
No - bod - y knows in A - mer - i - ca,   Puer - to Ri - co's in A -
Knobs on the doors in A - mer - i - ca,   Wall - to - wall floors in A -

1.2.
mer - i - ca!
mer - i - ca!

3.
mer - i - ca!

Chromatic Bells

The huapango *is a lively dance from the Caribbean that alternates between different meters. Two groups of bickering Puerto Rican girls sing the alternating thoughts about America.*

AMERICA, THE BEAUTIFUL

Katherine Lee Bates
(United States, 1859–1929)

Samuel A. Ward
(United States, 1847–1903)

1. O beau-ti-ful for spa-cious skies, For am-ber waves of grain, For pur-ple moun-tain maj-es-ties A-bove the fruit-ed plain! A-mer-i-ca! A-mer-i-ca! God shed His grace on thee, And crown thy good with broth-er-hood From sea to shin-ing sea!

2. O beau-ti-ful for pil-grim feet Whose stern im-pas-sion'd stress A thor-ough-fare for free-dom beat A-cross the wil-der-ness. God mend thine ev-'ry flaw, Con-firm thy soul with self-con-trol, Thy lib-er-ty in law.

3. O beau-ti-ful for he-roes prov'd In lib-er-at-ing strife, Who more than self their coun-try lov'd And mer-cy more than life. May God thy gold re-fine, Till all suc-cess be no-ble-ness, And ev-'ry gain di-vine.

4. O beau-ti-ful for pa-triot dream, That sees be-yond the years Thine al-a-bas-ter cit-ies gleam, Un-dimmed by hu-man tears. God shed His grace on thee, And crown thy good with broth-er-hood From sea to shin-ing sea!

Autoharp (21-bar), strum L
Guitar, strum 28 (measures 1-8 and 13-16) and 22 (measures 9-12)
Piano, accompaniment pattern XI

Inspired after a visit to the big sky country of the American West, a Wellesley professor of English wrote the poem she would later couple with the tune of an existing hymn. "America, the Beautiful" invites us to share the awe of Katherine Lee Bates, more than eighty years after her journey to the summit of Pike's Peak.

ANGELS WE HAVE HEARD ON HIGH

French Carol

♩ = 144

1. An - gels we have heard on high, Sweet - ly sing - ing o'er the plains,
2. Shep - herds, why this ju - bi - lee? Why your joy - ous strains pro-long?
3. Come to Beth - le - hem and see, Him whose birth the an - gels sing;
4. See Him in a man - ger laid, Whom the choirs of an - gels praise;

And the moun - tains in re - ply, Ech - o - ing their joy - ous strains.
What the glad - some tid - ings be, Which in - spire your heav'n - ly song?
Come, a - dore on bend - ed knee Christ, the Lord, the new - born King.
Mar - y, Jo - seph, lend your aid, While our hearts in love we raise.

Glo - - - - - - - - - - - - - - - - -

- ri - a in ex - cel - sis De - o, De - o.
ihn ehx - chehl - sihs day - oh day - oh

Autoharp, strum L
Guitar, strum 27

13

ARE YOU SLEEPING?

French Round

Autoharp (15-bar), strum C
Guitar, strum 12
Piano, accompaniment pattern II

Christmas version

1. Like a choir of angels singing
   O'er the dells, o'er the dells,
   Comes the sound of ringing, comes the sound of ringing,
   Christmas bells, Christmas bells.

2. "Christ is born!" their message bringing,
   Sound the bells, sound the bells!
   Hear them gaily ringing, hear them gaily ringing,
   Christmas bells, Christmas bells.

French version

Frère Jacques! Frère Jacques!
freh-reh jhah-keh freh-reh jhah-keh

Dormez vous? Dormez vous?
dor-mez vous dor-mez vous

Sonnez les matines, Sonnez les matines,
soh-nay lay mah-tee-neh soh-nay lay mah-tee-neh

Din, din don! Din, din, don!
dihn dihn dawn dihn dihn dawn

THE ASH GROVE

John Oxenford
(England, 1812—1877)

Welsh Folk Song

Autoharp (15-bar), strum J
Guitar, strum 20 or melody
Piano, accompany using chord roots
Soprano recorder

15

AT THE FOOT OF YONDER MOUNTAIN

American Folk Song

1. At the foot of yon - der moun - tain there runs a clear
2. Now___ why___ she won't have me, I well un - der -
3. I___ wish I were a clerk, and could write a fine
4. I___ wish I were a lark and with swift wings could

stream, At the foot of yon - der moun - tain there lives a fair
stand; She___ wants___ some free - hold - er, but I have no
hand, I'd___ write___ her a let - ter from this dis - tant
fly; Right___ to___ my love's win - dow this night I'd draw

queen. She's hand - some, she's prop - er, and her ways___ they are
land. Yet I___ can main - tain___ her on___ sil - ver and
land. I'd send it by the wa - ters just___ for to let her
nigh. I'd sit___ in the win - dow all___ night___ long and

sweet; I___ ask no bet - ter pas - time than to sit at her feet.
gold, And as man - y oth - er fine things as my love's house can hold.
know I___ think of pret - ty Mar - y wher - ev - er I go.
cry That for love of pret - ty Mar - y I glad - ly would die.

Autoharp (15-bar), strum J
Guitar, strum 15
Piano, accompaniment pattern VIII

16

B-A-BAY

American Folk Song

B - A - bay, B - E - bee, B - I - bid - die - by,

B - O - bo, bid-die - by - bo B - U - bu, Bid-die by - bo - bu! _____

Refrain

This is just a sil - ly song! The words don't mean a thing.

D.C. al Fine
(or make up a new verse)

Nev - er mind the sil - ly words, just o - pen up and sing. Oh!

Autoharp, strum C
Piano, accompaniment pattern III

This song uses the vowels A,E,I,O,U preceded by a consonant. Select different consonants and create new verses, such as:

D-A-day...
M-A-may...
P-A-pay...

17

BANKS OF THE OHIO

American Ballad

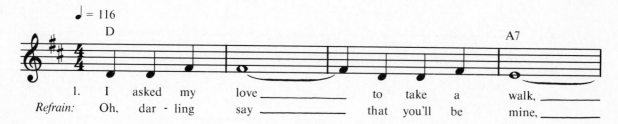

1. I asked my love _____ to take a walk, _____
Refrain: Oh, dar-ling say _____ that you'll be mine, _____

To take a walk, _____ just a lit-tle walk. _____
In no oth-er's arms, _____ en - twine, _____

Down be - side, _____ where the wa - ters flow, _____

Down by the banks _____ of the O - hi - o. _____

Autoharp (15-bar), strum N
Guitar, strum 25 or melody
Piano, accompaniment pattern XIII
Soprano recorder

2. I asked your mother for you, <u>dear</u>,
And she said you were too <u>young</u>;
Only say that you'll be <u>mine</u>,
Happiness together <u>we</u>'ll <u>find</u>. *(Refrain)*

3. <u>I</u> held a knife against her <u>breast</u>,
As gently in my arms she <u>pressed</u>,
She cried "Oh, Willie don't murder me,
I'm not prepared for eterni<u>ty</u>." *(Refrain)*

4. <u>I</u> took her by her lily white <u>hand</u>,
And led her down that bank of <u>sand</u>.
I plunged her in where she would <u>drown</u>,
And watched her <u>as</u> she <u>floated down</u>. *(Refrain)*

5. <u>I</u> started home 'tween twelve and <u>one</u>,
And cried "My God what have I <u>done</u>?"
I killed the one I love, you <u>see</u>,
Because she <u>would</u> not <u>marry me</u>. *(Refrain)*

6. <u>The</u> very next day at half past <u>four</u>,
The sheriff walked up to my <u>door</u>.
He said, "Young man, don't try to <u>run</u>,
You'll pay a <u>lot</u> for the <u>crime</u> you've <u>done</u>." *(Refrain)*

BARB'RA ALLEN

Anglo-American Ballad

♩ = 84

1. In Scar-let town where I was born, There was a fair maid dwell-in', Made
2. 'Twas in the mer - ry month of May, When flow - er buds were swell-in', Sweet
3. He sent his ser - vant to the town, To the place where she was dwell-in', Said

man - y a youth cry— "Well a day," Her name was Bar - b'ra Al - len.
Wil - liam on his— death-bed lay, For love of Bar - b'ra Al - len.
"Mas - ter bids you to come with me, If your name be Bar - b'ra Al - len."

Autoharp (21-bar), strum I
Guitar, strum 15 (try strum 14 on verses 4-7)

4. Then slowly, slowly, she came up
   And slowly, she drew near him,
   But all she said when she got there:
   "Young man, I think you're dyin'."

5. He turned his face unto the wall,
   For death was in him wellin';
   "Goodbye," he said, "to all my friends;
   Be good to Barb'ra Allen."

6. "Oh mother, oh mother, go dig my grave,
   And make it long and narrow;
   Sweet William died for love of me,
   And I will die of sorrow."

7. They buried her in the old church yard;
   Sweet William was laid beside her.
   And from his heart grew a red, red rose;
   From Barb'ra Allen's: a briar.

8. They grew and grew in the old church yard
   Till they could grow no higher;
   At last they formed a true lover's knot,
   And the rose grew 'round the briar.

The ballad is a sung story. Every narrative focuses on a single incident of universal appeal—romantic, gruesome, fabulous, or even miraculous. Each tale has several stanzas, with each stanza four (or five) phrases in length. Only in a few old ballads does the usually passive audience sing a final answering line. In old-style balladry, the tune is sung with great precision and economy. In adherence to the traditions of oral transmission, eccentricities are shunned in favor of an impersonal, yet intense, rendition.

THE BATTLE HYMN OF THE REPUBLIC

Julia Ward Howe
(United States, 1819—1910)

William Steffe
(United States, 1830—c. 1890)

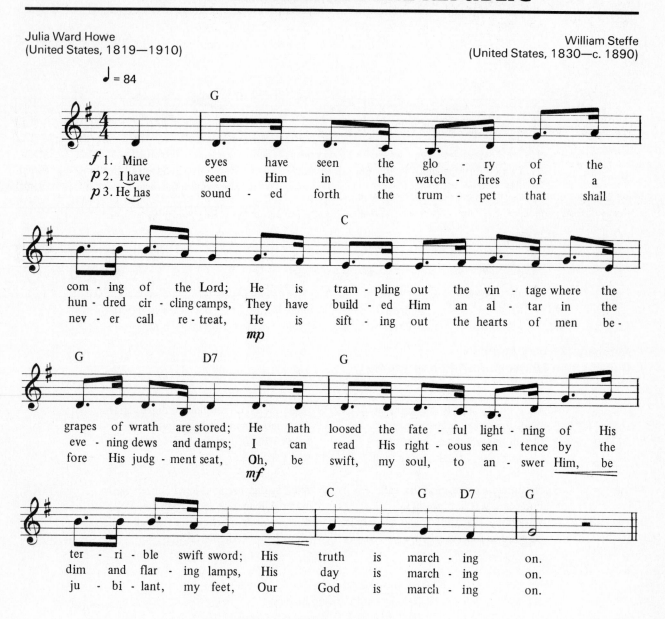

1. Mine eyes have seen the glory of the coming of the Lord; He is trampling out the vintage where the grapes of wrath are stored; He hath loosed the fateful lightning of His terrible swift sword; His truth is marching on.

2. I have seen Him in the watchfires of a hundred circling camps, They have builded Him an altar in the evening dews and damps; I can read His righteous sentence by the dim and flaring lamps, His day is marching on.

3. He has sounded forth the trumpet that shall never call retreat, He is sifting out the hearts of men before His judgment seat, Oh, be swift, my soul, to answer Him, be jubilant, my feet, Our God is marching on.

Refrain:

Glo - ry, glo - ry hal - le - lu - jah! Glo - ry, glo - ry hal - le - lu - jah!

Glo - ry, glo - ry hal - le - lu - jah! His truth is march - ing on.

last time ritard

Autoharp, strum L on the verse, strum O on the refrain
Piano, accompaniment pattern XVII, rolled chords (verse) and solid chords (refrain)

4. I have <u>read</u> a fiery gospel, writ in burnished rows of steel:
  "As ye <u>deal</u> with my condemners, so with <u>you</u> my grace shall <u>deal</u>;
  Let the <u>Hero</u>, born of woman, crush the <u>serpent</u> with His heel,
  Since <u>God</u> is <u>march</u>ing <u>on</u>." *(Refrain)*

5. In the <u>beauty</u> of the lilies Christ was born across the sea,
  With a <u>glory</u> in His bosom that trans<u>figures</u> you and <u>me</u>;
  As He <u>died</u> to make men holy, let us die to make men free,
  While <u>God</u> is <u>march</u>ing <u>on</u>. *(Refrain)*

6. He is <u>coming</u> like the glory of the morning on the wave,
  He is <u>wis</u>dom to the mighty, He is <u>honor</u> to the <u>brave</u>,
  So the <u>world</u> shall be His footstool, and the soul of wrong His slave,
  Our <u>God</u> is <u>march</u>ing <u>on</u>! *(Refrain)*

The ordeal of battle was all too familiar to soldiers who sang "John Brown's Body" as a Civil War marching song. But to Julia Ward Howe, wartime Washington, D.C., was a frenzied and frightening place to visit. After inadvertently witnessing a battle at a nearby army camp, Howe returned to her hotel. There she penned—in just a few hours—the now famous verses set to a hymn tune of William Steffe. Published in 1862, "The Battle Hymn of the Republic" quickly became a favorite with the Union army, and these new words replaced the "John Brown's Body" text.

BICYCLE BUILT FOR TWO

Harry Dacre

Autoharp, one strum each measure
Guitar, strum 16
Soprano recorder

BILL BAILEY

Hughie Cannon
(United States, 1877—1912)

Autoharp (15-bar), strum N
Chromatic Bells

BINGO

American School Song

There was a farm-er had a dog, and Bin-go was his name, O, B - i - n - g - o, B - i - n - g - o, B - i - n - g - o, and Bin-go was his name, O.

Guitar, strum 3
Piano, accompany using chord roots

Sing and play the traditional game for "Bingo." Omit a letter each time the song is repeated, inserting a clap where a letter should occur. Begin by omitting B, both the B and I, until all five letters are omitted and are replaced by five claps.

BIRD IN THE CAGE
(Kagome)

Japanese Song Game

Walking tempo

Ka - go - me,   Ka - go - me,   Ka - go - no na - ka - no
kah - goh - meh   *kah - goh - meh,*   *kah - goh - noh nah - kah - noh*

to - ri - wa,   I - tsu i - tsu de - ya - ru?
toh - ree - wah   *ih - tsoo ih - tsoo deh - yah - roo*

Yo - a - ke - no   ba - (n) - ni,   Tsu - ru to ka - me to
yoh - ah - keh - noh   *bah - (n) - nee*   *tsoo - roo toh kah - meh toh*

su - be - ta.   U - shi - ro - no sho - men da - re?
soo - beh - tah   *oo - shee - roh - noh show - mehn dah - reh*

Soprano recorder

English version

Kagome, Kagome,
Poor little bird in a bamboo cage;
Captive eyes and silent wings.
'Round and 'round the wild birds fly,
Calling and crying to *kagome*.
Guess my name and you can fly free!

English version by Patricia Hackett

Formation
Players form a circle and join hands. One player depicts the bird and sits or crouches in the center.

Game
Players walk in a circle while singing, stopping on the last word of phrase 4, "fly" (or "bani"). During phase 5 the teacher identifies one player, who sings phrase six as a solo. If the soloist's identity is correctly guessed by the bird, the two exchange roles. In case of an incorrect guess, the same bird remains in the center as the game is repeated.

BLACK IS THE COLOR

American Folk Song (Appalachian)

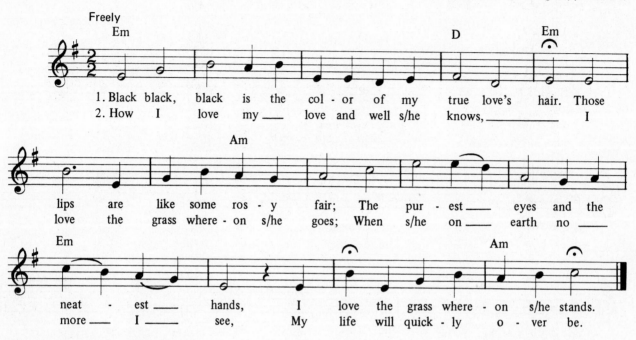

1. Black black, black is the col - or of my true love's hair. Those
2. How I love my ___ love and well s/he knows, _____ I

lips are like some ros - y fair; The pur - est ___ eyes and the
love the grass where - on s/he goes; When s/he on ___ earth no ___

neat - est ___ hands, I love the grass where - on s/he stands.
more ___ I ___ see, My life will quick - ly o - ver be.

Autoharp (21-bar), strum A (harp)
Guitar, free brush
Piano, accompaniment pattern XI
Soprano recorder

BLOW THE MAN DOWN

American Halyard Shanty

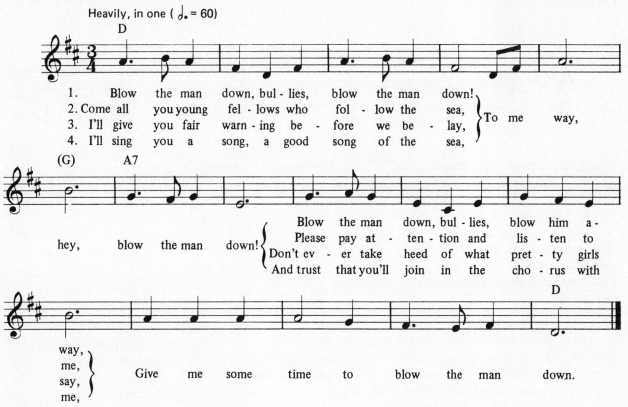

Autoharp (15-bar), strum once each measure
Guitar, strum 13
Piano, accompaniment pattern VI

The heavy, straining work on the great square-rigged merchant vessels was done to the strong rhythm of a sea shanty. These lusty work songs could time the group pull and also the interval of relaxation as the crew handled the halyards—the ropes used to hoist or lower a sail. In this halyard shanty, "blow the man down" probably means to "knock the man out" so he could be "shanghaied" to fill out a ship's crew.

BLUEBIRD

American Game Song

Autoharp (15-bar), strum C
Guitar, strum 5
Piano, accompaniment pattern III

Game
Children stand in a circle with hands joined and arms raised to form windows. One child is "it," (the bird), and he or she weaves inside then outside through the windows. On the last phrase he or she stands in place, facing one of the children in the circle. The singing stops, and the child who is it asks "What bird do you want to be?" The child in the circle answers, then becomes it for the next repetition of the song.

BLUETAIL FLY

American Minstrel Song

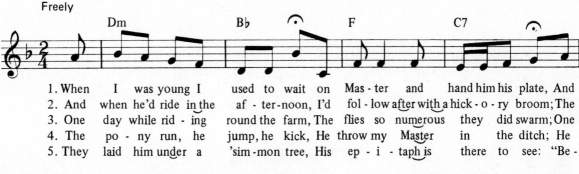

Freely

1. When I was young I used to wait on Mas-ter and hand him his plate, And
2. And when he'd ride in the af-ter-noon, I'd fol-low after with a hick-o-ry broom; The
3. One day while rid-ing round the farm, The flies so numerous they did swarm; One
4. The po-ny run, he jump, he kick, He throw my Master in the ditch; He
5. They laid him under a 'sim-mon tree, His ep-i-taph is there to see: "Be-

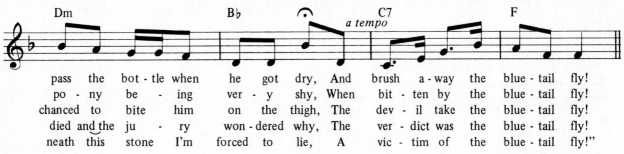

a tempo

pass the bot-tle when he got dry, And brush a-way the blue-tail fly!
po-ny be-ing ver-y shy, When bit-ten by the blue-tail fly!
chanced to bite him on the thigh, The dev-il take the blue-tail fly!
died and the ju-ry won-dered why, The ver-dict was the blue-tail fly!
neath this stone I'm forced to lie, A vic-tim of the blue-tail fly!"

Refrain:

Jim-my crack corn, and I don't care, Jim-my crack corn, and I don't care,

Jim-my crack corn, and I don't care, My Mas-ter's gone a-way.

Autoharp, strum freely until *a tempo,* **then strum C**
Piano, accompaniment pattern V until *a tempo*, **then III**

BOYSIE

Trinidad Lullaby

Rock, a - rock, a - rock, Boy - sie, Boy - sie can't sleep;

Rock, a - rock, a - rock, Boy - sie, Boy - sie can't sleep.

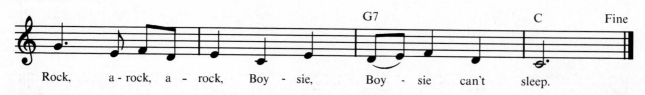

Look up - town, look down - town, find Boy - sie there;

Look up - hill, look down - hill, find Boy - sie there.

Autoharp, strum I
Piano, accompany using chord roots

BUFFALO DANCE

Collected by Patricia Hackett

Native American Song
(Southern Plains: Kiowa)

Strongly accented (♩ = 80)

Yoh hee yea, yoh hee yea. Yoh hee yea, yoh hee yea,

Large drum:

Yoh hee yea, yoh hee yea, Yoh hee yea, yoh hee yea, yoh hee yea.

Perform song three times

Solo on measures 1 and 2. All singers on repeat of measures 1 and 2. All singers on measures 3–9.

Traditional Native American music consisted almost entirely of song and was vital to Indian life. Music was associated with an individual's birth, coming of age, marriage, and so forth, and with the round of tribal events for the group. It was religious music with important ritual functions.

Equipment
One large drum, padded mallets, and chairs for six to eight drummers, and large sleighbells (tied to the ankles of the dancers).

Formation
Drummers sit in a circle around the drum, and the dancers form a large circle around them.

Dance
Only the drummers sing the "Buffalo Dance;" dancers do not sing. On the drum roll of measures 1 and 2 the dancers individually meander, as if they were bison grazing. During measures 3–9 the dancers face center, stand in place, and bounce on their heels. On the repeat of measures 3–9 the dancers move quickly to the center to form a tight circle around the drummers, and continue the bouncing movement.

Just prior to the second and third repetitions of the dance, drummers play a 2 to 3 measure drum roll, giving the dancers time to move away from the drum and back into a large circle.

BURY ME BENEATH THE WILLOW

American Country Song

1 and 5. Bur - y me be - neath the wil - low, 'Neath the weep-ing wil - low tree. __

When s/he hears his/her __ love is sleep - ing, May - be then s/he'll think of me.

Verse:

2. My
3. S/he
4. Place

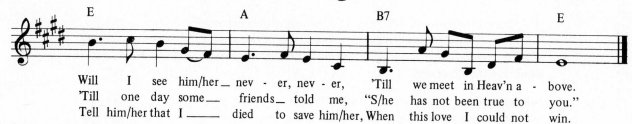

heart is sad and __ I am lone - ly, Think - ing of the one I love,
told me that s/he __ real - ly loved me, How could I think s/he'd be un - true,
on my grave a __ snow - white lil - y To prove that I was true to him/her,

Will I see him/her __ nev - er, nev - er, 'Till we meet in Heav'n a - bove.
'Till one day some __ friends __ told me, "S/he has not been true to you."
Tell him/her that I __ died to save him/her, When this love I could not win.

Guitar, strum 29 or 25

*On smaller notes, sing "loo."

BYE, BABY BUNTING

Nursery Song

Bye, ba - by bunt - ing, Dad - dy's gone a - hunt - ing;

Catch a lit - tle rab - bit skin To wrap the ba - by bunt - ing in.

Soprano recorder (play one half-step higher)

CHEH CHEH KOOLAY

African Song
(West Africa: Ghana)

Cheh cheh kool-ay. *Cheh cheh kool-ay.* Cheh cheh koh-fee sah.

Cheh cheh koh-fee sah. Kah-fee sah lang-ah. *Kah-fee sah lang-ah.*

Tah-tah shee lahn-gah. *Tah-tah shee lahn-ga.* Coom ah-dye-day. *Coom ah-dye-day.*

Game

Children form a circle around a leader. The leader sings the calls and makes the motions described below. The players in the circle respond by singing and imitating the caller. Players move constantly during the singing, twisting their bodies or bouncing up and down.

Cheh cheh koolay: Hands on head; all twist their bodies along with the beat as they sing.
Che che koh-fee sah: Hands on shoulders; twisting continues.
Kahfee sah lahn-gah: Hands on waist; twisting continues.
Tah tah shee lahn-gah: Hand on knees. All change to an up-and-down movement, bending the knees along with the beat.
Coom ah-dye-day: Hands on ankles; up and down movement continues. At the end of the song, players jump as they shout "hey!"

33

CHICKEN CHOWDER
Rag

Irene M. Giblin
(United States, dates unknown)

35

Chromatic bells
Piano, accompaniment pattern VI

Ragtime piano developed as music for the "sporting" life, but soon became popular in the parlors of genteel ladies. The transplantation was possible as piano rags began to be published in the Gay Nineties. Pianist-salespeople demonstrated rags and other sheet music for the amateur pianist in many ten-cent stores. Like the composers of rags, these clerks were accomplished pianists—and so were their customers. Skill is required to play melodies that have such wide ranges, and employ such persistent syncopations, as do rags. Melodies can traverse long scale passages or outline chords. The rather conventional harmony focuses on the primary chords in major keys. Nearly always there are four different parts (strains), often following the pattern AABBACCDD. Each strain is a symmetrical sixteen measures in length, with some rags including introductions and/or transitional passages. The young women played with the arched wrist and fingers of classical pianists, befitting a music that had traveled far from its folk origins. Many of these women composed piano rags that have been rediscovered in recent years.

CHILDREN, GO WHERE I SEND THEE

Black American Song

Guitar, strum 2

37

CHRISTMAS IS HERE!

Swedish Folk Song

♩ = 96

Nur är det jul i - gen, och nu är det jul i - gen, och
new air deh yule ee - yen oh new air deh yule ee - yen oh

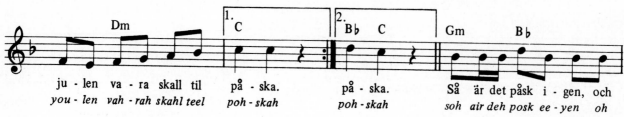

ju - len va - ra skall til på - ska. på - ska. Så är det påsk i - gen, och
you - len vah - rah skahl teel poh - skah poh - skah soh air deh posk ee - yen oh

så är det påsk i - gen. Och pås - ken va - ra skall til ju - la.
soh air deh posk ee - yen oh posk-ken vah - rah skahl teel you - lah

Autoharp, strum I
Chromatic bells
Piano, accompaniment pattern IX

English version
Christmas is here again, Oh, Christmas is here again,
Our happy days will last till Easter.
Then it is Eastertime, Oh, then it is Eastertime,
And Easter joy will last till Christmas.

CIELITO LINDO

Quirino Mendoza y Cortez
(Mexico)

1. E - se lu - nar que tie - nes, Cie - li - to
eh - seh loo - nahr keh tyeh - nehs syeh - lee - toh

Lin - do, Jun - to a la bo - ca,___
leen - doh hoon - toh a lah boh - kah

No se lo _____ des a na - die, Cie - li - to
noh seh loh dehs ah nah - dyeh syeh - lee - toh

Lin - do, Que a _____ mi me to - ca. _____
leen - doh keh ah mee meh toh - kah

Refrain:

¡Ay, ay, ay, ay! _____

Can - ta y no llo - res. _____ Por - que can - tan -
kahn - tah ee noh yoh - rehs pohr - keh kahn - tahn -

do se a - le - gran, Cie - li - to Lin - do Los___
doh seh a - leh - grahn syeh - lee - toh leen - doh lohs

___ cor - ra - zo - nes.___
koh - rah - soh - nehs

Autoharp (21-bar), strum J (verse) and strum H (refrain)
Chromatic bells
Guitar, strum 18

2. Si tu mama te dice.
   see too mah-mah teh dee-seh
   Cielito Lindo, 'Cierra la puerta,
   syeh-lee-toe leen-doh syeh-rah lah pwehr-tah
   Hace ruido a la llave,
   hah-seh rwee-doh ah lah yah-veh
   Cielito Lindo, Y dejala abierta. *(Refrain)*
   syeh-lee-toh leen-doh ee deh-hah-lah ahb-yehr-tah

English version

1. Night and day 'neath your window,
   Cie-lito Lindo, playing and singing.
   My guitar strumming from afar,
   Brings my song to you softly winging. *(Refrain)*

2. If your mot-her should tell you,
   Cie-lito Lindo, "Come from your window,"
   I'll wait by the garden gate,
   You're my fate, my Cielito Lindo *(Refrain)*

Spaniards found sophisticated musical instruments and a complex melodic system in Mexico at the time of the conquest. Modern Mexican folk music strongly reflects Spanish music in its melodies, dances, and instruments. European violins, harps, guitars, and trumpets all became popular in folk music. From 3 to 12 of these instruments make up today's mariachi ensemble of violins, trumpets, arpón *(harp)*, guitarron *(a large bass guitar)*, and jarana *(a smaller, 8-gut-stringed version of the guitar)*. Mariachi ensembles perform "Cielito Lindo," which is based on the jarabe, a popular dance in $\frac{6}{8}$ or a fast $\frac{3}{4}$ meter.

CIRCLE 'ROUND THE ZERO

Black American Game Song

Cir-cle round the ze - ro,   Find your lov-in' ze - ro,   Back, back   ze - ro,

Side, side   ze - ro,   Front, front ze - ro,   Tap your lov - in' ze - ro.

Autoharp, strum M
Guitar, strum 24
Piano, accompaniment pattern XII

Formation
Players in a circle, doing a patschen-clap motion throughout the game.

Game
Measures 1–2: A leader moves around the outside of the group, stopping behind a player on "your loving zero."
Measure 3: Back to back, the two players bump twice.
Measure 4: They bump hips twice.
Measure 5: The two players face each other, and clap hands twice.
Measure 6: On "tap," the leader taps his zero's shoulder and takes his or her place.

CLAPPING LAND

Danish Folk Song

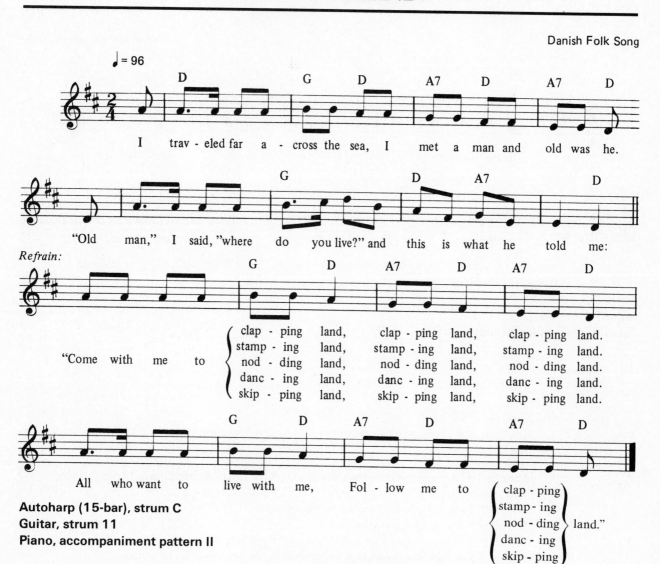

I trav-eled far a-cross the sea, I met a man and old was he.

"Old man," I said, "where do you live?" and this is what he told me:

Refrain:

"Come with me to
{
clap - ping land, clap - ping land, clap - ping land.
stamp - ing land, stamp - ing land, stamp - ing land.
nod - ding land, nod - ding land, nod - ding land.
danc - ing land, danc - ing land, danc - ing land.
skip - ping land, skip - ping land, skip - ping land.
}

All who want to live with me, Fol - low me to
{
clap - ping
stamp - ing
nod - ding
danc - ing
skip - ping
} land."

Autoharp (15-bar), strum C
Guitar, strum 11
Piano, accompaniment pattern II

On the refrain, do body rhythms along with the words "clapping land" and so forth.
For example, clap the rhythm of the words "clapping land," each time they occur.

COFFEE GROWS ON WHITE OAK TREES

American Play-Party Song

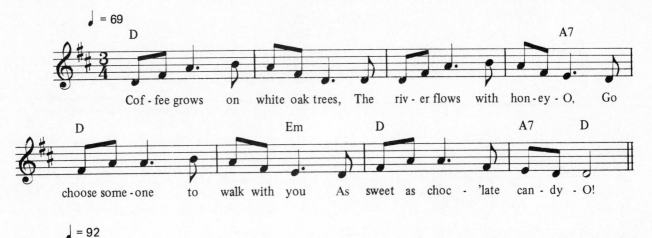

Cof - fee grows on white oak trees, The riv - er flows with hon - ey - O, Go

choose some - one to walk with you As sweet as choc - 'late can - dy - O!

1. Two in the mid-dle and I can't dance, Bet-sy!! Two in the mid-dle and I can't dance, Bet-sy!
2. Four   Four
3. Eight   Eight

Two in the mid - dle and I can't dance, Bet - sy! Hel - lo, Nan - cy Brown!
Four
Eight

Autoharp (15-bar), strum H (refrain) and strum D (verse)
Guitar, strum 16 (refrain) and strum 4 (verse)

Formation

Couples stand side by side with hands joined, forming two concentric circles; girls are on the inside. One boy stands in the center of the circle.

Dance

Measures 1–8: Couples walk clockwise in a circle. The boy in the center selects a girl from the circle to join him for measure 9 actions.

Measures 9–16: Couples skip around the circle. The boy in the center swings his partner, first by the right hand (measures 9–12) and then by the left hand (measures 13–16).

When the song is repeated, the two dancers in the center each select a partner from the circle as the couples walk clockwise. During measures 9–16, the four dancers in the centrer swing; those in the outside circle skip.

On the next repetition, 8 dancers will swing in the center, then 16, and finally 32. (The song's words change to "sixteen" or "thirty-two," as needed.) The dance is repeated until everyone is in the center.

43

COME, FOLLOW

English Round

With spirit

Come, fol - low, fol - low, fol - low, fol - low, fol - low, fol - low me!

Whith-er shall I fol - low, fol - low, fol - low, whith-er shall I fol - low, fol - low thee?

To the green - wood, to the green - wood, to the green-wood, green - wood tree.

Autoharp (21-bar), strum A
Guitar, strum 2

CONCERTO FOR ORCHESTRA
Second Movement Theme

Béla Bartók
(Hungary, 1881—1945)

Soprano recorder

The brilliant composer and pianist Béla Bartók was also a tireless collector of folk music. Near the turn of the century, he and his lifelong friend Zoltán Kodály set out with the earliest recording equipment to preserve and study the peasant music of Hungary and Eastern Europe. While the ancient scales and nonsymmetrical rhythms of this folk music may have influenced Bartók's own composition, his music is unique: Both lyrical and dynamic, it is full of original musical ideas expressed through distinctive harmonies, rhythms, forms, and instrumental sonorities. One of the great composers of our time, Bartók fled fascist Hungary in 1940. With his wife he emigrated to the United States, where they toured as pianists—but with meager financial success. Poverty stricken and dying of leukemia in 1945, Bartók was reputed to regret that he must die "with so much music left unsaid."

45

CONCERTO FOR VIOLIN IN E MINOR
Opus 64
Second Movement Theme

Felix Mendelssohn
(Germany, 1809—1847)

Soprano recorder

A wunderkind, Felix Mendelssohn was by the age of 11 already set on his career as a composer and pianist. In his Berlin home, Mendelssohn's wealthy family frequently assembled an orchestra for musical evenings which included his gifted sister, Fanny. By all accounts, Felix was refined and sensitive as an adult. He traveled widely, meeting and charming fellow artists—as well as the young Queen Victoria. Mendelssohn was a versatile composer, creating many melodic works with exquisitely refined orchestration. His short piano pieces—reflecting the ardor of the Romantic movement—were widely played in the homes of young Victorian women. We are also indebted to Mendelssohn as a conductor, for it was he who laid the foundation for the revival of the music of Bach.

THE CONDOR
(El Condor)

Moderately (♩ = 80-84)

Latin American Melody

El a - mor___ co - mo un con - dor ba - ja - ra, mi co - ra -
ehl ah - mohr coh-moh oon cohn-dohr bah - hah - rah mee coh - rah -
gus - tia y el do - lor me de - ja - ras, mi co - ra -
goos-teeyah ee el doh - lore may day - ha - rass mee coh - rah -

zón, gol - pea - ra, ___ des pues se i - ra. ___ Mm ___
ssohn gohl - pay - rah dehs pwes seh ee - rah
zón, su - fri - ra, ___ y mo - ri - ra. ___
ssohn soo - free - rah ee moh - ree - rah

La lu - na en el de - sier to bril - la - ra, Tu ven -
lah loo - nah ehn ehl dah -sseeair toh bree - yah - rah too ben -
El a - mor___ co - mo el con - dor vo - la - ra, Par - ti -
ehl ah - mohr coh-moh ehl cohn dohr boh - lah - rah pahr - tee -

dras, So - la - men - te un be - so, ___ me de - ja - ras. ___ Mm ___
drahss so - lah-men-teh oon beh - so meh day-ha - rass
ra, Y a - sí nun - ca más, ___ re - gre - sa - ras.
rah ee ah-see noon - cah mahs ray-gray-sah - rahss

___ Quién sa - be ma - ña - na vol - ve - ras ___ qué ha -
kyehn sah - bay mah-nyah-nah bowl-bay - rahss kay ah -

47

ras_____ no pen - sa - ras.   Yo sé que nun - ca vol - ve -
rahss   no behn - sah - rass   joh seh kay noon - cah - bowl - bay -

ras,   más pien - so que_____ no vi - vi - re,   co - mo po -
rahss   mahss beeyehn - so kay   noh bee - bee - ray   coh - moh poh -

dré._____   2. La an - dré._____   Mm _____
dray   *lah ahn - dray*

Autoharp, strum L
Guitar, strum 27

Translation

Like the condor, love descends to strike my heart, then takes flight again; like the bright moon, love comes, leaving but a kiss.

Who knows? Tomorrow love may return . . . or never. How can I go on, with such sadness and pain in my heart?

Like the condor, love descends to strike my heart, then take flight again.

Who knows? Tomorrow love may return . . . or never. How can I go on?

COUNTING SONG

African Children's Song
(Zimbabwe)

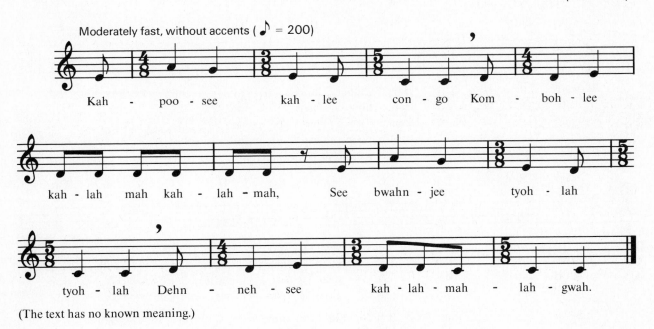

Moderately fast, without accents (♪ = 200)

Kah - poo - see   kah - lee   con - go   Kom - boh - lee

kah - lah   mah   kah - lah - mah,   See   bwahn - jee   tyoh - lah

tyoh - lah   Dehn - neh - see   kah - lah - mah - lah - gwah.

(The text has no known meaning.)

Even in games, African children sing in voices similar to those of their elders: wide, slightly nasal, and throaty. In this counting song, two phrases (a typical scheme) are repeated as the children sit on the ground in a row, both legs outstretched. Their enunciation while singing is slurred and unaccented, as the guesser (who remains standing) points to each leg in turn (on beat 1 of each measure). The leg on "-lah-gwah" at the end of each repetition is "out," and is tucked under the body. The song is repeated until only one leg remains out-stretched: that of the game's winner.

The simple texture of this counting song belies the multilayered, percussive sound common to much African music. Typically, a profusion of drums, xylophones, rattles, and metal bells play in solo, in ensemble, and as accompaniment for singing and dancing. Nearly everywhere south of the Sahara, the timbre most admired is a buzzing, rattling, percussive sound.

49

COVENTRY CAROL

Robert Croo
(fl. 1534)

English Melody
(1591)

Freely (𝅗𝅥 = 84-88)

Refrain: Lul - ly, lul - lay, thou lit - tle ti - ny child, Bye, bye, lul -
1. O sis - ters too, how may we do, For to pre -
2. Her - od, the king, in his rag - ing, Charg - éd he
3. Then woe is me, poor child for thee, And ev - er
Refrain: Lul - ly, lul - lay, *(and so forth)*

ly, lul - lay. Lul - lay, thou lit - tle ti - ny
serve this day, This poor young - ling for whom we do
hath this day His men of might, in his own
mourn and say, For thy part - ing nor say nor

child, *Refrain*, 1: Bye, bye, lul - ly, lul - lay.
sing, 2. All young chil - dren to slay.
sight, 3. Bye, bye, lul - ly, lul - lay.
sing,

Piano, accompany using chord roots

50

THE COWBOY'S LAMENT

American Cowboy Song

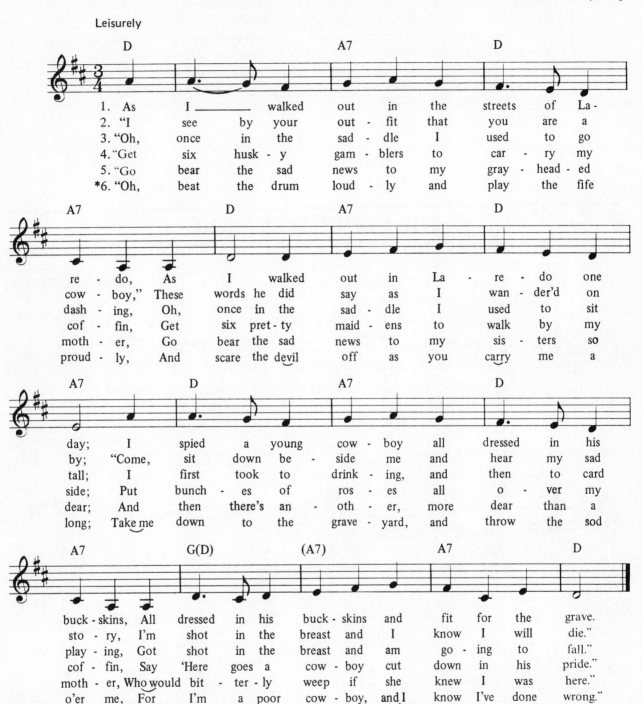

Leisurely

1. As I _____ walked out in the streets of La -
2. "I see by your out - fit that you are a
3. "Oh, once in the sad - dle I used to go
4. "Get six husk - y gam - blers to car - ry my
5. "Go bear the sad news to my gray - head - ed
*6. "Oh, beat the drum loud - ly and play the fife

re - do, As I walked out in La - re - do one
cow - boy," These words he did say as I wan - der'd on
dash - ing, Oh, once in the sad - dle I used to sit
cof - fin, Get six pret - ty maid - ens to walk by my
moth - er, Go bear the sad news to my sis - ters so
proud - ly, And scare the devil off as you carry me a

day; I spied a young cow - boy all dressed in his
by; "Come, sit down be - side me and hear my sad
tall; I first took to drink - ing, and then to card
side; Put bunch - es of ros - es all o - ver my
dear; And then there's an - oth - er, more dear than a
long; Take me down to the grave - yard, and throw the sod

buck - skins, All dressed in his buck - skins and fit for the grave.
sto - ry, I'm shot in the breast and I know I will die."
play - ing, Got shot in the breast and am go - ing to fall."
cof - fin, Say 'Here goes a cow - boy cut down in his pride."
moth - er, Who would bit - ter - ly weep if she knew I was here."
o'er me, For I'm a poor cow - boy, and I know I've done wrong."

*Verse 6 may be sung as a refrain throughout.

Autoharp (15-bar), strum H and J (verse 6, strum I high to low)
Guitar, strum 20 (verse 6, strum 14)
Piano, accompaniment pattern VII

51

The vernacular of the range was unprintable. It is said that when a cowboy sang in polite company, he would need to whistle nine out of ten verses! No one is certain just how cowboy songs originated or whether the tunes were composed by the men themselves. Most likely they were based on existing melodies, borrowed from popular ballads, railroad songs, or mountain songs of the late nineteenth century. After the cowboy's evening meal, the most musical of the group might strike up a solo as the men sat around the fire or chuck wagon. Hardly any one singer remembered all the verses, so other men might add stanzas to keep things going. Fortunately, a few collectors relished these songs that eased the loneliness of life on the trail, and preserved them—although in expurgated versions—for later generations.

THE CROCODILE SONG

Nova Scotia Folk Song

"The Crocodile Song" was taken from SONGS AND BALLADS OF NOVA SCOTIA by Helen Creighton. Dover Publications, New York, 1966.

Autoharp, strum G

DE COLORES

Traditional Mexican Song

♩ = 126-132

De _____ co - lo - res, _____ De co -
deh   coh - loh - rehs   deh coh

lo - res se vis - ten los cam - pos en la pri - ma -
loh - rehs seh vees - tehn lohs cahm - pohs ehn lah pree - mah -

ve - ra, _____
veh - rah

De _____ co - lo - res, _____ De - co -
deh   coh - loh - rehs   deh coh -

lo - res son los pa - ja - ri - tos que vie - nen de a -
loh - rehs sone lohs pah - hah - ree - tohs keh vee eh - nehn deh ah -

fue - ra, _____
fooeh - rah

De _____ co - lo - res, _____ De co - lo - res es
deh   coh - loh - res   deh coh - loh - res ehs

el ar - co i - res que ve - mos lu - cir, _____
ehl ahr - coh ee - rehs keh veh - mohs loo - seer

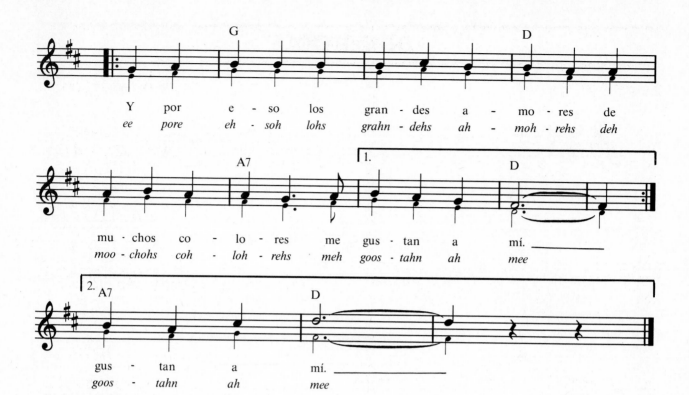

Y   por   e - so   los   gran - des   a - mo - res   de
ee   pore   eh - soh   lohs   grahn - dehs   ah - moh - rehs   deh

mu - chos   co - lo - res   me   gus - tan   a   mí. ____
moo - chohs   coh - loh - rehs   meh   goos - tahn   ah   mee

gus - tan   a   mí. ____
goos - tahn   ah   mee

Autoharp (15-bar), strum I (harp)
Chromatic bells
Guitar, strum 21
Piano, accompaniment pattern VIII

English version

When ____ the meadows,
When the meadows burst forth in the cool dewy colors
   of springtime:
When the swallows,
When the swallows come winging in clouds of bright
   colors from far off,
When ____ the rainbow,
When the rainbow spreads ribbons of color all over
   the sky;
Then I know why the splendors of true love are great and
   their colors, the best ones of all.
Then I know why the splendors of true love are great and
   their colors, the best ones of all.

English version by Alice Firgau

   In the 19th century, fashionable European dances such as the waltz, polka, and bolero provided the basis for popular Mexican and Latin American music. "De Colores" is a valse rancheras, associated with the states of Jalisco and Michoacan (northwest of Mexico City). Ranchera songs have a special Mexican flavor, and became popular favorites through their use in Mexican films of the 1930s and 1940s. "De Colores" was used as a theme song in the labor struggle of California farmworkers in the 1960s and was popularized by Joan Baez, the American folk singer. Many other Mexican songs have become internationally known, such as "Granada" Agustín Lara (1897—1970), and "La Bamba," Richie Valens' arrangement of a Mexican wedding song.

DON GATO

Margaret Marks

Mexican Folk Song (adapted)

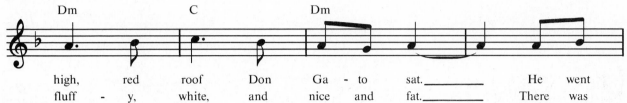

1. Oh, Se-ñor Don Ga-to was a cat,_____ On a
2. "I a-dore you!" wrote the la-dy cat,_____ Who was

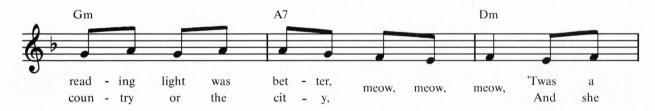

high, red roof Don Ga-to sat._____ He went
fluff-y, white, and nice and fat._____ There was

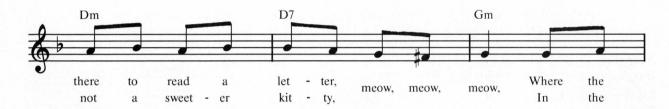

there to read a let-ter, meow, meow, meow, Where the
not a sweet-er kit-ty, meow, meow, meow, In the

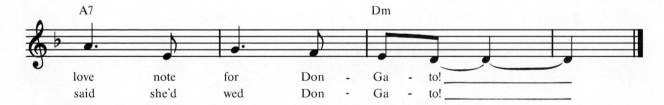

read-ing light was bet-ter, meow, meow, meow, 'Twas a
coun-try or the cit-y, meow, meow, meow, And she

love note for Don - Ga - to!_____
said she'd wed Don - Ga - to!_____

Autoharp, strum F (verses 1-5), harp (verse 6)

3. Oh, Don Gato jumped so happily
He fell off the roof and broke his knee,
Broke his ribs and all his whiskers, meow, meow, meow,
And his little solar plexus, meow, meow, meow,
¡ Ay carramba! cried Don Gato!

4. Then the doctors all came on the run
Just to see if something could be done
And they held a consultation, meow, meow, meow,
About how to save their patient, meow, meow, meow,
How to save Señor Don Gato!

5. But in spite of ev'rything they tried
Poor Señor Don Gato up and died,
Oh, it wasn't very merry, meow, meow, meow,
Going to the cemetery, meow, meow, meow,
For the ending of Don Gato!

Sing verse 6 slowly:

6. When the funeral passed the market square
Such a smell of fish was in the air,
Though his burial was slated, meow, meow, meow,
He became re-animated! Meow, meow, meow,
He came back to life, Don Gato!

DOODLE DOO DOO
(Waddaly Atcha)

Words and music by Kassel and Stitzel
(United States)

Wad-da-ly a-tcha, wad-da-ly a-tcha, Doo-dle-ee-doo,_ doo-dle-ee-doo;_ Wad-da-ly a-tcha, wad-da-ly a-tcha, Doo-dle ee-doo,_ doo-dle-ee-doo._ It's the sim-pl-est thing,_ noth-in' much to ___ it, ___ All you got to do is doo-dle-ee-doo it; ___ I like the rest, But the part I love best, It goes doo-dle-ee, doo-dle-ee-doo. Whoo!

Autoharp (15-bar), strum G (Banjo)
Piano, accompaniment pattern XII

DOWN BY THE STATION

American School Song

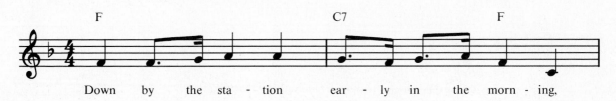

Down by the sta – tion ear – ly in the morn – ing,

See the lit – tle puf – fer – bil – lies all in a row.

See the en – gine driv – er pull the lit – tle han – dle,

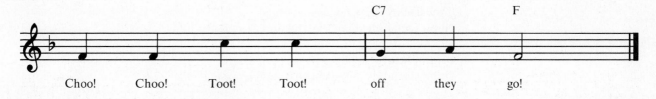

Choo! Choo! Toot! Toot! off they go!

Autoharp, strum G (twice each measure)

Create a pantomime for the song's words.

57

DOWN IN THE VALLEY

American Folk Song

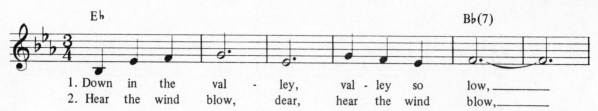

1. Down in the val - ley, val - ley so low, _____
2. Hear the wind blow, dear, hear the wind blow, _____

Hang your head o - ver, hear the wind blow. _____

Autoharp (15-bar), strum H
Guitar, strum 16 (play one half step higher)

3. If you don't love me, love whom you please,
   Throw your arms 'round me, give my heart ease.

4. Give my heart ease, dear, give my heart ease,
   Throw your arms 'round me, give my heart ease.

5. Write me a letter, send it by mail
   Send it in care of Birmingham Jail.

6. Birmingham Jail, love, Birmingham Jail,
   Send it in care of Birmingham Jail.

7. Build me a castle forty feet high,
   So I can see her, as she rides by.

8. As she rides by love, as she rides by,
   So I can see her, as she rides by.

9. Roses love sunshine, violets love dew,
   Angels in heaven know I love you.

10. Know I love you dear, know I love you,
    Angels in heaven know I love you.

THE DRUNKEN SAILOR

American Sea Shanty

Heavily (♩ = 100)

1. What shall we do with the drunk-en sail-or? What shall we do with the drunk-en sail-or? What shall we do with the drunk-en sail-or?

Ear-lye in the morn-ing. *Refrain:* Hoo-ray and up she ris-es, Hoo-ray and up she ris-es, Hoo-ray and up she ris-es, Ear-lye in the morn-ing.

Autoharp, strum A; 21-bar autoharp, drone (Dm+Dmaj and Cmaj+Cm)
Piano, accompaniment pattern XI
Chromatic bells

2. Give him a dose of salt and water, *(three times)*
   Earlye in the morning. *(Refrain)*

3. Put him in the bilge and make him drink it, *(three times)*
   Earlye in the morning. *(Refrain)*

4. Shave his chest with a rusty razor, *(three times)*
   Earlye in the morning. *(Refrain)*

5. Put him in the longboat till he's sober, *(three times)*
   Earlye in the morning. *(Refrain)*

6. Keep him there and make him bail her, *(three times)*
   Earlye in the morning. *(Refrain)*

7. Pull out the plug and wet him all over, *(three times)*
   Earlye in the morning. *(Refrain)*

8. Put him in the guard room till he's sober, *(three times)*
   Earlye in the morning. *(Refrain)*

9. That's what we do with the drunken sailor, *(three times)*
   Earlye in the morning. *(Refrain)*

Shantymen led work songs on eighteenth- and nineteenth-century sailing vessels. The shantyman needed a strong voice and a good memory; it was his responsibility to choose the right song for the job, to set the pitch and tempo, and to improvise if he ran out of verses before the task was done. It was not essential for the lines to rhyme; enough continuity was provided by the repetition of the refrain or by the response of the group as it answered each call of the shantyman. Irish, and later Blacks, were the most admired shantymen on American vessels.

59

DRY BONES

American Song

neck bone, the neck bone con-nect - ed to the back bone, The
back bone con-nect-ed to the thigh bone, the thigh bone con-nect-ed to the knee bone, The
knee bone con-nect - ed to the leg bone, the leg bone con-nect - ed to the
foot bone, Oh, hear the word of the Lord!_____

Piano, accompaniment III, then use XI measures 9-21 and measure 31 to the end

Play a different percussion instrument on the rest preceding each body part's name.
Play all instruments simultaneously during measures 23 to 30.

DUCK DANCE

Native American Song
(Florida: Seminole)

Chromatic bells

Background

"Duck Dance" is often the first dance or "mixer" at a powwow. A master of ceremonies typically begins the song and acts as dance leader.

Formation

Everyone sings the song, clapping a quarter-note beat, while standing or sitting in place. As the song is repeated, the dance leader moves randomly among the spectators and soon joins hands with one individual. The selected person dances (and sings) along with the leader, and selects a third person to join hands and join the line. This process continues until everyone is part of a serpentine line of singing dancers.

Dance

Beginning with the right foot, dancers slide feet along the floor, alternating right, left, right, and so forth.

THE DUCKLINGS
(Los Patitos)

Collected by Patricia Hackett

Salvadoran Folk Song

1. Los pa - ti - tos van al a - gua, Tien - en ga - na
   lohs pah - tee - tohs bahn ahl ah - wah tyehn - ehn gah - nah

de na - dar; En i - le - ras vien for - ma - das,
day nah - dahr ehn ee - lay - rahs b'yehn fohr - mah - dahss

Co - mo sa - ben ca - mi - nar. Va la pa - ta
coh - moh sah - behn cah - mee - nahr bah lah pah - tah

por di - lan - te, Los pa - ti - tos van de - tras.
pohr dee - lahn - tay Lohs pah - tee - tohs bahn day - trahss

Qua - tro cin - co, sies pa - ti - tos, Ni u - no me - nos ni u - no mas.
kwah - troh sin - koh sayees pah - tee - tohss nee oo - noh meh - nohs nee oo - noh mahss

Autoharp, strum C
Guitar, strum 11

63

2. Los patitos al estanque.
   lohs pah-tee-tohs ahl ehs-tan-kaye

   Ya se echeron a nadar.
   yah sayeh-chair-on ah nah-dah

   Como meten las cabezas,
   coh-moh meh-tehn lahs cah-bay-sahs

   Y la unelven a sacar.
   ee lah oon-ehl-behn ah say-cahr

   Quatro, cinco, sies patitos,
   kwah-troh, sin-koh, sayees pah-tee-tohs

   Ni uno menos, ni uno mas.
   nee oo-noh meh-nohs nee oo-noh mahs

   Los patitos van al aqua.
   lohs pah-tee-tohs bah nahl ah-kwah

   Tienen gana de nadar.
   t-yehn-ehn gah-nah- day nah-dahr

English version
Los patitos in the water,
How they love to dive and play!
Hear the mother call *patitos*,
Now it's time to swim away.
Mother leads and they will follow,
Los patitos all in line,
Four, and five, and six *patitos*,
Los patitos look so fine!

English version by Patricia Hackett

EENCY, WEENCY SPIDER

Traditional American Finger Play

Een - cy, ween - cy spi - der went up the wa - ter spout,
"Climb" up, touching one little finger to the thumb of the other hand. Then rotate wrists, alternately touching thumbs to little fingers.

Down came the rain and washed the spi - der out.
Bring hands down and out to sides

Out came the sun and dried up all the rain, And the
Make a big circle over head with arms

een - cy, ween - cy spi - der went up the spout a - gain.
"Climb" up again

Autoharp (15-bar), strum S
Guitar, strum 1 (play one half step higher)
Piano, accompany using chord roots

THE ENTERTAINER
Rag

Scott Joplin
(United States, 1868—1917)

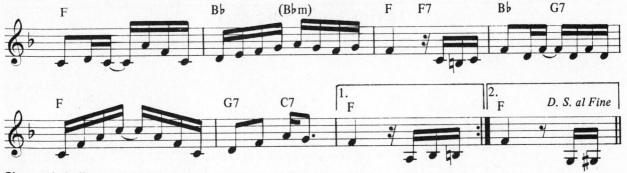

Chromatic bells

Near the turn of the century, a fellowship of pianists—mostly Black—entertained from New Orleans to Chicago. These piano "professors" were to develop one of the most engaging styles of the twentieth century.: the rag. They played dance music for the white underworld, "ragging the time" in the Black districts and the tenderloins of the Mississippi Valley. In 1899, the young Scott Joplin was in Sedalia, Missouri, at clubs like the Maple Leaf, creating his classic piano rags. Graceful and never too fast, these ragtime two-steps almost sound like "two different times at once." Over an unwavering, even "oom-pah" in the bass, syncopation throbs in the melody. These rags were an outgrowth of several styles that had gone before: the cakewalk, the minstrel show band, banjo music, and brass marching bands. After 1900, ragtime became the popular music of Broadway and of vaudeville for two decades, until blues and jazz swept the nation. Ragtime faded, but it was revived after World War II to charm and delight new generations.

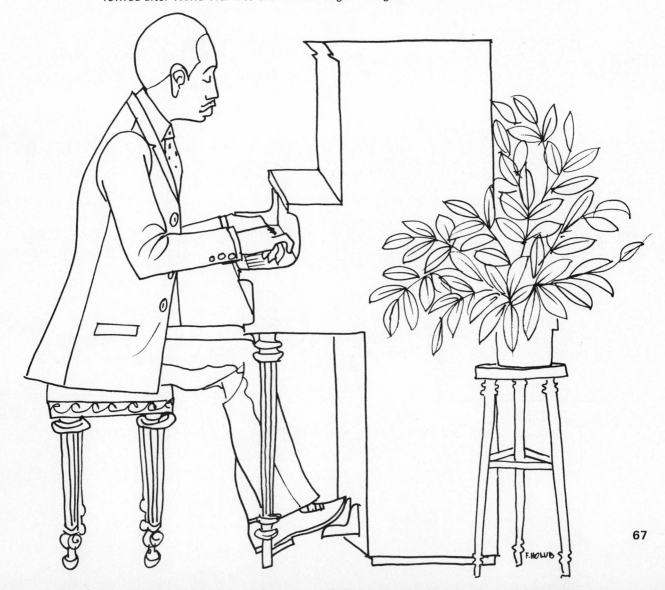

EPO I TAI TAI E

Collected by Marion A. Todd

Maori Song
(New Zealand)

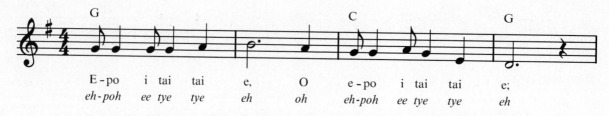

Autoharp, strum P
Guitar, strum 30

The song words mean "This is a strong man who fights like a bull."

EV'RY NIGHT WHEN THE SUN GOES DOWN

American Mountain Song

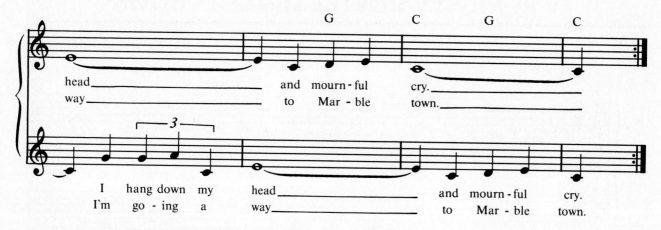

Autoharp, strum A (harp)
Guitar, strum 23
Piano, accompaniment pattern XVII

2. Oh, once I wore my apron low, _ _ _
   Oh, once I wore my apron low, _ _ _
   Oh, once I wore my apron low,
   Could hardly keep you from my door. _ _ _*(Refrain)*

3. And now my apron strings won't pin, _ _ _
   And now my apron strings won't pin, _ _ _
   And now my apron strings won't pin,
   You pass my door, and won't come in. _ _ _*(Refrain)*

4. I wonder what my mother will say, _ _ _
   I wonder what my mother will say, _ _ _
   I wonder what my mother will say,
   When I come home in a family way. _ _*(Refrain)*

5. She'll hang her head and bite her tongue, _ _ _
   She'll hang her head and bite her tongue, _ _ _
   She'll hang her head and bite her tongue,
   'Cause she done the same thing when she was young! _ _*(Refrain)*

6. I wish to the Lord my babe was born, _ _ _
   And sittin' on his papa's knee, _ _ _ _
   And me, poor girl, was dead and gone,
   With green grasses growing over me. _ _*(Refrain)*

EV'RYONE BUT ME

New England Folk Song

1. Oh, the fox and the hare, And the bad-ger and the bear, And the

squirrel in the wal - nut tree; And the fur - ry lit - tle rab - bits, So en -

gag - ing in their hab - its, Have all got a mate but me.

Autoharp (15-bar), strum A
Chromatic bells

2. Oh, the lark and the wren,
   And the cuckoo in the glen,
   And the owl in the hollow tree;
   And the jay bird and the hawk,
   With a cry and a squawk;
   Have all got a nest but me.

3. Oh, the fish and the frog,
   And the turtle and the dog,
   And the worm in the old oak tree;
   And the frisky little rat,
   And the big fat cat,
   Have all got a home but me.

Verses 2 and 3 by Patricia Hackett

THE FARMER IN THE DELL

American Game Song

1. The farm - er in the dell, The farm - er in the dell,
2. The farm - er takes a wife, The farm - er takes a wife,

Heigh ho, the der - ry O! The farm - er in the dell.
The farm - er takes a wife.

Autoharp (15 bar), strum S
Guitar, strum 37 (play one half step higher, using E and B7 chords)

3. The wife takes the child, . . .

4. The child takes the nurse, . . .

5. The nurse takes the dog, . . .

6. The dog takes the cat, . . .

7. The cat takes the rat, . . .

8. The rat takes the cheese, . . .

9. The cheese stands alone, . . .

Formation
Players form a circle. One player is selected as the farmer, and stands alone in the middle of the circle.

Game
Players forming the circle either stand in place as they sing (clapping steady beats), or, they skip around the circle. In each case they always stop singing and moving at the conclusion of each verse.

Verse 1: The farmer walks around inside the circle, and chooses a wife when the singing stops.
Verse 2: The wife and farmer walk around inside the circle, and the wife selects a child.
Verses 3-8: The last player to join those inside the circle chooses a person to become the next character mentioned in the song (nurse, dog, cat, rat, and cheese).
Verse 9: Everyone in the middle rejoins the outer circle except the cheese. The cheese stands alone during the singing of verse nine.
(When the game is played again, the cheese can be selected as the farmer.)

FLOWER DRUM SONG
(Feng Yang Hwa Gu)

Chinese Folk Song

♩ = 96

Dzwo_ shou_ lwo, you_ shou_ gu, shou na je lwo gu_
tzwoh show loowoh yoh show goo show nah juh loh goo

lai_ chang_ ge. Bye de_ ge er_ wo ye bu hwei chang,
lye chahng guh beeyeh duh guh ehr woh yeh boo hway chahng

jr hwei_ chang ge_ Feng_ Yang_ ge. Feng lai Feng Yang ge_ lai_
jer hway chahng guh fuhng yahng guh fuhng lye fuhng yahng guh lye

Refrain:

Ai ya ai you ya. Drrr! Ling ding Pyao yi pyao, Drrr! Ling ding Pyao yi pyao,
aye yah aye yoh yah der ling ding pyaow ee pyaow der ling ding pyaow ee pyaow

Drrr! Pyao! Drrr! Pyao! Drrr! Pyao! Drrr! Pyao! Pyao! Yo Drrr! Pyao! Pyao! Pyao yi pyao!
der pyaow der pyaow der pyaow der pyaow pyaow yoh der pyaow pyaow pyaow ee pyaow

English version
Sing the Feng Yang Song; Sing it loud and long.
Clash cymbals, beat drums, Strike the gong!
We are vendors trav'ling all day long,
Calling our wares with Feng Yang Song.
Feng yang, fong yong, beat gong, Strike the clappers well. *(Refrain)*

FOR HEALTH AND STRENGTH

Traditional Round

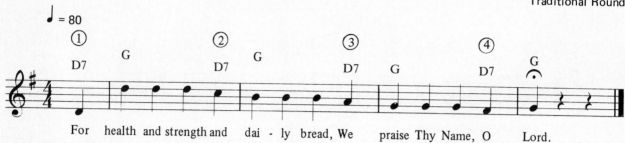

For health and strength and dai - ly bread, We praise Thy Name, O Lord.

Autoharp, strum L
Guitar, play melody
Soprano recorder

GIVE MY REGARDS TO BROADWAY

Words and music by George M. Cohan

♩ = 120

Bb   Eb   F7

Give my re - gards to Broad - way, Re -

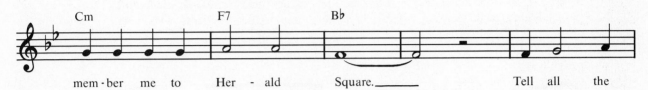

Cm   F7   Bb

mem - ber me to Her - ald Square._____ Tell all the

C7   F   C7

gang at For - ty Sec - ond Street that I will

F7   Bb

soon be there._____ Whis - per of how I'm

Eb   F7   Cm   F7

yearn - ing to min - gle with the old time

Bb   G7   Cm   G7

throng._____ Give my re - gards to old Broad -

Cm   Eb   Bb   F7   Bb

way and say that I'll be there, e're long._____

Autoharp (21-bar), strum A
Chromatic bells

Create a medley of turn-of-the-century songs, using "Give My Regards to Broadway," " Hello! Ma' Baby," and "While Strolling Through the Park." See the Alphabetical Index of Melodies for their page numbers.

GOLDEN RING AROUND THE SUSAN GIRL

American Folk Song (Appalachians)

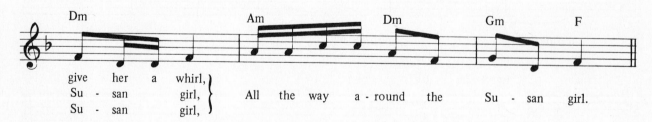

'Round and a - round, Su - san girl, Round and a - round, Su - san girl,

'Round and a - round, Su - san girl, All the way a - round, Su - san girl.

Autoharp (15-bar) strum E

THE GOLDEN VANITY

Anglo-American Ballad

♩ = 100

1. There once was a ship that sailed the low-land sea, And the name of the ship was the Gold-en Van-i-ty, And we feared she would be cap-tured by the Span-ish en-e-my, As she sailed up-on the low-land, low-land, low-land, We sailed up-on the low-land sea.

2. Then up stepped our cabin boy and brave-ly out spoke he, And he said to the captain, "What will you give to me If I swim up be-side the Span-ish en-e-my, And sink her in the low-land, low-land, low-land, And sink her in the low-land sea."

3. "I will give you sil-ver and I will give you gold, And my fair, love-ly daughter your bon-ny bride shall be If you swim up be-side the Span-ish en-e-my, And sink her in the low-land, low-land, low-land, And sink her in the low-land sea."

4. Then the boy spread his arms and o-ver-board sprang he, And he swam a-long side of the Span-ish en-e-my And with his brace and bit in her side he bored holes three, And sank her in the low-land, low-land, low-land, And sank her in the low-land sea.

Autoharp (21-bar), strum L
Guitar, strum 28

5. Then back again he swam, to the cheering of the crew,
   But our captain would not heed him, would not listen as he cried,
   "Oh messmates, draw me up, for I'm drifting with the tide,
   And I'm sinking in the lowland, lowland, lowland,
   I'm sinking in the lowland sea."

6. So his messmates drew him up, but up<u>on</u> the deck he <u>died</u>,
   And they <u>stitched</u> him in his hammock, which <u>was</u> so fair and wide,
   When they <u>slid</u> him overboard he just <u>drifted</u> with the <u>tide</u>,
   Then he <u>sank</u> into the <u>lowland</u>, <u>lowland</u>, <u>lowland</u>,
   He <u>sank</u> down in the <u>lowland</u> <u>sea</u>.

The English ballad tradition is very old. The artless simplicity of the text and tune suggests an origin with the illiterate folk of medieval villages and farms, though ballads have no known composers. But ballads were also sung by the minstrels of the Middle Ages, those professional entertainers who roamed the countryside or attached themselves to courts or great houses. Minstrels were legislated out of existence by Queen Elizabeth in sixteenth-century England and were succeeded by tavern poets, who composed new, topical texts for familiar ballad melodies. Printed on large sheets of paper called "broadsides," news and rumor were spread far and wide. Many of the old narrative ballads and broadsides crossed the Atlantic with British colonizers, and there they survived into the twentieth century. Folklorists discovered a living ballad tradition in the backwoods of the rural south, a tradition that had almost vanished in the British Isles.

GOOD KING WENCESLAS

John Neale (England, 1818—1866)

English Carol

Guitar, one strum each measure, or melody
Piano, accompany using chord roots
Soprano recorder

GOOD NIGHT
(Gute Nacht)

German Folk Song

Autoharp (21-bar), strum L
Guitar, strum 27

English version
Good night, good night, my tiny love,
Good night, sleep well my child.
Good night, good night, my tiny love,
Good night, sleep well my child.
May all good angels hover near those in the lovely heav'nly light,
Good night, good night, my tiny love,
Good night, sleep well my child.

GO TELL AUNT RHODY

American Lullaby

Simply

1. Go tell Aunt Rho - dy, Go tell Aunt Rho - dy,

Go tell Aunt Rho - dy; The old gray goose is dead.

Coda following verse 5:

Go tell Aunt Rho - dy, poor old Aunt Rho - dy,

Go tell aunt Rho - dy, The old gray goose is dead.

Autoharp, strum D
Piano, accompaniment pattern II

2. The <u>one</u> she's been savin', *(three times)*
   To <u>make</u> a feather <u>bed</u>.

3. She <u>broke</u> all the saw teeth, *(three times)*
   That <u>old</u> gray goose was <u>tough</u>.

4. The goslings are cryin', *(three times)*
   Be<u>cause</u> their mother's <u>dead</u>.

5. The <u>gander</u> is weepin', *(three times)*
   Be<u>cause</u> the goose is <u>dead</u>. *(Coda)*

82

GO TELL IT ON THE MOUNTAIN

Black American Spiritual

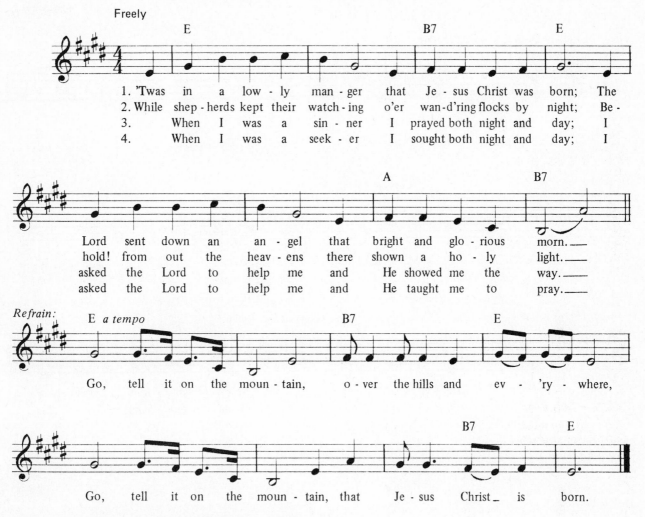

1. 'Twas in a low-ly man-ger that Je-sus Christ was born; The
2. While shep-herds kept their watch-ing o'er wan-d'ring flocks by night; Be-
3. When I was a sin-ner I prayed both night and day; I
4. When I was a seek-er I sought both night and day; I

Lord sent down an an-gel that bright and glo-rious morn.___
hold! from out the heav-ens there shown a ho-ly light.___
asked the Lord to help me and He showed me the way.___
asked the Lord to help me and He taught me to pray.___

Refrain:

Go, tell it on the moun-tain, o-ver the hills and ev-'ry-where,

Go, tell it on the moun-tain, that Je-sus Christ_ is born.

Guitar, free strum (verse) and strum 10(refrain)

In post–Civil War years, several Black American universities developed choirs which went on fund-raising tours throughout the nation. Audiences familiar only with stereotyped minstrel entertainment finally heard the great Black spirituals—in exciting concert arrangements. But spirituals flowered in rural America. Twentieth-century urban life gave rise to gospel music, a composite of the style of blues, spirituals, and tabernacle songs. The emotional fervor of gospel singing is often backed by strong rhythms on piano, guitar, or other instruments. Hand clapping, shouting, and demonstrative interplay, all contribute to the highly religious intensity of black gospel music. Much of this same energy and excitement can be heard in soul music, the secular equivalent of gospel.

GREETINGS OF PEACE
(Hevenu Shalom A'leychem)

Israeli Song

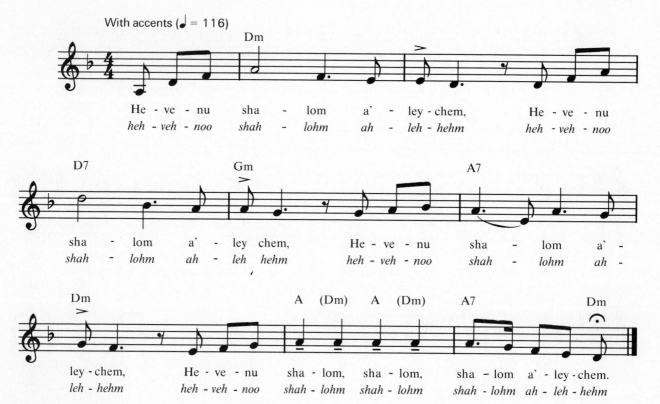

He - ve - nu sha - lom a' - ley - chem, He - ve - nu
heh - veh - noo shah - lohm ah - leh - hehm heh - veh - noo

sha - lom a' - ley chem, He - ve - nu sha - lom a' -
shah - lohm ah - leh hehm heh - veh - noo shah - lohm ah -

ley - chem, He - ve - nu sha - lom, sha - lom, sha - lom a' - ley - chem.
leh - hehm heh - veh - noo shah - lohm shah - lohm shah - lohm ah - leh - hehm

Autoharp, strum N
Guitar, strum 22

English version
We come to greet you in peace,
We come to greet you in peace,
We come to greet you in peace,
We come to greet you, greet you,
Greet you in peace.

GRINDING SONG

Adapted by Patricia Hackett

Native American Song
(California: Tachi Yokuts)

Split stick of dried elderberry:

Huh wil luh say nehm muh say pnt, hmm hmm. Say

qwehn nuh say nehm muh say pnt, hmm hmm.

Huh way way wuht nuh way wuht, hmm hmm.

More than one hundred different Native American groups lived amicably in the central two-thirds of California. No groups practiced agriculture, perhaps because food was usually plentiful. Acorns were a staple and were varied by game, shellfish, berries, seeds, and roots. Many California Indian songs are similar to the "Grinding Song" because they include only a few different pitches and are expressed in one to three short musical phrases. The "song" above is a short version of the original, which was much longer, with the three phrases alternating and repeating in no regular order.

GUANTANAMO LADY
(Guantanamera)

Lyric adaptation by Hector Angulo
based on a poem by José Martí
(Cuba, 1853—1895)

Original lyrics and music by
Jose Fernandez Dias (Joseito Fernandez)
Music adaptation by Pete Seeger
(United States, b. 1919)

♩ = 116-120

Refrain:

Guan-ta - na - me-ra,
gwahn-tah-nah-may-rah
gua -ji - ra,
gwah-hee-rah
Guan-ta - na - me-ra,
gwahn-tah-nah-may-rah

Guan - ta - na - me - ra,
gwahn - tah - nah - may - rah
gua - ji - ra,
gwah-hee-rah
Guan - ta - na - me - ra.
gwahn-tah - nah - may - rah

Fine

1. Yo soy un hom-bre sin-ce -ro,
   yoh soy oon ome-bray sin - say-roh
   De don - de cre-ce la pal -ma,___
   day don - day cray-say lah pahl - mah
2. Mi ver-so es de un ver - de cla ro,
   mee bare-soehs day oon bare-day clah - roh
   Y de un car - min en-can-di - do,___
   ee tah oon cahr - meen ehn-cahn-dee - doh
3. Con los po - bres de la ti - er - ra,
   cohn lohs poh -brace day lah tee - air - rah
   Qui-er - o yo mi suer-te e - char,___
   kee - air - oh yo mee swear-tay ay - chahr

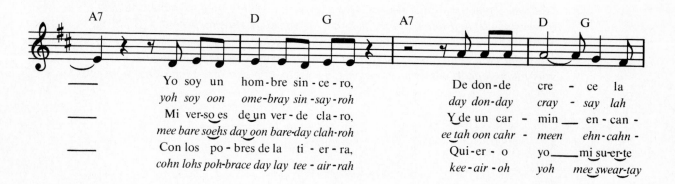

___ Yo soy un hom-bre sin -ce -ro,
    yoh soy oon ome-bray sin -say-roh
    De don-de cre - ce la
    day don-day cray - say lah
___ Mi ver-so es de un ver-de cla-ro,
    mee bare soehs day oon bare-day clah-roh
    Y de un car - min ___ en-can-
    ee tah oon cahr - meen ehn-cahn-
___ Con los po - bres de la ti - er - ra,
    cohn lohs poh-brace day lay tee - air-rah
    Qui-er - o yo___ mi su-er-te
    kee - air - oh yoh mee swear-tay

				D.C. al Fine
pal - ma,___	Y an-tes de mo-rir me quie - ro,		E-char mis ver-sos del al - ma.	
pahl - mah	*ee ahn-tays day moh-reer may keeaye - roh*		*aye-chahr mees bare-sohs dehl-ahl - mah*	
di - do,___	Mi ver-so es un cier-vo he - ri - do,		Que bus-ca en mon-te am-pa - ro.	
dee - doh	*mee bare-soehs oon seeair-voh ay - ree - doh*		*kay boos-cah ehn mohn-tay ahm-pah - roh*	
e - char,___	El ar-ro - yo de la si - er - ra,		Me com - place mas que el - mar.	
ay - chahr	*ehl ahrr-roh-yoh day lah see - air - rah*		*may cohm - plahs mahs kay ehl - mahr*	

Autoharp (15-bar), strum N (refrain) and free strum (verse)
Guitar, strum 25 (refrain) and 27 (verses)

Translation

1. I'm a sincere man from a land where palms grow,
   I want to pour forth the poems of my soul before I die.

2. My verses are light green and bright red . . .
   Like wounded fawns trying to hide in the mountain forest.

3. Let me be as one with all the humble people of the world,
   And take more pleasure from the calm mountain stream,
      than from the mighty ocean.

José Martí was born in Havana, Cuba. Poet, novelist, journalist, and revolutionary, Martí thought of himself as a citizen of the Americas. His dream was of a unified Latin America that would be able to thwart nineteenth-century North American imperialism. Involved in Cuba's struggle to gain independence from Spain, Martí was imprisoned, exiled, and finally killed as he landed with an armed group in Oriente Province—the same province where Fidel Castro's successful forces landed nearly sixty years later.

HANDGAME SONG

Collected by Patricia Hackett

Native American
(Southern Plains: Kiowa)

Aye kuh boo__ duh, aye kuh   boo__ duh,   Hay yah, aye kuh boo__duh.

Small drum:

The text is Kiowa "song words" whose meaning is not known, or forgotten.

Equipment for each of two teams

Two pairs of sticks. One of each pair is marked in the middle, to be covered by the hand during the game.

Guessing wand with fabric or feathers at the tip.

Ten counters (sticks) to display as each point is won.

Small drum and mallet.

Game

Two members of team 1 each hide two sticks: The sticks are grasped around the middle while behind the back, then displayed for the opposing team. Possible positions for the marked sticks are:

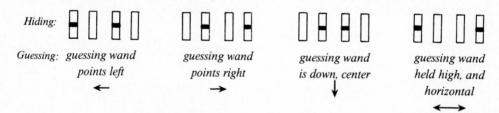

Hiding:

Guessing: guessing wand   guessing wand   guessing wand   guessing wand
                  points left   points right   is down, center   held high, and
                                                                                                          horizontal
                  ←   →   ↓   ↔

Singing is by the team hiding sticks; the other team consults among themselves, trying to make a correct guess.

Scoring

Points are scored by the hiding team when it deceives the guessers.

The opportunity to change possesion of the sticks (and score points) is achieved by a correct guess.

The first team to score ten points wins the game.

HANUKAH

Hebrew Melody

♩ = 120

C   F

Ha - nu - kah,   Ha - nu - kah,   hol - i - day so   fair,

Dm   G7   C

Glow - ing   light,   can - dles   bright,   hap - pi - ness we   share.

                                                                F

Gai - ly   dance,   gai - ly   sing   while   the   drey - dl   whirls,

G7   C

Round   and   round,   round   and   round,   see   how   fast   it   twirls.

Autoharp, strum C

*Hanukah, or Festival of Lights, is a Jewish celebration commemorating the rededica-
tion of the Temple in Jerusalem in 165 B.C. Special candles are lit on each of the eight
days, and there are parties and gifts. The dreydl is a top used in children's games.*

HAPPILY SINGING
(Alegria)

Puerto Rican Carol

Moderately and expressively (♩. = 52)

Ha - cia Be - lén se en-ca - mi - nan, Ma - rí-a con su a - man-te es-
ah -syah beh - lehn sehn-kah - mee - nah mah-ryah kohn soo ah - mahn-tehs-

po - so, Lle-van - do en su com-pa - ñí - a A to - do un Dios po-de-
poh-soh yeh-vahn - dwehn soo koem-pah - nyee-ah ah toh - thwoon dyohs poh-theh-

Refrain
ro - so. A - le - grí - a, a - le-grí - a, a - le - grí - a, A - le-
roh - soh ah - leh - gree - ah - leh-gree - ah - leh - gree - ah ah - leh-

rit. a tempo
grí - a, a - le-grí - a y pla - cer, Que la Vir - gen va de
gree - ah - leh-gree - ah ee - plah - sehr keh lah veer - hehn vah deh

pa - so Con su es - po - so ha - cia Be - lén.
pah - soh Kohn swehs - poh - soh ah - syah beh - lehn

Autoharp (15-bar), strum S
Guitar, strum 33

English version
On the roadway to the city,
Rides the Virgin on a donkey;
Traveling with her and dear Joseph
Is God's Spirit so almighty. *(Refrain)*
We are happily, happily singing,
Letting melody joyfully ring,
For sweet Mary, blessed Virgin,
Comes to Bethle'm this glad eve. *(Repeat refrain)*

HAPPY ARE THEY
(Hineh Ma Tov)

Israeli Echo Song

Autoharp (21-bar), strum C
Chromatic bells
Guitar, strum 7

Translation:
How good it is for brothers to dwell together!

Pronunciation guide:
Hineh = *hih-nay*
Ma tov = *mah-tove*
Uma = *oo-mah*
Naim = *nah-eem*

Shevet achim = *sheh-veht ah-heem*
Naim achad = *nah-eem ah-hahd*
Gam yachad = *gahm yah-hahd*

HAPPY ARE THEY
(Hineh Ma Tov)

Israeli Round

Autoharp, strum B
Chromatic bells
Guitar, strum 1

English version
Good is the time when we shall be
Living in peace as brothers. *(repeat lines 1 and 2)*
Hineh ma tov, Good the time shall be,
Shevet achim, Living in peace together. *(repeat lines 3 and 4)*

HAVA NAGILA

Israeli Dance Song

93

Autoharp (21-bar), strum L
Guitar strum, 22

Translation

Let us rejoice and be happy;
Let us sing and be happy.
Stir yourselves, friends, with a happy heart.

Formation

The hora is a line or circle dance without partners. Hands are on the neighbor's shoulders, and dancers move sideways to the left.

Dance

Begin with weight on right foot.
Beat 1: Step left with left foot;
Beat 2: Step on right foot, placing it behind left foot;
Beat 3: Step on left foot;
Beat 4: Hop on left foot, swinging right leg in front;
Beat 5: Set on right foot;
Beat 6: Hop on right foot, swinging left leg in front.

Repeat, gradually accelerating the tempo.

HAWAIIAN RAINBOWS

Modern Hawaiian Song

Ha - wai - ian rain - bows,
Slowly swing arms over the head from left to right to show the shape of a rainbow.

White clouds roll by;
Swing arms back from right to left, At the same time, roll one hand over the other to show clouds.

You show your col - ors
Swing arms from left to right. At the same time, make a rippling motion with the fingers as if pointing to all the colors of the rainbow.

A - gainst the sky.
Raise both hands high to the right (palms up). Move the left hand "across the sky" to the left side.

Ha - wai - ian rain - bows,
Slowly swing arms over the head from left to right to show the shape of a rainbow.

It seems to me,
Place the right hand under the left elbow and point the index finger of the left hand toward the chest ("it seems to me").

Reach from the moun - tain
Raise both hands high to the left.

Down to the sea.
Slowly lower hands toward the right knee and continue moving them out to the right ("Down to the sea").

Autoharp, strum A (harp)
Guitar, strum 27

Formation

Dancers kneel and sit low on their heels. To begin, they stretch both arms out to the left, with fingers pointing up and palm facing out. Each motion is smooth and flowing, and is performed slowly so it extends through two measures.

HEAD-SHOULDERS, BABY

Black American Game Song

1. Head — shoul-ders, Ba - by, one, two, three; Head —
2. Shoulders — chest,__ Ba - by, one, two, three; Shoulders —
3. Chest — knees,__ Ba - by, one, two, three; Chest —

touch   touch   clap   snap   clap   snap   clap   snap   and so on

shoul - ders, Ba - by, one, two, three; Head — shoul - ders, head —
chest, — Ba - by, one, two, three; Shoulders — chest, — shoulders —
knees, — Ba - by, one, two, three; Chest — knees, — chest —

shoul - ders, Head — shoul - ders, Ba - by, one, two, three.
chest, — Shoulders — chest, — Ba - by, one, two, three.
knees, — Chest — knees, — Ba - by, one, two, three.

Use both hands to touch the body parts named in the song. Touch, clap, and snap in a steady beat rhythm.

4. Knees-ankles, Baby, . . .
5. Ankles-knees, Baby, . . .
6. Knees-chest, Baby, . . .

7. Chest-shoulders, Baby, . . .
8. Shoulders-head, Baby, . . .

HE IS BORN

French Carol

Autoharp, one strum each measure. Strum 6 bass strings on the refrain, and all strings on the verse

HELLO, EV'RYBODY

Words by Charity Bailey
(United States, 1904—1978)
and Eunice Holsaert

American Folk Melody

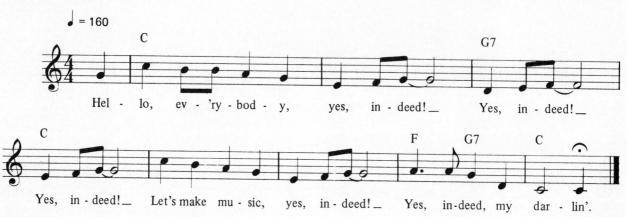

Hel - lo, ev - 'ry - bod - y, yes, in - deed! _ Yes, in - deed! _

Yes, in - deed! _ Let's make mu - sic, yes, in - deed! _ Yes, in - deed, my dar - lin'.

Autoharp, strum N
Piano, accompaniment pattern XI

HELLO! MA' BABY

Joseph E. Howard (United States, 1878-1961)
Ida Emerson (United States, late 19th-20th c.)

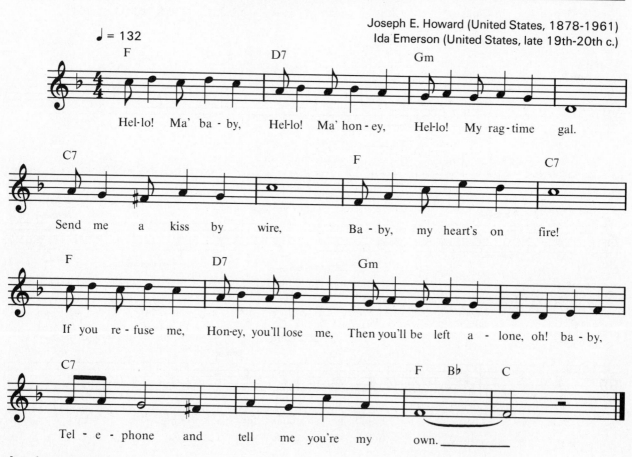

Hel-lo! Ma' ba - by, Hel-lo! Ma' hon - ey, Hel-lo! My rag - time gal.

Send me a kiss by wire, Ba - by, my heart's on fire!

If you re - fuse me, Hon-ey, you'll lose me, Then you'll be left a - lone, oh! ba - by,

Tel - e - phone and tell me you're my own. _____

Autoharp, strum P
Piano, accompaniment pattern XVI

HENG CHWUN FOLK SONG
(Everspring)

Chinese Folk Song
(Taiwan)

With movement (♩ = 80)

Yi nyan rung_ yi_____ you_ chwun_ tyan, Fan tu sya jung_____
yee nyehn roong yee yoh chwuun tyehn fahn too sshah juung

mang_ tyan_____ byan. Tyan li yang_ myau____ you_ lyu
mahng tyehn byehn thehn lee yahng myahoo yoh luu

lyu, Jya jya hu_ hu_ pu_ feng_____ nyan.
luu jyah jyah huu huu puu fuhng nyehn

English version
Earth gives our land everspring;
Soft breezes blow, birds all sing.
Bright sun and sky: fair each day;
Green fields are home: work, love, play.

English version by Patricia Hackett

HEY, HO! NOBODY HOME

Traditional Round

① Dm   C   Dm   C ② Dm   C   Dm   C

Hey, ho! no - bod - y home! Meat nor drink nor mon-ey have I none,

③ Dm   C   Dm   C   Dm C Dm   C

Still I will be ver - y mer - ry. — Hey, ho! no - bod - y home.

Autoharp, strum A
Chromatic bells

HEY, LIDEE

American Song

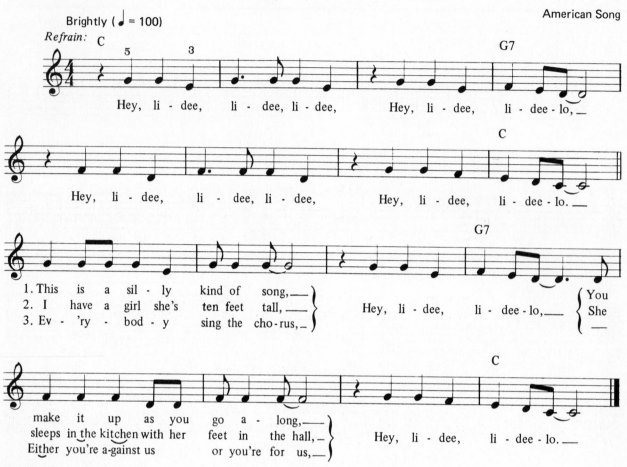

Autoharp, strum O
Guitar, strum 25
Piano, accompaniment pattern XI

Make up your own verses for this song.

HEY, TSWANA

African Round

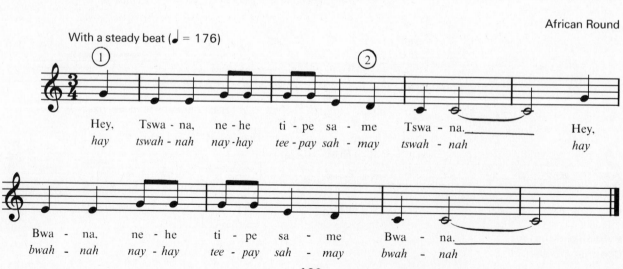

HILLS OF ARIRANG

Korean Folk Song

Autoharp, drone (Gmaj + Gm)
Guitar, strum 15
Soprano recorder

English version
    The words of Korea's oldest and most famous folk song speak of "crossing the hills of Arirang." These words that have come to suggest that to be truly happy, one must face and overcome life's difficulties.

        Arirang, Arirang, Arariyo,
        Arirang hills are still calling to me.
        All my trials, I know, can be o'ercome,
        Daily I go to cross Arirang hills.

        English version by Patricia Hackett

HOLD ON

Black American Song

With a strong beat (♩ = 80)

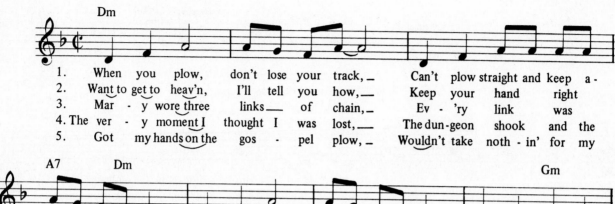

1. When you plow, don't lose your track,— Can't plow straight and keep a-
2. Want to get to heav'n, I'll tell you how,— Keep your hand right
3. Mar - y wore three links— of chain,— Ev - 'ry link was
4. The ver - y moment I thought I was lost,— The dun-geon shook and the
5. Got my hands on the gos - pel plow,— Wouldn't take noth - in' for my

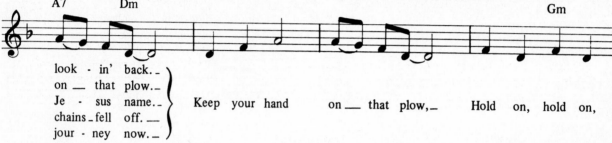

look - in' back.—
on — that plow.—
Je - sus name.—   Keep your hand on — that plow,— Hold on, hold on,
chains — fell off. —
jour - ney now.—

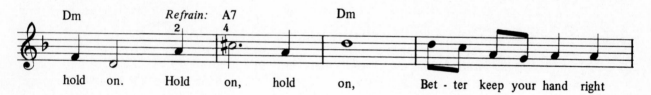

hold on.   Hold on, hold on,   Bet - ter keep your hand right

on ——— that plow, — Hold on, hold on, hold on.

Autoharp, strum A
Guitar, strum 10
Piano, accompaniment pattern XI

Originally a social and religious commentary, "Hold On" was easily adapted to the "Freedom Rider's Song" by Blacks attempting to desegregate public transportation in the South. Here are some of those verses:

1. Paul and Silas bound in jail,
   Had no money to go their bail,
   Keep your eyes on the prize,
   Hold on, hold on, hold on. *(Refrain)*

2. Freedom's name is mighty sweet,
   Soon one day we're gonna meet,
   Keep your eyes on the prize,
   Hold on, hold on, hold on. *(Refrain)*

3. The only chain that man can stand,
   Is that chain of hand in hand,
   Keep your eyes on the prize,
   Hold on, hold on, hold on. *(Refrain)*

4. We're gonna board that big Greyhound,
   Carryin' love from town to town,
   Keep your eyes on the prize,
   Hold on, hold on, hold on. *(Refrain)*

HOME ON THE RANGE

Dr. Brewster Higley
(United States)

Daniel E. Kelley
(United States)

Autoharp (15-bar), strum Q
Guitar, strum 33 or melody

THE HOPE
(Hatikvah)

Nephtali H. Imber
(1856—1909)

Traditional Melody

Maestoso (♩ = 80)

As long— as— deep with in— the— heart The soul of Ju-de-a is
Kol - od - ba - le-vav p' - ni - mah, ne-fesh y'-hu - di

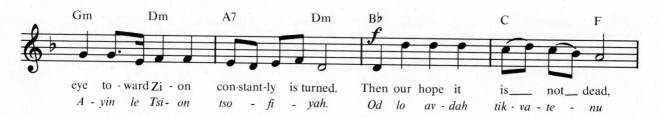

tur - bu - lent and strong, As long as to the East, for ward - ly, The
ho - mi - yah, U - l fa - a - tei miz-rach ka - di - mah,

eye to-ward Zi - on con-stant-ly is turned. Then our hope it is— not— dead,
A - yin le Tsi - on tso - fi - yah. Od lo av-dah tik-va-te - nu

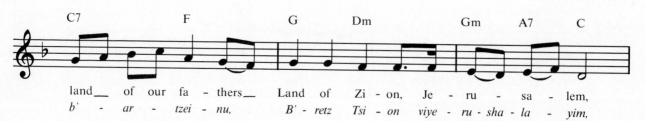

An - cient hope will soon be ful - filled, Free in our land, the
Ha - tik - va bat shnot al - pa - yim, L' - h'yot am chof - shi

land— of our fa - thers— Land of Zi - on, Je - ru - sa - lem,
b' - ar - tzei - nu, B' - retz Tsi - on viye - ru-sha-la - yim,

Free in our land, the land— of our fa - thers,— Land of Zi - on, Je - ru - sa - lem.
L'h' yot am chof -shi b' - ar - tzei - nu, B'e-retz Tsi - on viye - ru-sha-la - yim.

Autoharp, strum L

104

HOT CROSS BUNS

Traditional Song

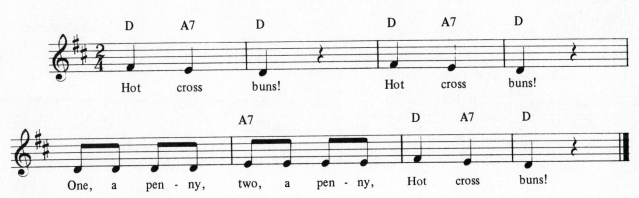

Hot cross buns! Hot cross buns!

One, a pen - ny, two, a pen - ny, Hot cross buns!

Autoharp (15-bar), strum C
Guitar, melody
Piano, accompany using chord roots

HUSH, LITTLE BABY

American Folk Song

Gently, with motion

1. Hush, lit - tle ba - by, don't say a word, Pa-pa's gon - na buy you a mock-ing-bird.
2. If that mock-ing - bird won't sing, Pa-pa's gon - na buy you a dia-mond ring.

Guitar, strum 12

3. If that diamond ring turns brass,
   Papa's gonna buy you a looking glass.

4. If that looking glass gets broke,
   Papa's gonna buy you a billy goat.

5. If that billy goat don't pull,
   Papa's gonna by you a cart and bull.

6. If that cart and bull turn over,
   Papa's gonna buy you a dog named
   Rover.

7. If that dog named Rover don't bark,
   Papa's gonna buy you a pony cart.

8. If that pony cart falls down,
   You'll be the saddest little child in town.

105

I AM THE MONARCH OF THE SEA
(from *H.M.S. Pinafore*)

William S. Gilbert
(England, 1836—1911)

Arthur S. Sullivan
(England, 1842—1900)

Sir Joseph: aunts. But when the breez - es blow, I gen - er - al - ly go be - low, And

Cousin Hebe: seek the se - clu - sion that a cab - in grants. And so do his sis - ters and his

Chorus: cous - ins and his aunts. And so do his sis - ters and his cous-ins and his aunts. And

so do his sis - ters and his cous - ins and his aunts. His

sis - ters and his cous-ins, Whom he reck-ons by the doz-ens, and his aunts._____

Autoharp, strum A
Piano, accompaniment pattern XVI
Chromatic bells

The comic operas of Gilbert and Sullivan delighted Victorian England with their satires of pomposity and hypocrisy. The lively charm of Sullivan's music and the brilliance of Gilbert's verse (which has been compared to that of Aristophanes) continue to provide amusement and pleasure whenever they are performed.

In H.M.S. Pinafore, *or* The Lass That Loved a Sailor *(1878), a humble sailor is in love with the Captain's daughter, who is being encouraged to marry the First Lord of the Admiralty. Describing his exalted position, the First Lord sings "I am the Monarch of the Sea." But the Captain's daughter confesses her love to the sailor, with whom she plans to elope.*

The lovers are betrayed, and all seems lost until it is learned that the Captain and the sailor were mixed up when babies. So the Captain's daughter is free to marry the sailor— who is really the Captain! Small wonder that Queen Victoria thought G & S plots "rather silly!"

I BOUGHT ME A CAT

Kentucky Folk Song

Autoharp, strum D (banjo)
Chromatic bells

I'D LIKE TO TEACH THE WORLD TO SING

Words and music by Bill Backer, Billy Davis,
Roger Cook and Roger Greenaway
(United States)

Autoharp (15 bar), strum 0
Guitar, strum 24
Piano, accompaniment pattern XV

* sing "loo" on smaller notes

109

IF YOU'RE HAPPY

American School Song

If you're hap-py and you know it,
{ clap your hands,
stamp your foot,
nod your head,
turn a - round,
touch your nose, }
If you're

hap-py and you know it,
{ clap your hands,
stamp your foot,
nod your head,
turn a - round,
touch your nose, }
If you're hap-py and you know it, then your

face will sure-ly show it, If you're hap-py and you know it,
{ clap your hands,
stamp your foot.
nod your head.
turn a - round.
touch your nose. }

Autoharp, strum N

I KNOW WHERE I'M GOING

American Folk Song

Autoharp, free rhythm
Guitar, one slow brush each measure
Piano, accompany using chord roots

I LOVE THE MOUNTAINS

American Round

♩ = 112

I love the moun - tains, I love the roll - ing hills,

I love the flow - ers, I love the daf - fo - dils,

I love the fire - side When all the lights are low,

Boom dee ah da, boom dee ah da, Boom dee ah da, boom dee ah da,

Boom dee ah da, boom dee ah da, Boom dee ah da, boom dee ah da

Autoharp, strum L or G
Chromatic bells

For harmony, sing phrases four and five
continuously during phrases one, two and three.

INDIAN FIDDLE MELODY

Collected by Patricia Hackett

Northwest India

Chromatic bells

INDIAN HYMN
(Ram Nam)

Religious Song from India

♩ = 96

Sri Ram   jai   Ram___ jai   jai___   Ram,_____   Sri   Ram _
shree rahm   jay   rahm   jay   jay   rahm   shree   rahm

jai   Ram___ jai   jai   Ram.   Jai   Si - ta,   Ram   jai___
jay   rahm   jay   jay   rahm   jay   see - dah   rahm   jay

jai   Ha - nu - man.   Sri   gu - ru   Ram   An - an - da   Bha - ga - van.
jay   hah - noo - mahn   shree goo - roo rahm ahn - ahn - dah bah - gah - vahn

Translation

Rama: victory to you! *(two times)*
Rama brought the monkey from Sri Lanka.
God is our real happiness and teacher.

This "Ram Nam" chant tells a portion of the epic tale *The Ramayana* and is used to aid meditation and concentration by repeating the name of Rama (Ram).

114

I NEVER WILL MARRY

American Ballad

Moderately

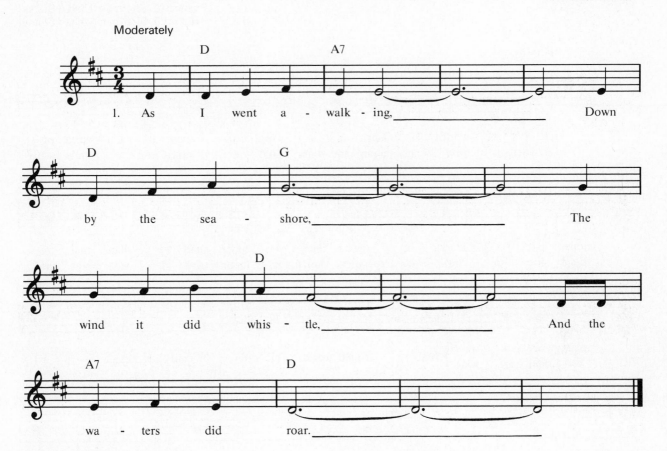

1. As I went a - walk - ing,_____ Down
by the sea - shore,_____ The
wind it did whis - tle,_____ And the
wa - ters did roar._____

Autoharp (15-bar), strum H
Guitar, strum 20 or melody
Piano, accompaniment pattern VIII

2. I saw a young maiden, Who sat on the sand,
A-reading a letter, That she held in her hand.

3. "My love has gone from me, The one I adore,
He's gone where I never Will see him no more."

4. I asked her to marry, With me, lest she weep,
She only could answer, "My love lies asleep."

5. "I never will marry, I'll be no man's bride,
I'll stay only single, All the days of my life."

IT'S A SMALL WORLD

Words and music by
Richard M. Sherman (United States)
Robert B. Sherman (United States)

Sing the verse and refrain simultaneously to create harmony.

Autoharp, strum A
Guitar, strum 7 (verse) and 24 (refrain)
Piano, accompaniment pattern XV
Chromatic bells

Refrain as sung in:

Germany:	Es ist eine kleine welt
Spain:	Es un mundo pequeño
Philippines:	Maliit na daigdig
Nigeria:	Ona kpo otete
Malaysia:	Bumi kita tidak besar

JAMAICA FAREWELL

♪ = 208

Caribbean Folk Song

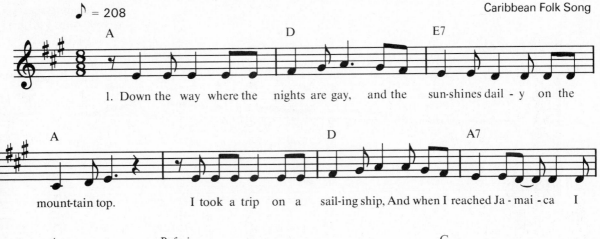

1. Down the way where the nights are gay, and the sun-shines dail - y on the

mount-tain top. I took a trip on a sail-ing ship, And when I reached Ja - mai - ca I

made a stop. *Refrain:* But I'm sad to say___ I'm on my way, ___

Won't be back for man - y a day.__ My head is down, my heart is

turn-ing a - round_ I had to leave a lit - tle girl in Kings-ton Town._

Guitar, strum 30
Piano, accompaniment pattern XVI

2. Sounds of laughter ev'rywhere
   And the dancing girls swaying to and fro.
   I must declare that my heart is there,
   Tho' I've been from Maine to Mexico. *(Refrain)*

3. Down at the market you can hear
   Ladies cry out while on their heads they bear
   Ackey, rice, salt fish are nice,
   And the rum is fine any time of year. *(Refrain)*

Many cultures have left their mark on the islands of the Caribbean, including those of Spain, France, Great Britain, North and South America, and the African nations. The music of Cuba, Jamaica, Haiti, and Trinidad reflect both African and Hispanic contacts, with the African traits especially strong. Instruments of African derivation dominate traditional Caribbean music making: drums of all sizes, iron bells, horns, stamping tubes, and even oversized thumb pianos. (As in Africa, voices supplied the desired effects in regions where instruments were banned or were unavailable.) Complicated rhythms are the "norm," with syncopations and cross rhythms performed in a strict, unvarying tempo.

JESU, JOY OF MAN'S DESIRING (excerpt)

Johann Sebastian Bach
(Germany, 1685—1750)

Soprano recorder

The Baroque was an exuberant and dynamic period (from about 1600 to about 1750) during which artists expressed a wide range of human feeling and ideas. Baroque music made extensive use of ornamentation and improvisation, and this era saw the beginning of idiomatic composition for specific instruments. Not only was our major/minor system crystallized in that period, but Baroque dance rhythms contributed to our modern predilection for the four-measure phrase. The towering genius of Johann Sebastian Bach brought the Baroque style to perfection with his creation of an immense quantity of sacred and secular music for varied instruments and voices. While Bach's music was neglected after his death, it was revived in the nineteenth century, and his spirit speaks to us as profoundly today as in his own time—truly a music for the ages.

JINGLE BELLS

Words and music by James Pierpont
(United States, 1822—1893)

D   G

1. Dash - ing through the snow   In a   one - horse o - pen sleigh;
2. A day   or two   a - go   I   thought I'd take a ride, And
3. Now the ground is white,   Go it while you're young,

A7   D

O'er the fields we   go,   laugh-ing all the way!   Bells on bob - tail ring, They're
soon Miss Fan - nie Bright, was seat - ed by my side! The   horse was lean and lank, Mis-
Take the girls   to - night, and sing this sleigh-ing song! Just   get a bob-tailed nag, Two-

G   D   A7   D

mak-ing spir - its bright. What   fun it is   to laugh and sing,   A sleigh - ing song to-night!
for-tune seemed his lot; He   got in - to a drift - ed bank, And we,   we got up - set!
for - ty   for his speed, Then   hitch him to an   o - pen sleigh, And crack! you'll take the lead!

Refrain:

Jin - gle bells!   Jin - gle bells!   Jin - gle   all   the way!

G   D   1.   A7   2.   A7   D

Oh, what fun   it is   to ride   in a   one-horse o - pen sleigh! __   one-horse o - pen sleigh!

Autoharp (15-bar), strum E
Guitar, strum 4 or 5
Piano, accompaniment pattern XVI

JOE TURNER BLUES

1. They tell me— Joe Turn-er's— come and gone,— They

tell me— Joe Turn-er's— come and gone.— He

left me— here to sing— this— song.

Depending on the singer, Joe Turner was either a sheriff or a good samaritan.

Autoharp (21-bar), strum G (twice each measure)
Guitar, strum 10

2. He <u>came</u> here with forty links of chain, *(two times)*
   He <u>left</u> me here to sing this <u>song</u>.

3. Joe <u>Turner</u>, he took my man away, *(two times)*
   He <u>left</u> me here to sing this <u>song</u>.

These subjective sorrow songs called the blues developed in the early twentieth century, with the migration of rural Blacks to the cities. The bluesman was considered a footloose, irresponsible figure. Perhaps his blues songs eased the pain and stress of adjustment to the new urban lifestyle. There has been much research and speculation, but no one has really identified the roots of blues. Whatever their origin, they were considered the devil's music by many faithful churchgoers. Blues are among the most unique and powerful musical expressions of twentieth-century America and had a profound influence on the development of jazz.

JOHNNY, I HARDLY KNEW YOU

Irish Melody

*Verse 1 may be sung as a recurring refrain.

Autoharp (21-bar), strum R
Guitar, strum 35

1. When Johnny comes marching home again, Hurrah! Hurrah!
   We'll give him a hearty welcome then, Hurrah! Hurrah!
   The men will cheer and the boys will shout,
   The ladies they will all turn out,
   And we'll shout for joy when Johnny comes marching home!

2. Let love and friendship on the day, Hurrah! Hurrah!
   Their choicest treasure then display, Hurrah! Hurrah!
   And let each one perform some part,
   To fill with joy the warrior's heart.
   And we'll shout for joy when Johnny comes marching home!

3. Get ready for the jubilee, Hurrah! Hurrah!
   We'll give the hero three times three, Hurrah! Hurrah!
   The laurel wreath is ready now
   To place upon his royal brow,
   And we'll shout for joy when Johnny comes marching home!

Words by Patrick S. Gilmore (Irish-American bandmaster)

JOHNNY HAS GONE FOR A SOLDIER

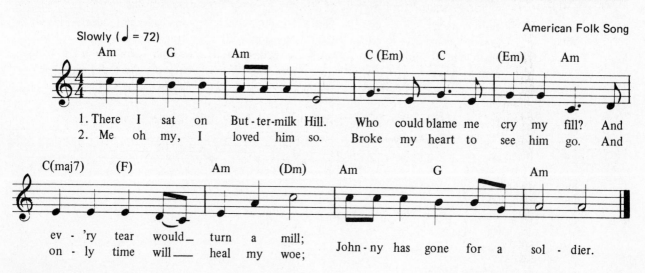

American Folk Song

Slowly (♩ = 72)

1. There I sat on But-ter-milk Hill. Who could blame me cry my fill? And
2. Me oh my, I loved him so. Broke my heart to see him go. And

ev - 'ry tear would— turn a mill; John-ny has gone for a sol - dier.
on - ly time will— heal my woe;

Autoharp, strum A (harp)
Guitar, strum 27
Soprano recorder

JOSHUA FOUGHT THE BATTLE OF JERICHO

Black American Spiritual

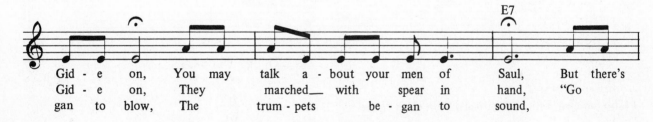

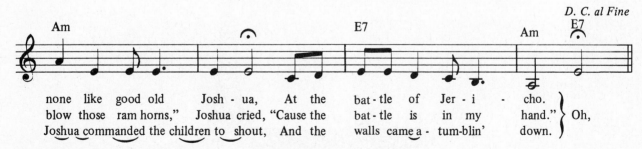

Autoharp, strum L (refrain) and free strum (verse)
Guitar, strum 2

JOY TO THE WORLD

Isaac Watts
(England, 1674—1748)

George Frederic Handel
(Germany, 1685—1759)

1. Joy to the world, the Lord is come! Let earth re- ceive her King. Let ev- 'ry heart pre- pare Him room, And heav'n and na- ture sing, And heav'n and na- ture sing, And heav'n and heav'n and na- ture sing!

2. Joy to the world, the Sav- ior reigns, Let men their songs em- ploy. While fields and floods, rocks hills and plains, Re- peat the sound- ing joy, Re- peat the sound- ing joy, Re- peat, re- peat, the sound- ing joy!

Autoharp, strum C
Piano, accompaniment pattern II on each chord symbol

124

KA MATE

Maori Action Song
(New Zealand)

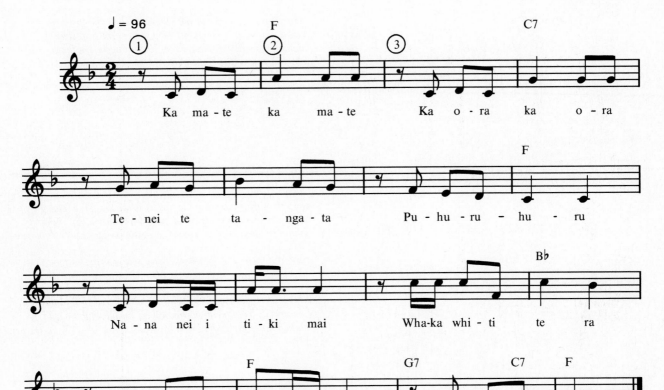

Ka ma-te ka ma-te Ka o-ra ka o-ra

Te nei te ta — nga-ta Pu-hu-ru-hu-ru

Na-na nei i ti-ki mai Wha-ka whi-ti te ra

U-pa-ne kau-pa-ne Whi-ti te ra.

Autoharp, strum C
Piano accompaniment pattern III

Pronunciation guide

a as in *a*-bout
e as in n*e*t
i as in p*i*t
u as in p*u*t
au as in *a*-bout
ei as in *ei*ght
ng as in si*ng*

Dancers form a row.

Actions: All actions are performed crisply. Perform foot movements throughout. The weight is on the left foot, while the right foot stamps the ground, the left knee bending slightly. Stamp on each beat. Keep the back straight during all movements.

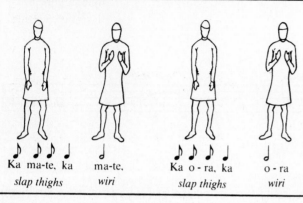

Wiri: Bend the arms at the elbow, angling the forearms slightly forward, with palms facing. Perform a quivering motion: move the wrist and palm, not the fingers. The fingers move as extensions of the quivering palm. (ma-te)

Ka ma-te, ka   ma-te,   Ka o - ra, ka   o - ra
slap thighs   *wiri*   *slap thighs*   *wiri*

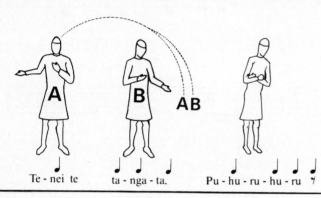

Drop the forearm so that the fingers point straight ahead. Move the hand forward and backward alternately, beginning with the right hand. (Te-nei-te ta-nga-ta)

Feet: Make a quarter turn to the left, pivoting on the left foot, stamping 4 times with the right foot (Pu-hu-ru-hu-ru)

Arms: Close the right fist; bend the elbow and bring the forearm up. Slap the forearm and the outside with the left hand 4 times, coinciding with the foot stamps (Pu-hu-ru-hu-ru)

Te - nei te   ta - nga - ta,   Pu - hu - ru - hu - ru

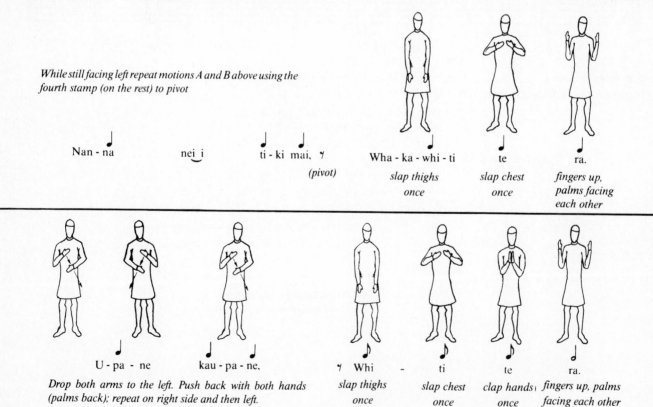

While still facing left repeat motions A and B above using the fourth stamp (on the rest) to pivot

Nan - na   nei i   ti - ki mai,   Wha - ka - whi - ti   te   ra.
             (pivot)   *slap thighs*   *slap chest*   *fingers up,*
                               once   *once*   *palms facing*
                                         each other

U - pa - ne   kau - pa - ne,   Whi - ti   te   ra.
                                  slap thighs   *slap chest*   *clap hands*   *fingers up, palms*
Drop both arms to the left. Push back with both hands   *once*   *once*   *once*   *facing each other*
(palms back); repeat on right side and then left.

126

KANG DING CITY
(Kang Ding Ching Ge)

Chinese Folk Song

Gently (♪ = 92)

Pau ma lyou, lyou de shan — shang, Yi dwo lyou, lyou de yun, Ah!
pow mah leeoh leeoh duh shahn shahng yee dwoh leeoh leeoh duh yuhn ah

Dwan, dwan lyou, lyou de jau — dzai, Kang Ding lyou, — lyou de cheng, Ah!
dwahn dwahn leeoh leeoh duh jahaoo dsigh kahng dihng leeoh leeoh duh chuhng ah

Ywe lyang, wan, — wan, — Kang Ding lyou, — lyou de cheng, Ah!
yooeh leeahng wahn wahn kahng dihng leeoh leeoh duh chuhng ah

Chromatic bells

English version
Crescent moon floating in the sky,
Silver clouds on the mountain,
Bright, bright stars in a night of calm,
Kang Ding, city of the moon, Ah!
Kang Ding! Kang Ding! shining home,
Kang Ding, city of the moon, Ah!

English version by Patricia Hackett

KISO RIVER SONG

Japanese Folk Song

Chromatic bells
Soprano recorder

English version
Kiso is fair,
Trees along the river,
Kiso to Ontake mountain.
Floating our logs,
Woodsmen work dawn to darkness,
Yoi, yoi, yoi!

English version by Patricia Hackett

128

KOOKABURRA
(Khukhabara)

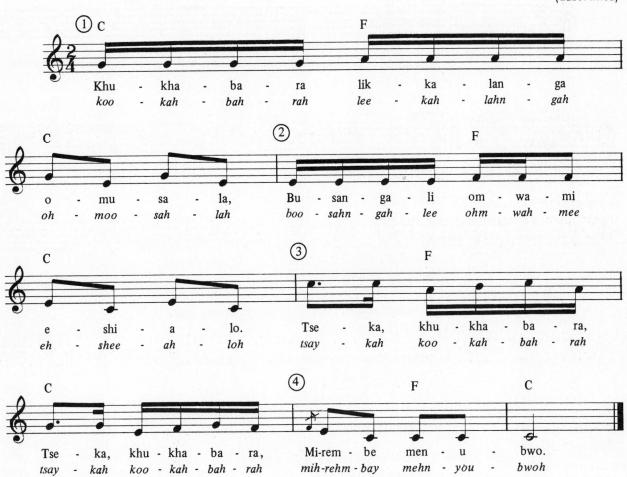

Khu - kha - ba - ra lik - ka - lan - ga
koo - kah - bah - rah lee - kah - lahn - gah

o - mu - sa - la, Bu - san - ga - li om - wa - mi
oh - moo - sah - lah boo - sahn - gah - lee ohm - wah - mee

e - shi - a - lo. Tse - ka, khu - kha - ba - ra,
eh - shee - ah - loh tsay - kah koo - kah - bah - rah

Tse - ka, khu - kha - ba - ra, Mi-rem - be men - u - bwo.
tsay - kah koo - kah - bah - rah mih-rehm - bay mehn - you - bwoh

Autoharp, strum C

English version
Kookaburra sits in the old gum tree,
Happy, happy king of the bush is he!
Laugh, kookaburra, laugh, kookaburra!
Happy your life must be!

The kookaburra is an Australian bird with a raucous cry that sits in eucalyptus trees and "laughs" noisily. The version from Kenya uses the Swahili dialect of the Luhya people (Luo tribe).

KUM-BAH-YAH

Black American Song

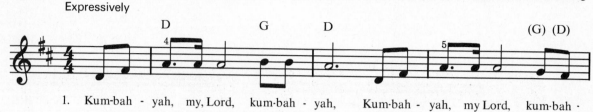

1. Kum-bah - yah, my, Lord, kum-bah - yah, Kum-bah - yah, my Lord, kum-bah -
yah, Kum-bah - yah, my Lord, kum-bah - yah, Oh, Lord,____ kum-bah - yah.

Autoharp (15-bar), strum L
Guitar, brush a steady beat or play melody
Piano, accompaniment pattern XI

2. Someone's prayin', Lord, Kum-bah-yah, *(three times)*
   Oh, Lord, kum-bah-yah.

3. Someone's singin', Lord, Kum-bah-yah, *(three times)*
   Oh, Lord, kum-bah-yah.

4. Someone's cryin', Lord, Kum-bah-yah, *(three times)*
   Oh, Lord, kum-bah-yah.

5. Someone's dancin', Lord, Kum-bah-yah, *(three times)*
   Oh, Lord, kum-bah-yah.

6. Someone's shoutin', Lord, Kum-bah-yah, *(three times)*
   Oh, Lord, kum-bah-yah.

LADY, COME

English Round

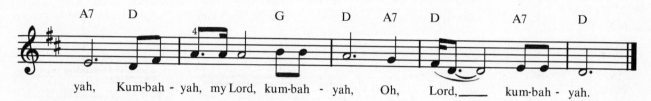

La - dy, come, can't you see?

John fell off the white oak tree.

Autoharp, strum A
Piano, accompaniment pattern XI

LA RASPA

Mexican Folk Dance

♩ = 100

The work of the day is done, And un-der the set-ting sun, The

mu - sic is bright and gay, Just hear those mu - si - cians play! Their

voic - es are sing - ing a hap - py song, This is fi - es - ta day. And

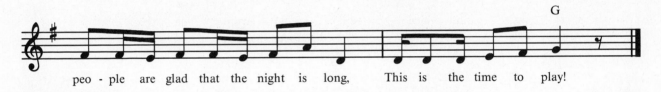

peo - ple are glad that the night is long, This is the time to play!

Chromatic bells

Formation
Form a circle with boys and girls alternating.

Dance
Hands placed on hips as the dance begins.
The following movement fits one measure; perform it four times to fit measures 1–4:

a) Hop on left foot and simultaneously extend the right foot
   forward, heel down and toe up
b) Hop on the right foot and simultaneously extend the left
   foot forward, heel down and toe up
c) Feet pause
d) Clap own hands

Measures 5-6: Partners link right elbows and skip clockwise in a circle in place.
Measures 7-8: Partners link left elbows and skip counterclockwise in a circle in place.

131

LAREDO

Mexican Folk Song

Slowly

Ya me voy, para el La - re - do, mi bien Te
yah meh voye pahrah ehl lah - reh-doh mee byehn teh

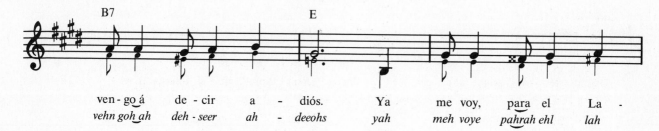

ven - go á de - cir a - diós. Ya me voy, para el La - la
vehn goh ah deh - seer ah - deeohs yah meh voye pahrah ehl lah

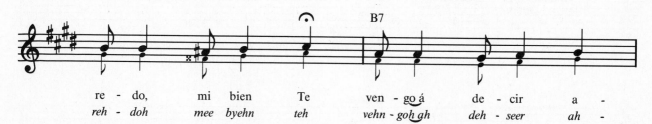

re - do, mi bien Te ven - go á de - cir a -
reh - doh mee byehn teh vehn - goh ah deh - seer ah -

diós. De a - llá te man - do de - cir, ___ mi bien, Co -
deeohs deh a - yah teh mahn-doh deh - seer ___ mee byehn coh -

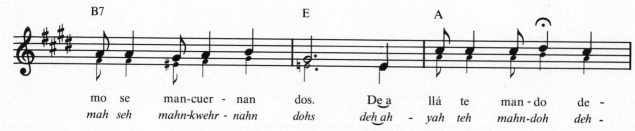

mo se man-cuer - nan dos. De a llá te man - do de -
mah seh mahn-kwehr - nahn dohs deh ah - yah teh mahn-doh deh -

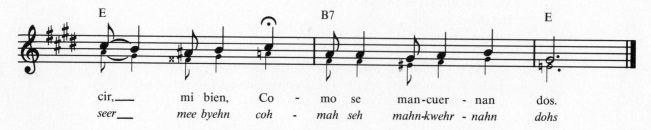

cir, ___ mi bien, Co - mo se man-cuer - nan dos.
seer ___ mee byehn coh - mah seh mahn-kwehr - nahn dohs

Guitar, strum 31

132

2. Toma esa llavita de oro, mi bien,
   tohmah ay-sah yah-vee-tah deh oh-roh mee byehn
   Abre mi pecho y verás:
   ah-breh mee peh-coh ee veh-rahs
   Lo mucho que yo te quiero, mi ben,
   loh moo-choh keh yoh teh keh kyeh-roh mee byehn
   Y el mal pago que ma dás.
   ee elh mahl pah-goh keh meh dahs

English version

1. I'm off for Laredo, farewell my love,
   I'm sorry to cause you pain;
   I promise to send a letter, my love,
   To say when we'll meet again.
   Don't follow across the prairie, my love,
   Don't follow me where I go,
   But wait till I send a message, my love,
   Till then I will miss you so.

2. I've brought you a hand-sewn saddle, my love,
   A blanket and bridle fine;
   So when you go past the bunkhouse, my love,
   The cowboys will know you're mine.
   I've brought you a key of silver, my love,
   Attached to a golden chain,
   To lock up your heart forever, my love,
   If never we meet again.

English version by Margaret Marks

Mexican folk music has special characteristics. Melodies often empasize the first and third scale tones, and are frequently harmonized in 3rds or 6ths. There is no ornamentation or improvisation. Triple meter is frequently used. A composition often begins slowly, gradually accelerating to the main body of the composition, and at the end, accelerating again. The vocal style is also distinctive, because the voice is tense and nasalized, and at a high pitch—often going into falsetto.

LIKE AS A FATHER

Luigi Cherubini
(Italy, 1760—1842)

Like as a fa - ther pi - tieth his chil - dren,
So the Lord has mer - cy, so the Lord has mer - cy,
So the Lord has mer - cy on them that fear, On them that
fear Him; Like as a fa ther pi - ti - eth,
Pi - tieth his chil - dren, The Lord has mer - cy, The Lord has
mer - cy on them that fear Him; Like as a fa - ther
pi - tieth his chil - dren, So the Lord hath mer - cy,
The Lord hath mer - cy on them that fear Him.

LITTLE BIRD
(Pateachka)

Collected by Patricia Hackett

Russian Game Song

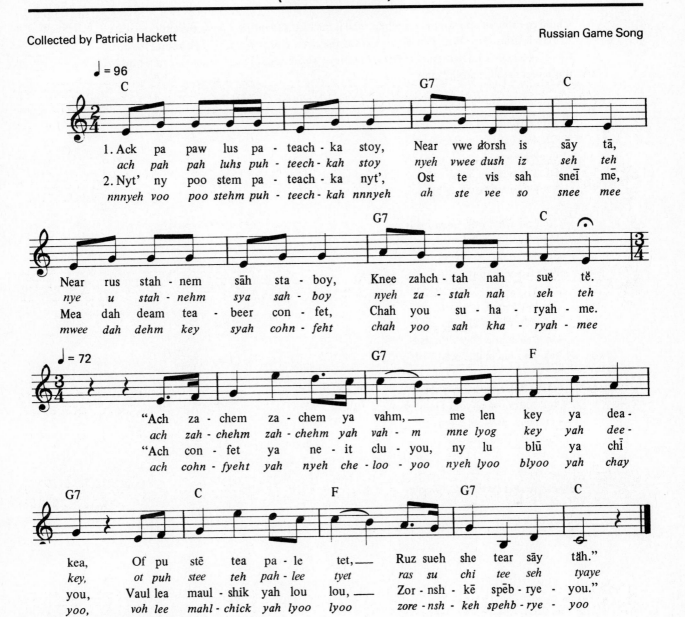

Autoharp, strums C and H
Piano, accompaniment patterns III and VII

135

Game

Children form a circle around one child, who is the bird. On the first verse, the children walk in a circle around the bird. During the refrain, the circle children stand in place and the bird faces a selected child in the circle. These two players exchange places so there is a new bird in the center for the second verse.

English version

1. Oh, Pateachka, in the net,
   Look how we have caught you!
   Oh, Pateachka, in the net,
   Look how we have caught you!

   "Tell me why, why, must I stay?
   I am small and I'm wild;
   Let me go far, far away,
   Like a free, happy child."

2. Oh, Pateachka, stay with us,
   Take our tea and candy!
   Oh, Pateachka, stay with us,
   Take our tea and candy!

   "Oh, I don't want any sweets,
   And I don't want your tea!
   Let me go now, set me free,
   As a wild bird must be!"

English version by Patricia Hackett

LITTLE DONKEY
(Shau Mau Lyu)

Taiwan Children's Song

Lively (♩ = 112)

Wo you yi jr syau mau lyu, wo tsung lai ye bu chi,
woh you ee jer ssyow mahoo leeoo woe tssong lye yay boo chee

You yi tyan wo syin sye lai chau chi je chyu gan ji, Wo
yo ee tyehn woh seeihn syey lye chaoo chee juh chuh gahn jee woh

shou li na je syau pi byan Wo syin li jen de yi,
show lee nah juh sheeaou pee byahn woh sshihn lee jehn deh yee

Bu jr dzen me, hwa la la la la, wo shwai le yi shen ni.
boo jer tzuhn muh hwah lah lah lah lah woh shwye luh yee shuhn nee

Autoharp, strum E
Chromatic bells

English Version
Walking, walking by my side, A donkey, grey and brown;
Riding, riding, on his back, I'm going into town.
He's running, running, crazy brute: Be careful, or I'm downed;
Falling, falling, *Hwa la la la la*, I'm dumped onto the ground!

English version by Patricia Hackett

Traditional Chinese performance styles continue on Taiwan, as well as in Chinese-American communities in the United States. On mainland China many old folk tunes are used in choral settings, with new texts promoting national values. This extramusical function for music is at least as ancient as Confucius (500 B.C.). Chinese music has long been valued as a vehicle for social and political education, but enjoyed for its programmatic and allegorical qualities.

LONDON BRIDGE

Children's Game Song

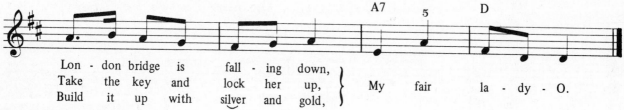

1. Lon - don bridge is fall - ing down, fall - ing down, fall - ing down,
2. Take the key and lock her up, lock her up, lock her up,
3. Build it up with silver and gold, silver and gold, silver and gold,

Lon - don bridge is fall - ing down,
Take the key and lock her up,   } My fair la - dy - O.
Build it up with silver and gold,

Autoharp (15-bar), strum E
Guitar, strum 4 or 5
Piano, accompaniment pattern III

Formation

Two players face each other, join hands, and raise their arms to form a bridge (arch). One player represents gold, the other, silver. Remaining players make a line, each placing arms on the waist or shoulders of the person ahead.

Game

As they sing verse 1, players in line walk under the bridge. On the words "lady-O" the bridge is lowered over the player underneath.

During verse 2 the players forming the bridge sway gently from side to side, arms encricling their captive.

During verse 3 there is a whispered conference in which the captive chooses silver or gold, and goes to stand behind the player representing this choice.

The song and game repeat until all players are captured. A tug-of-war is the traditional conclusion to the game, and it determines the victorious group.

A LONDONDERRY AIR

Words by Thomas Moore
(Ireland, 1779—1852)

Irish Folk Melody

Freely (♩ = 56-60)

My gen-tle harp, once more I __ wak-en The sweet-ness of thy slum-b'ring __

strain, __ In tears our last fare-well __ was __ tak-en, And now __ in __

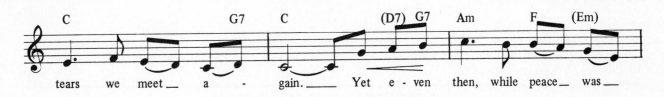

tears we meet __ a - gain. __ Yet e-ven then, while peace __ was __

sing-ing Her hal-cyon song o'er land __ and __ sea, __ Through joy and

hope to oth-ers __ bring-ing, She on-ly brought __ new __ tears __ to __ thee. __

Autoharp (15-bar), free strum
Piano, accompaniment pattern XI on each chord change

Danny Boy Text

1. Oh, Danny Boy, the pipes, the pipes are calling,
   From glen to glen, and down the mountain side;
   The summer's gone, and all the roses falling;
   It's you, it's you must go and I must bide.

   But come ye back when summer's in the meadow,
   Or when the valley's hushed and white with snow; __
   It's I'll be there in sunshine or in shadow,
   Oh, Danny Boy, Oh, Danny Boy, I love you so.

2. But come ye back when all the flow'rs are dyin',
   If I am dead, as dead I well may be,
   Ye'll come and find the place where I am lyin,
   And kneel and say an Ave Verum for me.

   And I shall hear, tho' soft you tread above me,
   And all my grave will warmer, sweeter be, __
   For you will bend and tell me that you love me,
   And I shall sleep in peace until you come to me.

LONDON'S BURNING

Traditional Round

① *Call:* Lon-don's burn-ing, *Response:* Lon-don's burn-ing, *Call:* Look out! *Response:* Look-out! ②

③ *Call:* Fire! Fire! *Response:* Fire! Fire! *Call:* Pour on wa-ter, *Response:* Pour on wa-ter!

Chromatic bells

LONESOME ROAD

American Folk Song

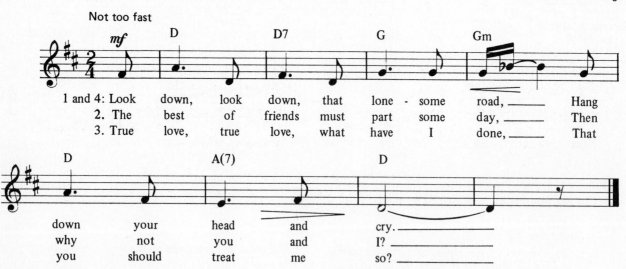

Not too fast

| D | D7 | G | Gm |

1 and 4: Look down, look down, that lone - some road, _____ Hang
2. The best of friends must part some day, _____ Then
3. True love, true love, what have I done, _____ That

| D | A(7) | D |

down your head and cry. _____
why not you and I? _____
you should treat me so? _____

Autoharp (15-bar), strum C
Guitar, strum 2 or 10
Piano, accompaniment pattern V

LOOBY LOU

Children's Game Song

Refrain:

Here we go loo - by loo, _____ here we go loo - by light, _____

Here we go loo - by loo, _____ all on a Sat - ur - day night. _____

Verse:

1. I put my right hand in, _____ I take my right hand out; _____ I

give my right hand a shake, shake, shake! And turn my self a - bout! _____

Guitar, strum 36

2. I put my left hand in, I take my left hand out,
   I give my left hand a shake, shake, shake,
   And turn myself about!

3. I put my right foot in, I take my right foot out,
   I give my right foot a shake, shake, shake,
   And turn myself about!

4. I put my left foot in, I take my left foot out,
   I give my left foot a shake, shake, shake,
   And turn myself about!

5. I put by big head in, I take my big head out,
   I give my big head a shake, shake, shake,
   And turn myself about!

6. I put my whole self in, I take my whole self out,
   I give my whole self a shake, shake, shake,
   And turn myself about!

Dance

Form a circle and join hands.

During the refrain dancers skip around the circle, stopping when the verse begins, and drop hands.

On each verse dancers pantomime the actions indicated by the lyrics. For example, on "I put my right hand in" dancers hold their right hands toward the center of the circle and shake them several times during "shake, shake, shake." After turning around in place, dancers join hands and prepare to skip once again in a circle.

141

LOST MY GOLD RING

Game Song
(Jamaica)

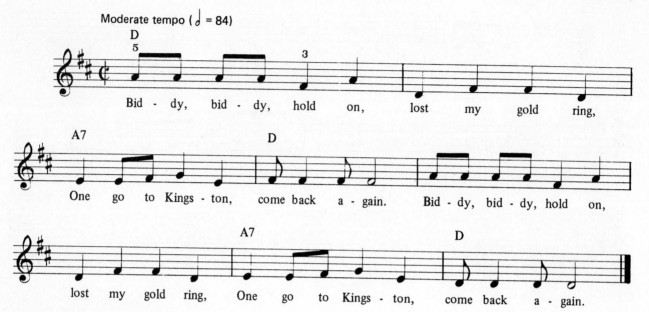

Autoharp (15-bar), strum A
Piano, accompany using chord roots

Formation
Players stand in a circle. Each player's hands are held cupped together at waist level. A hider (called master) stands in the center of the circle, and a guesser outside the circle.

Game
The master goes from player to player with hands cupped, concealing a gold ring. The guesser moves around the outside of the circle, following the master from player to player. The master pretends to pass the ring to each player, and at some point does so. If the guesser correctly discovers who has received the ring, the player holding the ring becomes the new guesser, and the guesser becomes the master.

LOVELY EVENING

German Round

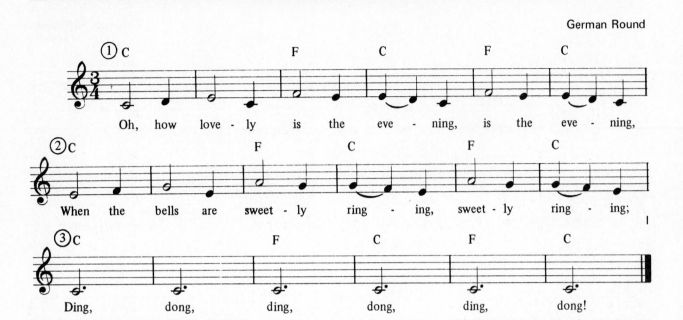

① C   F   C   F   C

Oh, how love - ly is the eve - ning, is the eve - ning,

② C   F   C   F   C

When the bells are sweet - ly ring - ing, sweet - ly ring - ing;

③ C   F   C   F   C

Ding, dong, ding, dong, ding, dong!

Autoharp, strum H
Guitar, strum 16
Piano, accompaniment pattern VIII

German version
O wie wohl ist mir am Abend, mir am abend,
oh vee vohl ihst meer ahm ah-bend meer ahm ah-bend

Wenn zur Ruh die Glocken läuten, Glocken läuten;
vehn tsoor roo dee gloh-kehn loy-ten gloh-kehn loy-ten

Bim, bam, bim, bam, bim, bam!

Spanish version
Fray Martin al campanario, campanario,
fray mer-teen ahl cahm-pah-nah-ree-oh cahm-pah-nah-ree-oh

Subey toca, la campana, la campana,
soo-beh-ee toh-cah lah-cahm-pah-nah lah-cahm-pah-nah

Tan, tan, tan, tan, tan, tan!
tahn tahn tahn tahn tahn tahn

LOVE SOMEBODY

American Folk Song

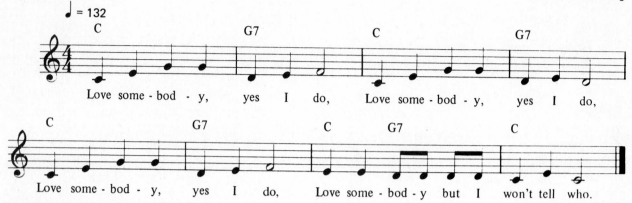

Autoharp, strum O
Piano, accompaniment pattern XII

LULLABY
(Abiyoyo)

African Folk Song

LULLABY
(Nen, Nen)

Japanese Folk Song

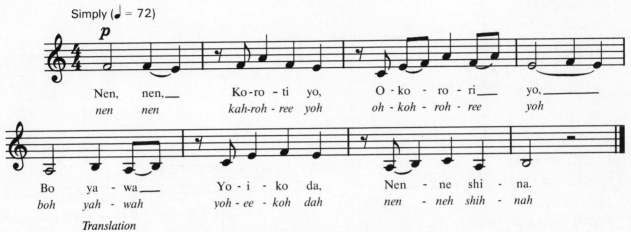

Simply (♩ = 72)

p

Nen, nen,___ Ko - ro - ti yo, O - ko - ro - ri___ yo,___
nen nen *kah-roh - ree yoh* *oh - koh - roh - ree* *yoh*

Bo ya - wa___ Yo - i - ko da, Nen - ne shi - na.
boh yah - wah *yoh - ee - koh dah* *nen - neh shih - nah*

Translation

Hush and go to sleep, my good child. Your nurse has gone, and now I keep watch.

MARY HAD A BABY

Black American Spiritual

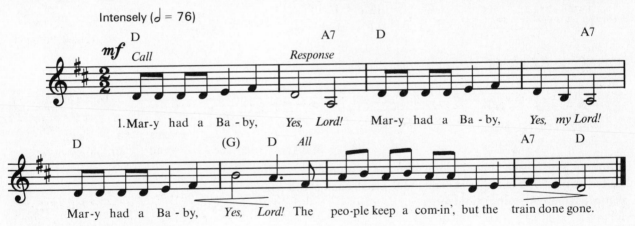

Intensely (♩ = 76)

D   A7   D   A7

mf *Call*   *Response*

1. Mar-y had a Ba - by, *Yes, Lord!* Mar-y had a Ba - by, *Yes, my Lord!*

D   (G)   D *All*   A7   D

Mar-y had a Ba - by, *Yes, Lord!* The peo-ple keep a com-in', but the train done gone.

Guitar, strum 4 or play melody
Piano, accompaniment pattern XVII

2. Where was He born? *Yes, Lord!* *(three times)*
The people keep a-comin', but the <u>train</u> done <u>gone</u>.

3. <u>Born</u> in a manger, *Yes, <u>Lord</u>!* *(three times)*
The people keep a-comin', but the <u>train</u> done <u>gone</u>.

4. <u>What</u> you gonna call Him? *Yes, <u>Lord</u>!* *(three times)*
The people keep a-comin', but the <u>train</u> done <u>gone</u>.

5. <u>Call</u> Him King Jesus, *Yes, <u>Lord</u>!* *(three times)*
The people keep a-comin', but the <u>train</u> done <u>gone</u>.

MATTHEW, MARK, LUKE AND JOHN

Elizabethan Folk Song (England)

1. Mat - thew, — Mark, and — Luke — and — John, — Bless'd the — bed — that —
2. God is the branch and — I — the — flow'r, — Pray God, — send — me a

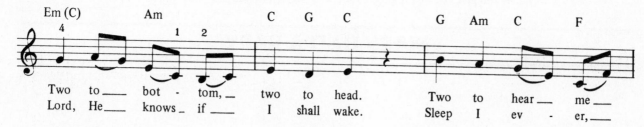

I lie — on. Four — an - gels — to — my — bed; —
bless - ed — hour. I go to bed, some — sleep — to — take; The

Two to — bot - tom, — two to head. Two to hear — me —
Lord, He — knows — if — I shall wake. Sleep I ev - er, —

when I pray, Two to bear — my — sins a - way.
sleep I never; God re - ceive — my — soul for - ev - er.

Autoharp, brush each chord change with pad of thumb
Guitar, strum 27; beginning at measure 8, brush each chord change
Piano, accompany using chord roots

MAYO NAFWA

African Folk Song
(Zambia)

African musicians are renowned for their metronomic sense, their ability to maintain a beat and tempo through performance. The beats may be accented regularly—ONE, two, three, ONE, two, three—but African music often moves in irregular meters, as in "Mayo Nafwa": ONE, two, ONE, two. ONE, two, three, ONE, two, three, ONE, two, ONE, two. "Mayo Nafwa" incorporates many other traits of African musical style: a single melodic phrase is repeated again and again; the phrase descends through a wide range; it ends on the lowest sung tone. "Mayo Nafwa" is sung by a group, responding to a leader's call; the group often sings in harmony. The Bemba people sing this song about a child who has lost his mother. The singers ask what they can do to help the child.

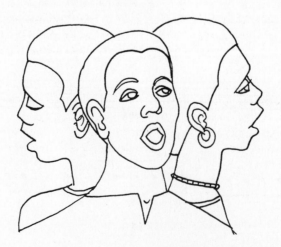

MEAN OLD BEDBUG BLUES

Transcribed by Patricia Hackett

As sung by Bessie Smith
(United States, 1894—1937)

1. Yes, bed-bug sure is e-vil,— they don't mean me no good; —
2. When I lay down at night, — I wonder how can a poor gal sleep; —
3. Bedbug's as big as a jack-ass,— will bite you and stand and grin; —

Yes, bed-bug sure is e-vil,— they don't mean me no good; —
When I lay down at night, — I wonder how can a poor gal sleep; —
Bedbug's as big as a jack-ass, — will bite you and stand and grin; —

Thinks he's a wood-peck-er and I'm — a chunk of wood. —
When some is holdin' my hand, oth-er's eat-in' my feet. —
Will drink all the bed bug poi-son, turn a-round and bite you a gain. —

Guitar, strum 10

Blues allow thoughts to be sung that could never be spoken—hence the graphic language of many lyrics. Blues are solo songs in which the first phrase is repeated twice (or three times) and concluded by a different phrase. AAB, AAAB, and AB schemes are heard. Each phrase is twelve beats (four bars) long. Blues are not call-and-response music; but because a sung phrase often pauses after six or eight beats, there is a space (of four to six beats) that is filled by instrumental improvisation. Early blues were self-accompanied solos, often with guitar.

The legendary Bessie Smith was known in her lifetime as the "Empress of the Blues." Tall and handsome, she rose from grinding Southern poverty to become America's greatest blues artist. Her voice was full of throaty, expressive coloration, always "bending" the rhythm and the pitch.

The blues can hardly be captured in musical notation as they express their poignant themes—exorcizing pain in the face of hard times or injustice.

MERRILY WE ROLL ALONG

Traditional Song

Mer - ri - ly we roll a - long, Roll a - long, roll a - long,

Mer - ri - ly we roll a - long, O'er the deep blue sea.

Autoharp, strum D
Piano, accompaniment pattern II

MERRY CHRISTMAS ROUND

Composer unknown

Joyfully

Mer - ry Christ-mas to you all, with a bright and cheer-ful call, __ Mer - ry

Christ-mas to you all, with a bright and cheer-ful call. Heigh oh, _____ Let it

ring, an ech - o bring. Heigh oh, _____ Mer - ry Christ-mas to you all, with a

bright and cheer-ful call, _ Mer - ry Christ-mas to you all, with a bright and cheer - ful

call. Heigh oh, _____ Let it ring, an ech - o bring. Heigh oh. _____

150

MEXICAN HAT DANCE
(El Jarabe)

Mexican Dance Melody

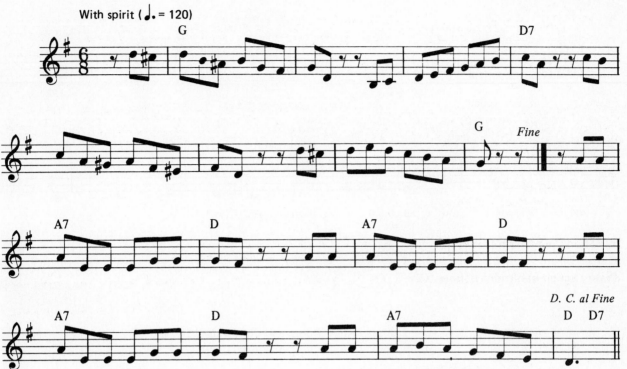

Autoharp (15-bar), strum S
Chromatic bells

The jarabe is one of the oldest Mexican folk dances. Apparently of Spanish derivation, it enacts a man's pursuit of an elusive female. The "Mexican Hat Dance" above is only that portion in which the woman dances around the sombrero of her partner.

MICHAEL, ROW THE BOAT ASHORE

Black American Spiritual

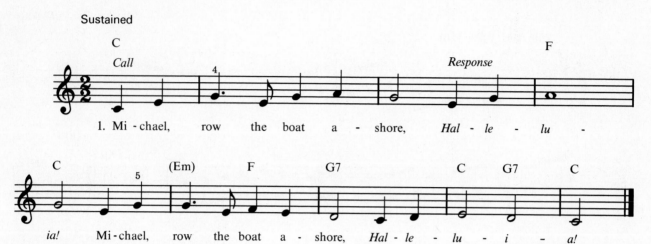

Autoharp, play melody rhythm
Guitar, strum 22 or 27
Piano, accompaniment pattern XIII

2. Jordan River is deep and wide, *Halleluia!*
   Jordan River is deep and wide, *Halleluia!*

3. Gabriel, blow the trumpet horn, *Halleluia!*
   Gabriel, blow the trumpet horn, *Halleluia!*

4. Trumpet sounds the world around, *Halleluia!*
   Trumpet sounds the world around, *Halleluia!*

5. Michael, haul the boat ashore, *Halleluia!*
   Michael, haul the boat ashore, *Halleluia!*

MISS MARY MACK

Black American Play Song

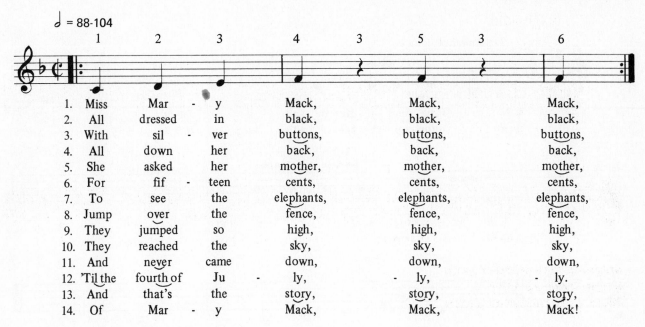

♩ = 88-104

1	2	3	4	3	5	3	6

1. Miss Mar - y Mack, Mack, Mack,
2. All dressed in black, black, black,
3. With sil - ver buttons, buttons, buttons,
4. All down her back, back, back,
5. She asked her mother, mother, mother,
6. For fif - teen cents, cents, cents,
7. To see the elephants, elephants, elephants,
8. Jump over the fence, fence, fence,
9. They jumped so high, high, high,
10. They reached the sky, sky, sky,
11. And never came down, down, down,
12. 'Til the fourth of Ju - ly, - ly, - ly.
13. And that's the story, story, story,
14. Of Mar - y Mack, Mack, Mack!

Motions for each beat

1. Cross own hands across chest, hit own shoulders.
2. Slap thighs.
3. Clap own hands.
4. Clap partner's right hand.
5. Clap partner's left hand.
6. Clap both partner's hands.

MISTER FROG WENT A-COURTIN'

Anglo-American Ballad

Autoharp (15-bar), one strum each measure (drone, Dmaj and Dm)
Guitar, strum 2

3. He said, "Miss Mouse are you within?" Um-hm! Um-hm!
   He said, "Miss Mouse are you within?"
   "Yes, Sir, here I sit and spin," Um-hm! Um-hm!

4. He took Miss Mouse upon his knee, Um-hm! Um-hm!
   He took Miss Mouse upon his knee,
   Said, "Miss Mouse, will you marry me?" Um-hm! Um-hm!

5. She said "I cannot tell you, Sir," Um-hm! Um-hm!
   She said "I cannot tell you, Sir,"
   Till my Uncle Rat comes home, Um-hm! Um-hm!

6. So Uncle Rat gave his consent, Um-hm! Um-hm!
   So Uncle Rat gave his consent,
   And made a handsome settlement, Um-hm! Um-hm!

7. Then Uncle Rat, he went to town, Um-hm! Um-hm!
   Then Uncle Rat, he went to town,
   To buy Miss Mouse a wedding gown, Um-hm! Um-hm!

8. Oh, where will the wedding supper be? Um-hm! Um-hm!
   Oh, where will the wedding supper be?
   Away down yonder in a hollow tree, Um-hm! Um-hm!

9. The first to come was a little bee, Um-hm! Um-hm!
   The first to come was a little bee,
   He carried a Bible on his knee, Um-hm! Um-hm!

10. The next to come was a little white moth, Um-hm! Um-hm!
    The next to come was a little white moth,
    She spread out the tablecloth, Um-hm! Um-hm!

11. The next to come was a great big snail, Um-hm! Um-hm!
    The next to come was a great big snail,
    Carried a fiddle on his tail, Um-hm! Um-hm!

12. Mister Frog came swimming across the lake, Um-hm! Um-hm!
    Mister Frog came swimming across the lake,
    He got swallowed up by a big black snake, Um-hm! Um-hm!

13. There's bread and cheese upon the shelf, Um-hm! Um-hm!
    There's bread and cheese upon the shelf,
    If you want any more you can sing it yourself, Um-hm! Um-hm!

In English speaking lands, songs of the nursery are often related to the ballad tradition. The marriage of frog and mouse is a narrative folk song from the reign of Elizabeth I, originally a biting satire which made use of the Queen's habit of referring to her ministers by animal nicknames. After losing its popularity and timeliness, modified versions of "Mister Frog Went a-Courtin'" joined other tunes in the nursery. It resides there with many animal tales and fables, as well as songs about once current events. Children continue to sing counting-out songs and games: ancient rituals re-enacted, with their ceremonial texts now tangled and garbled, the original meanings obscured or forgotten in naïve transformations.

MISTER SUN

Traditional American Song

With an easy swing

Oh, Mis - ter Sun, Sun, Mis - ter Gold - en Sun,

Please shine down on me. Oh, Mis - ter Sun, Sun,

Mis - ter Gold - en Sun, Hid - ing be - hind a tree.

These lit - tle chil - dren are ask - ing you To

please come out so we can play with you. Oh, Mis - ter Sun, Sun,

Mis - ter Gold - en Sun Please shine down on me.____

Autoharp, strum G (banjo)
Piano, accompaniment pattern XVI

*Perform this song three times. The first two times, the melody is performed as written. The last time, the second-to-last measure is sung three times before going on to the final measure.

Invent a pantomime to depict the song's words.

MISTY

Johnny Burke
(United States, 1908—1964)

Errol Garner
(United States, 1921—1977)

Look at me, I'm as help-less as a kit-ten up a
way and a thou-sand vi-o-lins be-gin to

tree, ___ And I feel like I'm cling-ing to a cloud, I can't ___ un-der-stand, ___ I get
play, ___ Or it might be the sound of your "hel-lo," That mu - sic I hear ___ I get

mist - y just hold - ing your hand. ___ Walk my
mist - y the mo - ment you're

near. You can say that you're lead - ing me on, ___ but it's just what I want you to do, ___ Don't you no - tice how

hope-less - ly I'm lost, That's why I'm fol - low - ing you. ___ On my

own would I wan - der through this won - der - land a - lone? ___ Nev - er know - ing my

right foot from my left, my hat — from my glove? — I'm too mist - y and too much in

love. _____ I'm just too mist - y, _____ and too much in love. _____

MOON REFLECTIONS
(Kojo Notsuki)

Doi Bansui
(Japan)

Taki Lentaru
(Japan)

♩ = 100

Am ... **Dm** ... **E7**

Ha - ru ko - ro - no,   Ha na no - en,
hah - roo koh - roh - noh   hah nah no - ehn

Am ... **Dm** ... **E7** ... **Am**

Me - gu - ru - sa   ka - zu - ki,   Ka - ge - sa - shi - ta.
meh - goo - roo - sah   kah - zoo - kee   kah - gay - sah - shee - tah

p ... **Dm** ... **E7** ... **Dm** ... **E7**

Chi - yo - no ma - tsu - ga - e,   Wa - ke i - de - shi,
chee - yoh - noh mah - tsoo - gah - aye   wah - kay ee - deh - shee

Am ... **Dm** ... **E7** ... **Am**

Mu - ka shi - no hi - ka - ri,   I - ma i - zu - ko.
moo - kah shee - noh hee - kah - ree   ee - mah ee - zoo - koh

Autoharp, strum A (use only upper and middle octave strings, brushed from high to low)
Guitar, strum 27

English version
Branches sway, moon shines, Blossoms twist and climb,
'Round an ancient castle wall, Where we pause tonight.
Ghostly rays slant through the trees, Shadows float and glide.
As we raise our cups to drink, Look! the moon inside!

English version by Patricia Hackett

MORNING HAS BROKEN

Eleanor Farjeon
(United States, 1881—1965)

Welsh Melody

With movement

1. Morn - ing has bro - ken Like the first morn - ing, Black-bird has
2. Sweet the rain's new fall, Sun - lit from heav - en, Like the first
3. Mine is the sun light! Mine is the morn - ing, Born of the

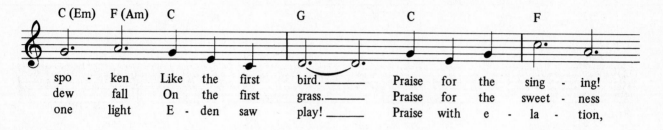

spo - ken Like the first bird._____ Praise for the sing - ing!
dew fall On the first grass._____ Praise for the sweet - ness
one light E - den saw play! _____ Praise with e - la - tion,

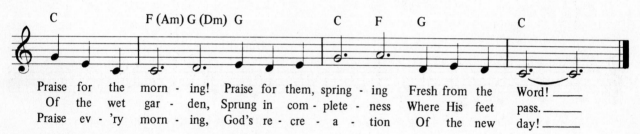

Praise for the morn - ing! Praise for them, spring - ing Fresh from the Word! _____
Of the wet gar - den, Sprung in com - plete - ness Where His feet pass._____
Praise ev - 'ry morn - ing, God's re - cre - a - tion Of the new day!_____

Autoharp, strum three steady beats each measure
Guitar, strum 16
Piano, accompany using chord roots

MORNING SONG
(Las Mañanitas)

Mexican Folk Song

♩ = 84

E

1. Es – tas son las ma – ña – ni – tas, Que can –
ehs – tahs sohn lahs mah-nyah – nee – tahs keh cahn –

B7

E   **A**   **E**

ta ba el Rey Da – vid, A las mu – cha – chas bo –
tah bah ehl roy dah – veed ah lahs moo – chah – chahs boh –

B7   **E** **A** **B7** **E**   *Refrain*

ni – tas Se las can – ta – mos a – quí. Des –
nee – tahs seh lahs cahn – tah – mohs ah – kee dehs –

B7   **E**   **A7**   **E**

pier – ta, mi bien, des – pier – ta Mi – ra que ya a man – ne – ció; Ya los
pyehr – tah mee byehn dehs – pyehr – tah mee – rah keh yah ah mahn-nah – seeohs yah lohs

A   **E**   **E A B7 E**

pa – ja – ri – llos can – tan, La lu – na ya se me – tió.
pah – hah – ree – yohs cahn – yahn lah loo – nah yah seh meh – tyeeoh

Mexican-Americans often sing "Las Mananitas" for birthday celebrations.

Chromatic bells
Guitar, strum 15

161

2. Si el sereno de la esquina
   Me quisiera hacer favor,
   De apagar su linternita
   Mientras que baja mi amor. *(Refrain)*

3. Ahora si, señor sereno
   Le agredezco su favor,
   Encienda su liternita
   Que ya ha bajado mi amor. *(Refrain)*

English version
   Hear us sing *las mañanitas*,
   As the morning light appears,
   And the gentle bird will join
   In the happy music he hears.
   Oh, wake up and see the sunshine,
   Oh, wake up and meet the day,
   Hear, the morning bird is singing,
   The silver moon's gone away.

English version by Lupe Allegria

Pre-Hispanic music of Mexico was always associated with ritual and ceremony, and was a communal expression rather than an individual one. Instrumental performance was always combined with singing, and certain instruments (such as the four-hole flute) were thought to have supernatural powers. The defeat of the Aztec chief Cuauhtemoc by Cortez (1521) marked the end of the pre-Hispanic period.

The arrival of the Spaniards profoundly changed music in Mexico. During the colonial period (1521—1810) music was used to help convert the people to Christianity. Very soon, European musical instruments and music education were introduced. During this period, Mexican composers wrote much religious music based on European models.

After independence from Spain in 1810, music in Mexico was still influenced by European music—particularly Italian opera. Composers such as Tomás Leon (1826—93) adapted European techniques and forms. However, in the 20th century, Carlos Chávez (1899—1978) and other composers have developed a classical style deeply rooted in Mexican folk music.

MY DANCING DAY

English Carol

With movement (♩. = 76)

1. To - mor - row shall be ___ my danc - ing day: I
2. Then was ___ I born of a vir - gin pure, Of
3. In a man - ger laid ___ and wrapped ___ I was, So
4. Then af - ter - wards ___ bap - tized ___ I was; The

would ___ my true ___ love did ___ so chance To ___ see the
her ___ I ___ took flesh - ly sub - stance; Thus ___ was I
ver - y poor ___ this was ___ my chance, Be - twixt an
Ho - ly Ghost ___ on me ___ did glance, My ___ Fa - ther's

leg - end of ___ my play,
knit to man's ___ na - ture,   } To call my true ___ love
ox and a sil - ly poor ass,
voice heard from ___ a - bove,

to ___ my dance: Sing O my ___ love, O ___ my love, my

love, my love; This have I done ___ for my ___ true love.

Autoharp (15-bar), one strum each measure
Guitar, strum 13

As we know it today, the carol is a joyful yet reverent song celebrating Christmas. But the carol was originally secular (probably the circle dance song popular in Europe during the Middle Ages), with profane texts describing love, politics, hunting, drinking, and the like. In the fifteenth century, religious reformers took these lively, rhythmic carol melodies and supplied them with pious texts—perhaps jealous that the devil seemed to have all the good tunes. Each stanza unfolded the story of Christmas or of other holy days. Early carols included a refrain, which sometimes resisted change by retaining its worldly text, as in "My Dancing Day." Sadly, these merry songs were soon suppressed altogether by dour Puritans and have only been rediscovered in this century.

MY NIPA HOME
(Bahay Kubo)

Philippine Folk Song

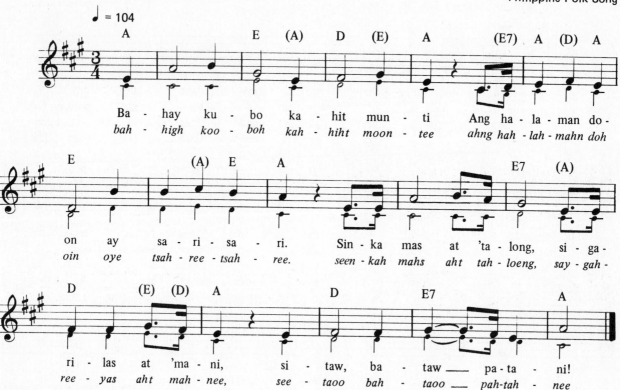

Ba - hay ku - bo ka - hit mun - ti Ang ha - la - man do -
bah - high koo - boh kah - hiht moon - tee ahng hah - lah - mahn doh

on ay sa - ri - sa - ri. Sin - ka mas at 'ta - long, si - ga -
oin oye tsah - ree - tsah - ree. seen - kah mahs aht tah - loeng, say - gah -

ri - las at 'ma - ni, si - taw, ba - taw ___ pa - ta - ni!
ree - yas aht mah - nee, see - taoo bah - taoo ___ pah - tah - nee

Guitar, strum 16
Piano, accompaniment pattern VII

The people of the Philippines have been in contact with Spanish culture for more than 300 years, and today nearly all of their music reflects this Iberian influence. Guitars, pianos, and ensembles of steel strings (rondella) play Philippine folk melodies with harmonies and rhythms borrowed from the music of western Europe. "Bahay Kubo" for example, uses the major chords and triple meter of Spanish music, yet it is considered a typical Philippine folk song. In contrast, there are Moslem peoples in the southern Philippine Islands who retain a distinctive, florid song style, along with ensembles of flutes, zithers, and gongs which resemble Indonesian orchestras. In a few mountain regions, isolated groups still preserve a folk music that has origins in remote and ancient hills of the Malaysian mainland.

English version

My nipa home is very small,
But it houses the foods that I grow, one and all.
There is room for the beans, for the corn, and the rice,
And lots of coconut, too!

English version by Patricia Hackett

164

MY WHITE HORSE
(Mi Caballo Blanco)

Words and Music by
Francisco Flores del Campo
(Chile)

Es mi caballo blan - co, com - o un a - man - e - cer.
ehs mee cah - bahl - yoh blahn - coh coh - mo oon ah - mahn - eh - sare

Siem - pre jun - ti - tos va - mos, es mi a - mi - go mas fi - el.
Syem - pray hoon - tee - tohs bah - mohs ehs mee ah - mee - goh mahs fy - ehl

Mi ca - ba - llo, mi ca - ba - llo, se va y se va.
mee cah - bahl - yoh mee cah - bahl - yoh say bah ee say bah

Mi ca - ba - llo, mi ca - ba - llo, se va y se va.
mee cah - bahl - yoh mee cah - bahl - yoh sah bah ee say bah

Ah, ah, ah, ah.

Ah, ah, ah, ah.

Autoharp (21-bar), strum H
Guitar, strum 16
Piano, accompaniment pattern VII

English version
My horse is like the sunrise, My horse is white as dawn.
We always ride together Singing as we ride along.
___ Mi caballo, ___ mi caballo, He's galloping on,
___ Mi caballo, ___ mi caballo, into the dawn.
Ah!   —   —   —
Ah!   —   —   —

English version by Samuele Maqui

Most Latin American folk music shows the influence of Spain and Portugal. Although there are places where African influences dominate—and in remote regions of the Andes or Upper Amazon the music is strongly Indian—nearly everywhere in Latin America there are hybrid styles: mestizo *(Native American and Spanish),* mulato *(African and European)* and zambo *(African and Native American).* Pre-Hispanic flutes and panpipes are still played in Bolivia, Chile, Ecuador, and Peru, and indigenous Indian dances have been woven into Christian celebrations. Afro-Hispanic music, with its intense, percussive rhythms, permeates life in parts of Brazil, Colombia, and Venezuela. But nearly everywhere in Latin America, Hispanic musical traits tend to dominate. Guitars, violins, and harps accompany melodies which are sometimes harmonized in the parallel thirds of Portugal.

NAVAHO RIDING SONG

Native American Song

Chromatic bells

NOBODY'S BIS'NESS

Caribbean Folk Song (Virgin Islands)

With an easy swing ($\quarternote$ = 92)

No - bod - y's bis-'ness if I do or if I don't, No - bod-y's bis-'ness but my

own. If no-bod-y's with me I can go it all a-lone, No-bod-y's bis-'ness but my

own. *Refrain:* When you've got it all the world is with you, When it's gone you're all a-lone,

1. No - bod - y's bis-'ness but my own.

2. No - bod - y's bis-'ness but my own.

Autoharp, strum P (verse) and L (refrain measure 9)
Piano, accompaniment pattern XV
Chromatic bells

NURSERY SONG

Collected by Patricia Hackett

Simply (♩ = 100)

Yang wa ____ wa   Syan syi ____ syi
yahng wah wah   ssyow ssyee ssyee

Yu le yi ge yang wa ____ wa.
you luh ee guh yahng wah wah

Ni tsung na li lai,   Ni wang na li chu.
nee tssong nah lee lye   nee wahng nah lee choo

Yu le yi ge yang wa ____ wa.
you luh ee guh yahng wah wah

English version
Smiling doll, smiling doll,
Yes, I have a smiling doll.
Tell me where you're from,
Tell me where you go.
Yes, I have a smiling doll.

O CHRISTMAS TREE
(O Tannenbaum)

Traditional German Carol

Moderately

O Tan - nen-baum, O Tan - nen-baum, Wie treu sind dei - ne
oh tah - nehn-baoom oh tah - nehn-baoom vee troy zihndt die - nuh

Blät - ter! O Tan - nen-baum, O Tan - nen-baum, Wie
blay - tehr oh tah - nehn baoom oh tah - nehn - baoom vee

treu sind dei - ne Blät - ter! Du grünst nicht nur zur
troy zihdt die - nuh blay - tehr doo groonst nihkt noor tzoor

Som - mer - zeit, Nein, auch im Win - ter wenn es schneit. O
zuhm - mehr - zite nine aook ihm vihn - tehr vehn ehs shnite oh

Tan - nen-baum, O Tan - nen-baum, Wie treu sind dei - ne Blät - ter!
tah - nehn-baoom oh tah - nehn-baoom vee troy zihndt die - nuh blay - tehr

Autoharp, strum H

English version
O Christmas tree, O Christmas tree,
With faithful leaves unchanging;
O Christmas tree, O Christmas tree,
With faithful leaves unchanging.
Not only green in summer's heat,
But also winter's snow and sleet,
O Christmas tree, O Christmas tree,
With faithful leaves unchanging;

O COME, ALL YE FAITHFUL
(Adeste Fideles)

Attributed to John F. Wade
(England, 18th century)

Autoharp, play melody rhythm
Soprano recorder

Latin lyrics and pronunciation
Adeste, fideles, laeti triumphantes,
uh-dehs-teh fee-deh-lehs lay-tee tree-oom-phan-tehs
Venite, venite in Bethlehem!
veh-nee-teh veh-nee-teh een beth-leh-hehm
Natum videte, Regem Angelorum,
nah-toom vee-deh-teh reh-jehm ahn-jeh-loh-ruhm
Venite, adoremus! Venite adoremus!
veh-nee-teh ah-doh-reh-moos veh-nee-teh ah-doh-reh-moos
Venite adoremus Dominum.
veh-nee-teh ah-doh-reh-moos doh-mee-noom

171

O COME, O COME EMMANUEL

Adapted by Thomas Helmore
(England, 1811—1890)

1. O come, O come, Em - man - u - el, And ran - som cap - tive Is - ra - el, That mourns in lone - ly ex - ile here Un -
2. O come, Thou Wis - dom from on high, And or - der all things far and nigh; To us the path of knowl - edge show, And
3. O come, De - sire of na - tions, bind All peo - ples in one heart and mind; Bid en - vy, strife, and quar - rels cease; Fill

til the Son of God ap - pear. Re - joice! Re - joice! Em -
cause us in her ways to go. Re - joice! Re - joice! Em -
the whole world with heav - en's peace.

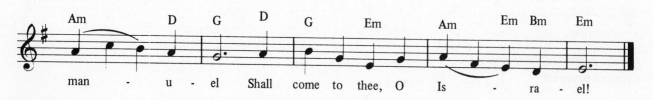

man - u - el Shall come to thee, O Is - ra - el!

Piano, accompany using chord roots on each change of chord
Soprano recorder

172

ODE TO JOY
(from Symphony No. 9 in D major)

Ludwig van Beethoven
(Germany, 1770—1827)

Freud - e, schoen - er Goet - ter - funk - en, Toch - ter aus E - ly - si - um,
froy   deh shuu - nehr guu - tehr - foon - ken   tahk - tehr aoos aye - lee - see - oom

Wir be - tre - ten feu - er - trunk - en. Himm - li - sche, dein Heil - ig - tum!
veer bee - tray - tehn foy - er - troon - kehn him - lih - sheh dine hy - lihg - toom

Dein - e Zaub - er bind - en — wie - der, Was die — Mo - de streng ge - theilt; Al -
dye - nuh tsow - ber bihn - dehn vee - dehr vahs dee moh - dah strehng guh - thighlt ah -

- le Men - schen wer - den Brud - er, — Wo dein sanf - ter Flueg - el weilt.
- leh men - shehn vare - dehn brew - dehr voh dine sahn - ftehr flee - gehl vyelt

Piano, accompaniment pattern XI
Soprano recorder

English version

Joyful, joyful, we adore thee,
God of glory, Lord of love;
Hearts unfold like flow'rs before thee,
Op'ning to the sun above.
Melt the cloud of sin and sadness,
Drive the dark of doubt away.
Giver of immortal gladness,
Fill us with the light of day.

English version by Henry Van Dyke

OH, MARY, DON'T YOU WEEP

Black American Spiritual

Oh, Mar - y, don't you weep, don't you mourn,

Oh, Mar - y, don't you weep, don't you mourn, Phar - aoh's arm - y got

drownd - ed, Oh, Mar - y, don't you weep.

Guitar, strum 10

OH, MY LITTLE BOY

American Folk Song

Oh, my lit - tle boy, Who made your breech - es?

Oh, my lit - tle boy, Who made your breech - es?

Oh, my lit - tle boy, Who made your breech - es?

"Mom - my cut 'em out, and Dad - dy sewed the stitch - es."

Authoharp, strum D
Piano, accompaniment pattern II

OLD BRASS WAGON

American Dance Song

Dance tempo

1. Cir - cle to the left, old brass wag - on, Cir - cle to the left,

old brass wag -on, Cir-cle to the left, old brass wag-on, You're the one, my dar - lin'.

Autoharp, strum D (banjo)
Chromatic bells

2. Circle to the right, old brass wagon, *(three times)*
   You're the one my darlin'.

3. Swing, oh, swing, old brass wagon, *(three times)*
   You're the one my darlin'.

4. Skipping all around, old brass wagon *(three times)*
   You're the one my darlin'.

Formation
Form a single circle of partners, girls on boys' right.

Dance
Verse 1: All circle left.
Verse 2: All circle right.
Verse 3: Partners face each other, join hands, and swing once around.
Verse 4: Girls stand on boys' right, forming an inner circle; partners link arms and
skip clockwise around the circle.

OLD HUNDREDTH
(Psalm 100, altered)

William Kethe
(1561)

Louis Bourgeois
(France, c. 1510—?)

Piano, accompany using chord roots
Soprano recorder

OLD JOE CLARK

American Folk Song

Lively

1. Old Joe Clark, he had a house, six - teen sto - ries high,
2. I went up to Joe's new house, stepped right in the door,
3. Old Joe Clark, he had a dog, dumb as he could be,
4. Old Joe Clark had a mean old cat, never did sing or pray,

Ev - 'ry sto - ry in the house, smelled like ap - ple pie.
Joe was sleepin' on a feath - er bed, I had to sleep on the floor.
Barked a lady - bug up a stump, a pig up a hol - low tree.
Stuck her head in the milk - ing pail, washed her sins a - way!

Refrain:

'Round and 'round, old Joe Clark, 'round and 'round, I say;

'Round and 'round, old Joe Clark, dance your cares a - way.

Autoharp, (15-bar), strum E; (21-bar), strum C (drone: play Dmaj and Dm simultaneously throughout)
Guitar, strum 12
Piano, accompaniment pattern II

5. Old Joe Clark, he had a wife, name of Mary Lou;
   She had two great big brown eyes, the other two were blue. *(Refrain)*

6. Old Joe Clark, he built a house, told his friends "It's neat!"
   He built the floors above his head, the ceilings under his feet. *(Refrain)*

7. Old Joe Clark had a violin, played it all the day,
   Never did he fiddle around, all he'd do was play. *(Refrain)*

OLD MacDONALD

American Folk Song

1. Old Mac - Don - ald had a farm, E - I - E - I - O, And on that farm he had some chicks, E - I - E - I - O. With a chick - chick here, and a chick-chick there, Here a chick, there a chick, ev - 'ry where a chick-chick, Old Mac - Don - ald had a farm, E - I - E - I - O.

Chromatic bells

2. Old MacDonald had a farm, E-I-E-I-O,
   And on that farm he had some ducks, E-I-E-I-O,
   With a quack-quack here, and a quack-quack there,
   Here a quack, there a quack, ev'rywhere a quack quack,
   Old MacDonald had a farm, E-I-E-I-O.

3. Old MacDonald had a farm, E-I-E-I-O,
   And on that farm he had some pigs, E-I-E-I-O,
   With an oink-oink here, and an oink-oink there,
   Here an oink, there an oink, ev'rywhere an oink-oink,
   Old MacDonald had a farm, E-I-E-I-O.

4. Old MacDonald had a farm, E-I-E-I-O,
   And on that farm he had some turkeys, E-I-E-I-O,
   With a gobble-gobble here, and a gobble-gobble there,
   Here a gobble, there a gobble, ev'rywhere a gobble-gobble,
   Old MacDonald had a farm, E-I-E-I-O.

OLD PAINT

American Cowboy Song

Not too fast

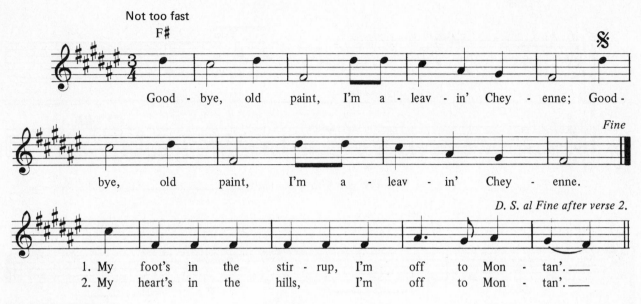

Good - bye, old paint, I'm a - leav - in' Chey - enne; Good -

bye, old paint, I'm a - leav - in' Chey - enne.

Fine

D. S. al Fine after verse 2.

1. My foot's in the stir - rup, I'm off to Mon - tan'. ___
2. My heart's in the hills, I'm off to Mon - tan'. ___

Chromatic bells

OLD SMOKY

American Ballad

With feeling

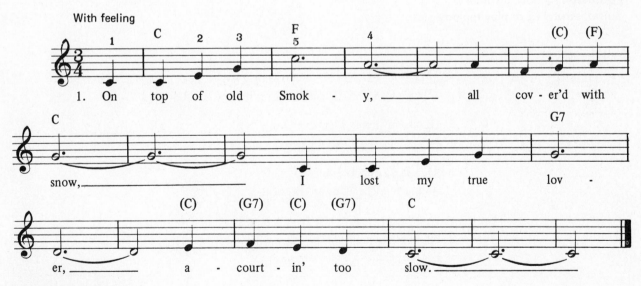

1. On top of old Smok - y, ___ all cov - er'd with

snow, ___ I lost my true lov -

er, ___ a - court - in' too slow. ___

Autoharp, strum H
Guitar, strum 19
Piano, accompaniment pattern VII

2. A-courtin' is pleasure, but partin' is grief,
   A falsehearted lover, is worse than a thief.

3. S/he'll hug you and kiss you, and tell you more lies,
   Than cross ties on the railroad, or stars in the skies.

4. On top of old Smoky, all covered with snow,
   The wild birds will hear me, sing a song of my woe.

179

OLD TEXAS

American Cowboy Song

Autoharp (15-bar), strum E
Guitar, strum 12 or play melody

2. They've plowed and fenced my cattle range,
   And the people there are all so strange.

3. I'll take my horse, I'll take my rope,
   And hit the trail upon a lope.

4. Say *adios* to the Alamo,
   And turn my head toward Mexico.

5. I'll make my home on the wide, wide range,
   For the people there are not so strange.

6. The hard, hard ground shall be my bed,
   And my saddle seat shall hold my head.

O MUSIC, SWEET MUSIC

Traditional Round

Autoharp, strum I
Guitar, strum 14
Soprano recorder

ORANGES AND LEMONS

English Folk Song

♩ = 104

"Oran - ges and lem - ons," say the bells of St. Clem - ents.
"Give me five far - things," say the bells of St. Mar - tins;

"When will you pay me?" say the bells of Old Bai - ley;

"When I grow rich," say the bells of Shore - ditch.

"When will that be?" ___ say the bells of Step - ney; ___

"I do not know," ___ says the great bell of Bow. ___

Here comes the can - dle to ___ light you to bed, And

here is your pil - low to ___ cov - er your head.

Chromatic bells
Soprano recorder

OUR LAND
(Artza Alinu)

Israeli Dance Song

Ar-tza a - li - nu, ar-tza a - li - nu, ar-tza a - li – nu.

Ar-tza a - li - nu, ar-tza a - li - nu, ar-tza a - li – nu.

La la la la la la la la la la la, La la la la la

la la la la la la, La la la la la la la; La la la la la

la la. La la la la la la la. La la la la la la la.

Autoharp, strum N or P

Translation
> We have come to our land.

Dance the hora along with "Our Land." See directions
accompanying "Hava Nagila."

OVER THE RAINBOW

E. Y. Harburg

Harold Arlen
(United States, 1905—1986)

Piano, accompaniment pattern XIII; measures 19–27, XVII

OVER THE RIVER AND THROUGH THE WOOD

Lydia M. Childs
(United States, 1802—1880)

American Song

Autoharp (15-bar), strum S

Create a dramatization or pantomime to depict the song's words.

THE OWL
(El Tecolote)

Mexican Folk Song

Chromatic bells
Guitar, strum 16 or 20

Translation   The owl stays up until sunrise. You have all day; why do you fly at night? Poor little bird is tired of flying!

PAT-A-PAN

Bernard de la Monnoye

Burgundian Carol (France)

♩ = 138

mf

Dm   A(7)   Dm

1. Wil - lie, take your lit - tle drum, Rob - in, bring your flute and
2. Men of old in an - cient days Gave the King of Kings their
3. God and man are now as one They com - bine as flute and

A(7)   Dm

come! ⎫
praise! ⎬ Play - ing on the flute and drum, Tu - re - lu - re - lu, pat - a - pat - a -
drum. ⎭

A7   Dm   A7   Dm   A7   Dm   *f*

pan, Play - ing on the flute and drum, ⎧ We will cel - e - brate this day!
                                         ⎨ Let us cel - e - brate as they!
                                         ⎩ Sing and dance for joy this day!

Autoharp, strum O
Guitar, strum 26
Piano, accompaniment pattern XI
Soprano recorder

French song text

1. Guillaume prends ton tambourin,
   Toi, prends ta flûte, Robin;
   Au son de ces instruments,
   Tu-re-lu-re-lu, pat-a-pat-a-pan,
   Au son de ces instruments,
   Je dirai Noë gaîment.

2. C'était la mode autrefois
   De louer le Roi des rois,
   Au son de ces instruments,
   Tu-re-lu-re-lu, pat-a-pat-a-pan,
   Au son de ces instruments,
   Il nous en faut faire autant.

3. L'homme et Dieu sont plus d'accord
   Que la flûte et le tambour.
   Au son de ces instruments,
   Tu-re-lu-re-lu, pat-a-pat-a-pan,
   Au son de ces instruments,
   Chantons, dansons, sautons en.

PAVANA

Arranged by Patricia Hackett

Sixteenth-century Italian Dance

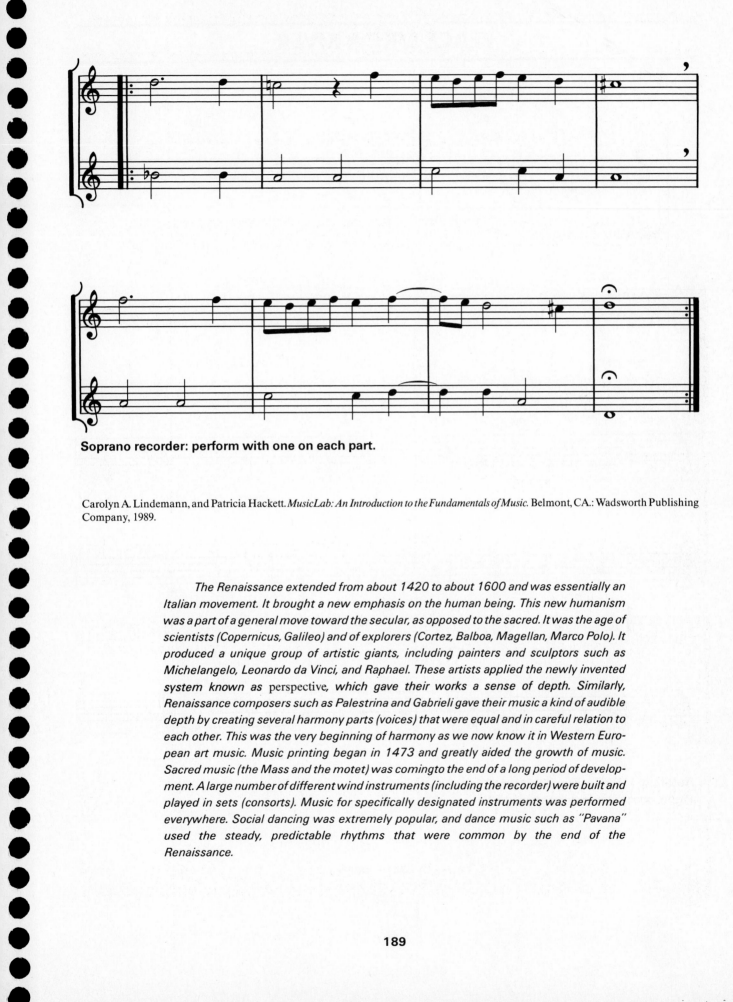

Soprano recorder: perform with one on each part.

Carolyn A. Lindemann, and Patricia Hackett. *MusicLab: An Introduction to the Fundamentals of Music.* Belmont, CA.: Wadsworth Publishing Company, 1989.

The Renaissance extended from about 1420 to about 1600 and was essentially an Italian movement. It brought a new emphasis on the human being. This new humanism was a part of a general move toward the secular, as opposed to the sacred. It was the age of scientists (Copernicus, Galileo) and of explorers (Cortez, Balboa, Magellan, Marco Polo). It produced a unique group of artistic giants, including painters and sculptors such as Michelangelo, Leonardo da Vinci, and Raphael. These artists applied the newly invented system known as perspective, *which gave their works a sense of depth. Similarly, Renaissance composers such as Palestrina and Gabrieli gave their music a kind of audible depth by creating several harmony parts (voices) that were equal and in careful relation to each other. This was the very beginning of harmony as we now know it in Western European art music. Music printing began in 1473 and greatly aided the growth of music. Sacred music (the Mass and the motet) was coming to the end of a long period of development. A large number of different wind instruments (including the recorder) were built and played in sets (consorts). Music for specifically designated instruments was performed everywhere. Social dancing was extremely popular, and dance music such as "Pavana" used the steady, predictable rhythms that were common by the end of the Renaissance.*

PEACE LIKE A RIVER

Traditional American Song

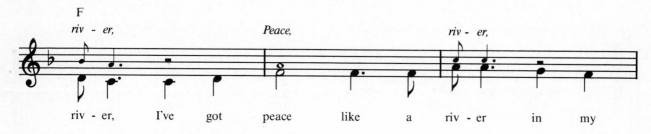

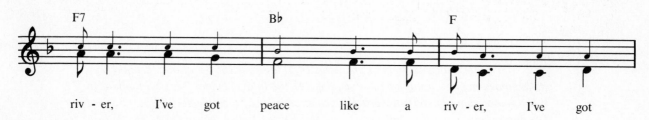

Autoharp (15-bar), strum A (harp)
Piano, accompaniment pattern XVII

2. I've got joy like a fountain...
3. I've got love like the ocean...

PEER GYNT SUITE NO. 2
Fourth movement theme:
"Solveig's Song"

Edvard Grieg
(Norway, 1843—1907)

Andante (♩ = 80-84)

Soprano recorder

PHILIPPINE WELCOME SONG
(Umupo Po)

Philippine School Song

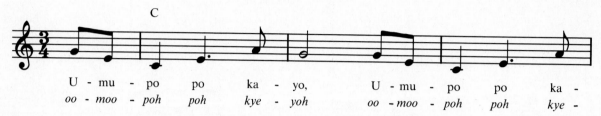

U - mu - po po ka - yo,   U - mu - po po ka -
oo - moo - poh poh kye - yoh   *oo - moo - poh poh kye -*

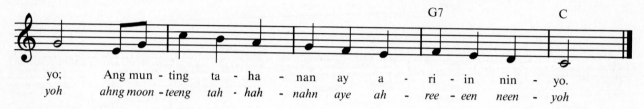

yo; Ang mun - ting ta - ha - nan ay a - ri - in nin - yo.
yoh ahng moon - teeng tah - hah - nahn aye ah - ree - een neen - yoh

Autoharp, strum J
Piano, accompaniment pattern VI

English version
Have a seat, please, dear guest,
Have a seat, please, dear guest.
Feel at home, O dear friend,
In this small, humble home.

English version by Patricia Hackett

PIPE DANCE SONG

Collected by Patricia Hackett

Native American Song
(Plains: Sauk-Fox)

*Begin in a moderate tempo. Sing three times, gradually accelerating throughout, to ♩ = 200.

Translation

My friend (Twee-ah-way-ha)
Takes care of horses' feet (Nee-kuh-na-way)

Formation

Two or three dancers are encircled by spectators. A group of drummers sits around a drum placed just outside the circle. Drummers sing and play; dancers do not sing.

Dance

During the drum roll the dancers stand in place and quiver, swaying the torso. On the steady beats (measures 3–11) dancers do the war dance, using the traditional toe-heel step. As they dance they hold the bowl of the calumet pipe in one hand, stem outward. They offer it (symbolically) to the various spectators in the circle, but do not actually give away the pipe.

PIZZA, PIZZA, DADDY-O!

Black American Game Song

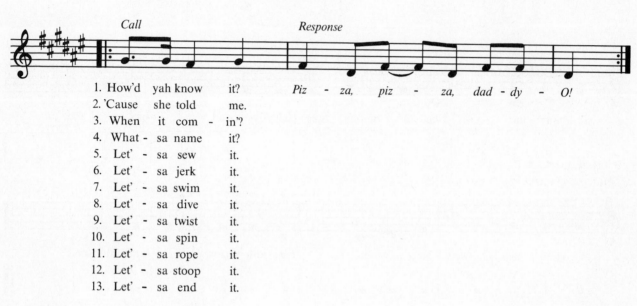

1. How'd yah know   it?   Piz - za,   piz - za,   dad - dy - O!
2. 'Cause she told   me.
3. When   it com - in'?
4. What - sa name   it?
5. Let' - sa sew   it.
6. Let' - sa jerk   it.
7. Let' - sa swim   it.
8. Let' - sa dive   it.
9. Let' - sa twist   it.
10. Let' - sa spin   it.
11. Let' - sa rope   it.
12. Let' - sa stoop it.
13. Let' - sa end   it.

Response

End it,   end_ it, dad-dy   O!

Formation
Players stand in a circle facing the center. One player stands in the center.

Game
Players begin by singing the name of the player in the center, who then leads 1–13 calls and the motions.

On "Pizza, pizza, daddy-o!" all players sing and perform a five-beat foot pattern:
Beat 1: Jump, landing with feet apart;
Beat 2: Jump, landing with right foot crossed in front of left;
Beat 3: Jump, landing with feet apart;
Beat 4: Jump, landing with left foot crossed in front of right;
Beat 5: Jump, landing with feet together.

The song stops when the center player sings "let's end it." The center player then spins in a circle with eyes closed, arm and pointer finger extended. She stops, her finger identifying the next center player.

PLANTING RICE

Philippine Folk Song

With movement (♩ = 76)

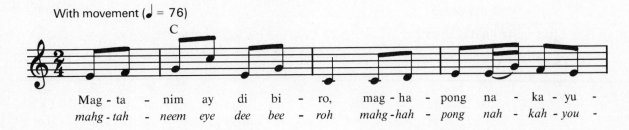

Mag - ta - nim ay di bi - ro,   mag - ha - pong na - ka - yu -
mahg - tah - neem eye dee bee - roh   mahg - hah - pong nah - kah - you -

ko,   'Di man lang ma - ka - ta - ya,   'Di man lang ma - ka - u - po.
koh   dee mahn lang mah - kah - tah - yah   dee mahn lang mah - kah - oo - poh

Autoharp, strum E
Piano, accompaniment pattern III

English version
Planting <u>rice</u> is never fun,
Work from dawn till set of <u>sun</u>;
Cannot stand and cannot sit,
Cannot rest for just a <u>bit</u>.

Formation
Dancers form a circle, facing clockwise. The left arm is extended outward from the body in a half circle, as if cradling a basket of rice seedlings.

Dance Steps
The dancer begins with weight on the left foot, ready to move clockwise. Four quick steps RLRL (♪♪♪♪) begin on the upbeat of the song. The quick steps alternate with one slow step R (♩) on the downbeat of each measure.

Arm Movements
The dance pantomimes taking rice seedlings from a basket and planting them in the ground. During the quick steps, the right hand gathers seedlings from the basket. The dancer bends at the waist on the long step, extending the right arm downward toward the center of the circle (as if planting the seedlings).

PRAISE SONG
(Hava Nashira)

With movement

Israeli Round

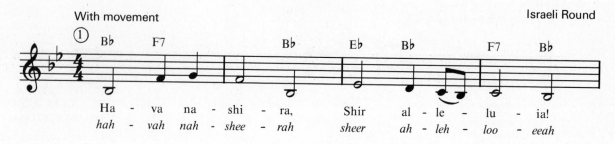

Ha - va na - shi - ra, Shir al - le - lu - ia!
hah - vah nah - shee - rah sheer ah - leh - loo - eeah

Ha - va na - shi - ra, Shir al - le - lu - ia!

Ha - va na - shi - ra, Shir al - le - lu - ia!

Autoharp (15-bar), strum L

English version
Now let us praise Him, Sing alleluia! *(sing three times)*

196

PRAYER SONG OF THE PEYOTE RELIGION

Collected by Patricia Hackett

Native American Song

A gourd rattle and a small drum plays this rhythm throughout: ♩♫

PRECIOUS LORD

Thomas A. Dorsey
(United States, 1899—)

With feeling

Pre - cious Lord, take my hand, Lead me on, help me stand; _____ I am tired, I am weak, I am worn. _____ Through the storm, through the night, Lead me on to the light, _____ Take my hand, _____ pre-cious Lord, _____ lead me home.

Autoharp, strum L
Guitar, strum 22
Piano, accompaniment pattern XVII

QUARTET FOR FLUTE AND STRINGS IN A MAJOR
K. 298
First movement theme

Wolfgang Amadeus Mozart
(Austria, 1756—1791)

Soprano recorder

The term Classical *was never meant to distinguish art music from popular music. Instead, it specifically designates the music of the Viennese Classical period, from about 1700 to about 1830. During this era, Haydn, Mozart, and Beethoven greatly expanded the repertoire of instrumental music with works of exceptional clarity, balance, and constraint. These eighteenth-century classical ideals were brilliantly synthesized by Mozart, who as a child prodigy was exhibited by his teacher-father throughout the capitals and courts of Europe. As a mature composer, Mozart was versatile, using his creative genius to fashion operas and symphonies as well as chamber and choral music of luminous grace.*

QUARTET IN F MAJOR
Opus 3, number 5
Second movement theme

Franz Joseph Haydn
(Austria, 1732—1809)

Andante cantabile (♩ = 76)

(Original key: C major)

Soprano recorder

QUINTET FOR CLARINET AND STRINGS IN A MAJOR
K. 581
Fourth movement theme

Wolfgang Amadeus Mozart
(Austria, 1756—1791)

Allegretto (♩ = 72)
(Original key: A major)

Soprano recorder

THE RAILROAD BOY

American Folk Song

1. She went up stairs_____ and made her bed,
With - out a word_____ to moth - er said.

Autoharp, strum C
Guitar, strum 4
Piano, accompaniment pattern V

2. Her mother dear she could not tell,
That railroad boy she loved so well.

3. He took another on his knee,
And now he's gone away from me.

4. She stayed upstairs and gave up hope,
They found her hanging by a rope.

5. "Oh, on my breast put a snow white dove,
And tell the world I died of love."

6. They dug her grave so wide and deep,
Put marble stone at her head and feet.

RAIN

American Play Song

Rain, rain, go a - way! Come a - gain some oth - er day.

Soprano recorder (play one half step higher)

RAISINS AND ALMONDS

Israeli Folk Song

To my lit - tle one's cra - dle in the night,_____ Comes a

new lit - tle goat_____ snow - y white._____ The

goat will trot to the mar - ket,_____ While

moth - er her watch_____ will keep, _____ To

bring you back rai - sins and al - monds._____

Sleep, my lit - tle one, sleep._____

Autoharp, strum B (harp)
Chromatic bells
Piano, accompaniment pattern XVII, play two chords each measure

English version by Sylvia and John Kolb

RAJASTHAN FOLK MELODY

Collected by Patricia Hackett

Northwest India

Chromatic bells

India is a huge country with one of the oldest civilizations in the world. From the beginning music has been a part of that culture. All kinds of music (and dance) are found: classical, religious, folk, and popular. The music of north India (Hindustani) is different from that of south India (Carnatic), but their origins are similar. Both styles share the same four main elements of Indian music: drone, melody, rhythm, and improvisation. Music and religion are linked, because music has long been associated with devotion and the temple. Beginning in the fourteenth century, classical Hindustani music was supported by Muslim courts and the upper class. A tremendous variety of instruments are found, including many plucked strings (sitar, sarod, vīnā, tambura), drums (tabla, mridangam, tavil), and winds (bansuri, shahnai, nagaswaram). The European violin is used in south India. "Rajasthan Folk Melody" is performed on the shahnai, an oboelike instrument.

RECREATION OF THE BALARI WOMEN

African Folk Song
(West Africa: Republic of the Congo)

Hay yah wil lee, yah koo lahm bee lahm bway, Way
kihn zoo pway kwan jee, Yah koo lahm bee lahm bway.

The ancient musical traditions of Africa continue to endure. South of the Sahara, music remains an important social and personal expression. In traditional African life, music marked the important rites of passage of an individual: birth, puberty, marriage, and death. For these occasions the professional musician was paid for services. At other times cohesive, blended voices of a group accompanied communal work efforts such as cultivating, harvesting, and canoeing. In these songs everyone conformed to an established, orderly plan of work and singing. Music was important in religious celebrations and in work, but also for sheer entertainment. This song is the good-natured complaint of a young bride who does not have enough utensils to cook properly. When singing without musical instruments, the singer provides her own accompaniment of body sounds: hand clapping or patting, slapping of thighs or upper arms, or finger snapping. Using body percussion while you sing, keep a steady beat (♩) until you become agile enough to try ♫ or ♬.

205

RIDING IN THE BUGGY

American Folk Song

1. Rid-ing in the bug-gy, Miss Ma - ry Ann, Miss Ma - ry Ann, Miss Ma - ry Ann,
2. I got a house in Bal - ti - more, Bal - ti - more, Bal - ti - more,

Rid - ing in the bug - gy, Miss Ma - ry Ann, She's a long ways from home.
I got a house in Bal - ti - more, And it's six sto - ries tall.

Refrain:

Who moans for me? Who moans for me?

Who moans for me, my la - dy, Who moans for me?

Autoharp, strum M
Chromatic bells
Guitar, strum 25
Piano, accompaniment pattern XV

RING AROUND THE ROSY

American Play Song

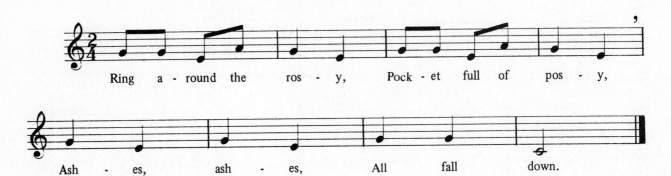

Ring a - round the ros - y, Pock - et full of pos - y,

Ash - es, ash - es, All fall down.

Soprano recorder

"Ring Around the Rosy" may describe characteristics of the plague that struck Europe in the 14th century: a rose-colored "ring" was an early sign that a blotch was about to appear on the skin; "a pocket full of posies" was a device to ward off stench and infection; "ashes, ashes" is a reference to "ashes to ashes, dust to dust," or perhaps to the sneezing "a-choo, a-choo" that afflicted the lungs of some victims—ending, inevitably, in "all fall down."

RISE, SUGAR, RISE!

American Folk Song

With spirit

Go - in' 'round the cir - cle two by two, Go - in' 'round the cir - cle two by two,

Go - in' 'round the cir - cle two by two, Rise, su - gar, rise!

Autoharp (15-bar), strum A

Make up your own verses and movements for the song

RITSCH, RATSCH

Swedish Folk Song

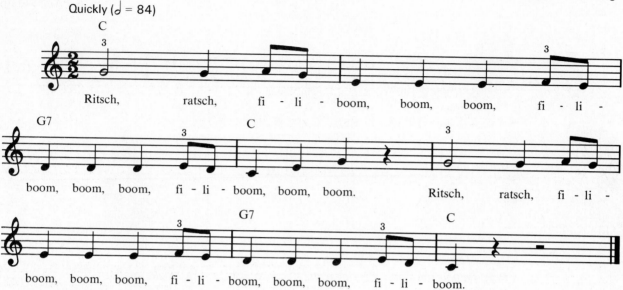

Ritsch, ratsch, fi - li - boom, boom, boom, fi - li - boom, boom, boom, fi - li - boom, boom, boom. Ritsch, ratsch, fi - li - boom, boom, boom, fi - li - boom, boom, boom, fi - li - boom.

Autoharp, strum L (banjo)
Piano, accompaniment pattern XI

ROCK-PASSING SONG

African Play Song
(West Africa: Ghana)

Ob - wi - sa - na sa na - na, Ob - wi - sa - na sa,
ohb wih sah nah sah nah nah

Ob - wi - sa - na sa na - na, Ob - wi - sa - na sa.

Translation
"Oh, Gramma, I just hurt my finger on a rock."

Formation
Players sit in a circle, each holding a pebble.

Game
Players sing during the game. Use the right hand to pass the pebble and to pick it up. On beat 1, place the pebble in front of the player on the right. On beat 2, pick up the pebble that is now in front of each player. Alternate these two movements throughout the song.

On the last note of the song there should be a pebble in front of each player. Any player with no pebble, or with several, must leave the game circle.

ROCKY MOUNTAIN

American Folk Song

1. Rock-y moun-tain, rock-y moun-tain, Rock-y moun-tain high,

When you reach that rock-y moun-tain Hang your head and cry.

Refrain:

Do, do, do, do, Do re-mem-ber me,

Do, do, do, do, Do, re-mem-ber me.

Autoharp (15-bar), strum C or D

2. Rocky mountain, rocky mountain,
Rocky mountain sky,
When you reach that rocky mountain,
Spread your wings and fly. *(Refrain)*

ROLL OVER

American Play Song

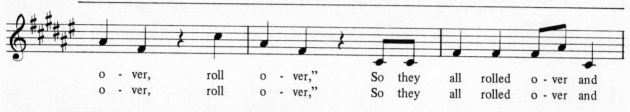

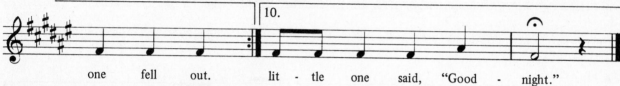

Autoharp, strum A (play one half step lower)
Chromatic bells
Guitar, strum 2 (play one half step lower)

Formation

Ten players stand side by side in a line.

Game

Players sing during the game. On the words "roll over" players rotate their forearms one over the other. On "they all rolled over" each player turns around in place, and the child on the right end of the line falls down (or kneels). The same actions are repeated nine times until only one player remains standing during verse 10. This player sings a solo "Good night" and the game ends.

RONDE
from *The Third Little Music Book* (1551)

Anonymous
Compiled by Tilman Susato
(Belgium, d. c.1561)

Chromatic bells
Soprano recorder

ROUND DANCE

Collected by Patricia Hackett

Native American Dance Song
Southern Plains (Kiowa)

♩. = 69

Soloist initially; all singers on repeat

Yah yah yah yah yoh hai yah, Yah, yah hay yah hay

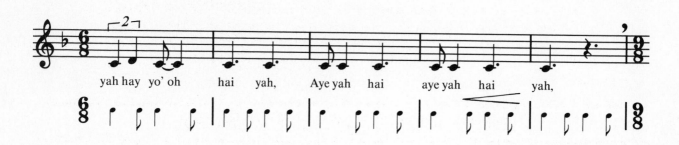

yah hay yo' oh hai yah, Yah yah yah hay yoh hai yah hay

yah hay yo' oh hai yah, Aye yah hai aye yah hai yah,

Yah yah yah hay yoh hai yah, Yah yah yah hay yoh - hai yah hay

yah hay   yo' oh   hai   yah   Aye yah   hai   aye yah   hay   yah.

Sing three times, each repetition louder than the preceding.

Formation

Four or five drummers sit around a large drum. Drummers sing and play for the dancers, who do not sing. Dancers form a circle, facing inward. Women hold their arms at waist level, one palm over the other. Men's arms hang in a natural position by their sides.

Dance

Dancers move sideways, in a clockwise direction, sliding along with the dotted quarter note beat of the song. Slide the left foot to the left, then slide the right foot close to the left foot, using just a little lift to do so. Alternate this footwork throughout.

The song is repeated three times, and on the last repetition dancers (and drummers) stop exactly on the last word of the song.

Today, Indian music is still a lively art, though it serves a different function than in earlier times. Many traditional ceremonies have become anachronistic in the modern world. Thus if the songs from these ceremonies continue to be sung, they reflect the desire to affirm an Indian identity—culturally and socially. Many urban Indian groups share a modern musical tradition (Pan-Indian) which reflects strong influences of the Plains Indians. The Kiowa "Round Dance" is popular throughout the Western states and is sometimes used as a mixer, as a friendship dance, or to honor selected tribal members.

ROW, ROW, ROW YOUR BOAT

Traditional Round

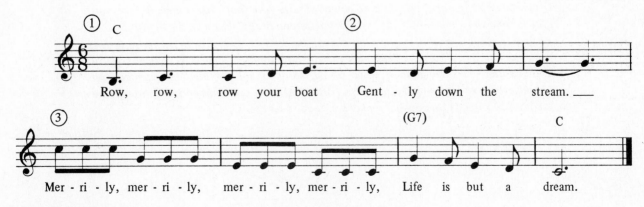

Row,   row,   row your boat   Gent - ly down the   stream. ___

Mer - ri - ly, mer - ri - ly,   mer - ri - ly, mer - ri - ly,   Life is but a   dream.

Autoharp, strum B

ROYAL GARDEN BLUES

Clarence Williams
(United States, 1893—1965)
Spencer Williams
(United States, 1889—1965)

Autoharp, improvise a strum
Chromatic bells
Piano, accompaniment pattern XV

1. "Hon, don't you hear that trombone moan?
   Just listen to that saxophone,
   Gee, hear that clarinet and flute,
   Cornet a-jazzin' with a mute,
   Makes me just throw myself away,
   When I hear 'em play.

2. That weepin' melancholy strain,
   Say, but it's soothin' to the brain.
   Just wanna get right up and dance,
   Don't care, I'll take most any chance,
   No other blues I'd care to choose,
   But Royal Garden Blues."

In 1924 the legendary Leon "Bix" Beiderbecke (United States, 1903—1931) recorded "Royal Garden Blues" with the Wolverines. Bix was on cornet, with five other musicians on trombone, clarinet, banjo, drums, and piano. This was Chicago-style jazz; music that had moved upriver from New Orleans after Storyville, the infamous red light district, was shut down in 1917. Bix grew up listening to early recordings by the Original Dixieland Jass Band, little dreaming that he would one day sit in with the greats: King Oliver, Louis Armstrong, and Jimmie Noone. Theirs was "hot" jazz; music full of short phrases and changing harmonies as in "Royal Garden Blues" (but with the rhythms never played as straight as they are written above). Beiderbecke's exquisite cornet tone was accompanied by self-taught fingerings that helped create a distinctive, lyrical style of improvisation. Bix died a young man of 28, admired and imitated by jazzmen, but appreciated by only a handful of listeners. Fortunately, his genius has endured through the magic of recordings that delight millions of today's jazz fans.

SAIL AWAY, LADIES

American Play-Party Song

♩ = 104

D (C) D G A7 D

Ain't no use to sit and cry, Sail a-way, la-dies, sail a-way.

D (C) D G A7 D

You'll be an an-gel bye and bye, Sail a-way, la-dies, sail a-way.

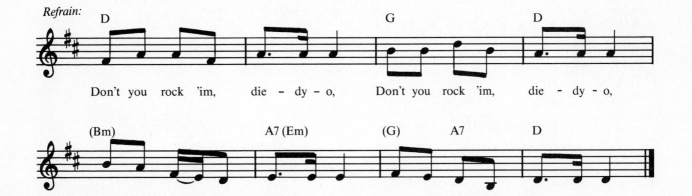

Refrain:

D G D

Don't you rock 'im, die – dy – o, Don't you rock 'im, die – dy – o,

(Bm) A7 (Em) (G) A7 D

Don't you rock___'im, die – dy – o, Don't you rock 'im, die – dy – o.

Autoharp (15-bar), strum C (banjo)
Guitar, strum 8

2. I've got a home in Tennessee, Sail away, ladies, sail away.
   That's the place I wanna be, Sail away, ladies, sail away. *(Refrain)*

3. Ever I get my new house done, Sail away, ladies, sail away.
   I'll give the old one to my son, Sail away, ladies, sail away. *(Refrain)*

4. Come along boys and go with me, Sail away, ladies, sail away.
   We'll go down to Tennessee, Sail away, ladies, sail away. *(Refrain)*

ST. PAUL'S STEEPLE

English Melody

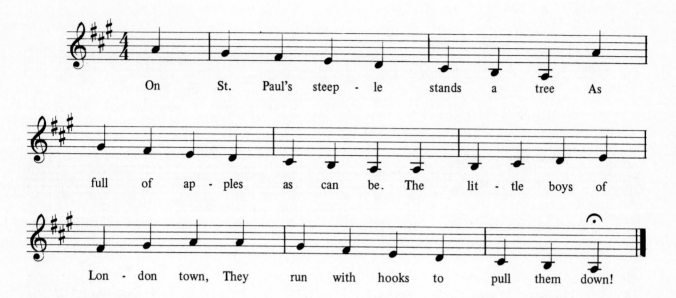

On St. Paul's steep - le stands a tree As

full of ap - ples as can be. The lit - tle boys of

Lon - don town, They run with hooks to pull them down!

Chromatic bells

SAKURA
(Cherry Blossoms)

Japanese Folk Song

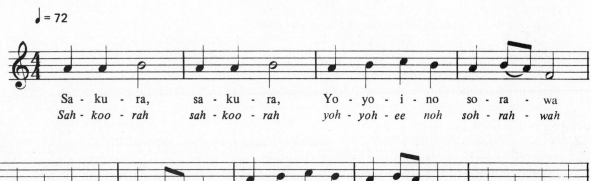

Autoharp, strum A
Guitar, strum 2

Optional accompaniments to
play during each measure:

Single pitches   A   D

Chords   Am   Dm

English version

Sakura, sakura
Cherry blossoms fill the sky,
Petals drifting ev'rywhere!
Are they mist or are they cloud,
Wafting fragrance on the breeze?
Sakura, sakura;
Let all go to see.

English version by Patricia Hackett

217

Formation
The following movements can be performed while seated or standing.

Starting position
Palms together in a prayerlike position in front of the chest.

Movements
All movements should be large, flowing, and graceful.
Measure 1: Raise the right arm overhead in a circular movement up and to the right, stopping just above the shoulder level, palm up. The left hand remains at chest level.
Measure 2: Raise the left arm overhead in a circular movement up and to the left, stopping just above the shoulder level, palm up. The right hand remains just above shoulder level, palm up.
Measure 3: Bring palms quickly together in front of the chest. Then repeat the measure 1 movement.
Measure 4: Repeat the measure 2 movement.
Measure 5: Bring arms together overhead, forming a large circle.
Measure 6: Hold the measure 5 position.
Measure 7: Hold both arms to the right side, with the right arm slightly higher. Hold arms vertically, away from the body. Turn head to the *left*.
Measure 8: Hold the measure 7 position.
Measure 9: Hold both arms to the left side, with the left arm slightly higher. Hold palms vertically, away from the body. Turn head to the *right*.
Measure 10: Hold the measure 9 position.
Measure 11: Repeat the measure 1 movement.
Measure 12: Repeat the measure 2 movement.
Measure 13: Repeat the measure 1 movement.
Measure 14: Repeat the measure 2 movement.

A refined, highly cultivated art music flowered in Japan, with its roots in ancient court and Buddhist ritual music. At the same time, a lively stream of folk music served the people, accompanying their work, dance, and local ceremonies. While indigenous music flourished during the isolation of the Edo period (1615–1868), the twentieth century push toward modernization brought with it the influence of Western music. In the wake of World War II, the practice of traditional music and arts was retained mostly by the elderly or more conservative elements of society. Resurgent nationalism is reversing this trend, but even now, traditional music is heard less often on the media than at the business dinner. There, the elderly executive may sing a song such as "Sakura" for the pleasure of his guests.

SALLY BROWN

American Capstan Shanty

Feel each beat (♩ = 80)

1. I shipped on board of a Liv - er - pool lin - er, ____
2. Sal - ly Brown is a nice young la - dy, ____
3. She's tall and dark but not too shad - y, ____
4. Her mother don't like a tar - ry sail - or, ____
5. She wants her to mar-ry a one - eyed cap - tain, ____

Refrain:

'Way, hey ____ roll and go. And we'll go all night and we'll

go 'till morn - in'. I spend my mon-ey a - long with Sal - ly Brown.

Autoharp (21-bar), strum C
Piano, accompaniment pattern   III

American sea shanties borrow their tunes from almost anywhere: from the English and Irish seamen, from balladry and from the music hall, and from the Blacks who signed onto ships at Gulf ports. Using these melodies, the men fashioned their own irreverent and pungent texts. The shantyman might bellow out verses gibing his mates or shout sarcastic slurs on the ancestry of hard-driving masters. The sailor's life on sea and land was often a topic, in texts that could singe the timbers of cabin walls. A lady of easy virtue is the subject of this capstan shanty, sung to the slow, processional tempo of feet in sea boots. "Sally Brown" would be sung while the anchor was being raised. The cable attached to the anchor was wound around the capstan; a barrellike device turned by bars inserted into its toothed rim.

SALLY, GO 'ROUND THE SUN
Version 1

American Folk Song

Sal - ly, go 'round the sun,_____ Sal - ly, go

'round the moon,_____ Sal - ly, go 'round the

chim - ney pot Mon - day af - ter - noon. Boom!

Autoharp (15-bar), one strum each measure

SALLY, GO 'ROUND THE SUN
Version 2

Collected by John Lomax
in Atmore, Alabama (1934)

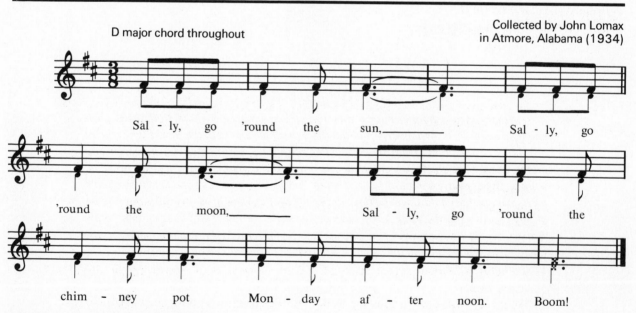

Sal - ly, go 'round the sun,_____ Sal - ly, go

'round the moon,_____ Sal - ly, go 'round the

chim - ney pot Mon - day af - ter noon. Boom!

Autoharp, one strum each measure
Guitar, one strum each measure

Formation Players form a circle and join hands.

Game Players walk to the right while singing the song. On "boom" they do a little jump and change direction. Hands remain joined. On the next repetition of the song, players circle left.

When version 1 is sung as a round, form two concentric circles. Each circle moves in a different direction. The circle performing part 2 of the round starts moving after four measures.

SALTY DOG

American Mountain Song

Salt - y dog, salt - y dog, I don't wan - na be your
man at all, Hon - ey, let me be your salt - y dog. ____
Down in the wild - wood sit - ting on a log, sing - ing a song a - bout a
salt - y dog, Hon - ey, let me be your salt - y dog. ____

Guitar, strum 25
Piano, accompaniment pattern XVI

Formation
Partners in a double circle, all facing clockwise. Partners hands are joined or their arms are around each other's waist.

Dance
Measures 1–2: Place left heel forward, then left toe backward, then run forward three quick steps (left, right, left).
Measures 3–4: Place right heel forward, then right toe backward, then run forward three quick steps (right, left, right).
Measures 5–6: With the left foot take a two-step (step, close, step, pause) diagonally forward to the left.
Measures 7–8: With the right foot take a two-step (step, close, step, pause) diagonally forward to the right.
Measures 9–10: Step and then hop on the left foot, and then run three quick steps forward (right, left, right).
Measures 11–12: Same as measures 9–10.
Measures 13–14: Same as measures 5–6.
Measures 15–16: Same as measures 7–8.

SANDY LAND

American Play-Party Song

Autoharp (15 bar), strum D (banjo)
Guitar, strum 29
Piano, accompaniment pattern IV

2. <u>Raise</u> my 'taters in sandy land, *(three times)*
   <u>La</u>dies, fare you <u>well</u>.

3. <u>Swing</u>, oh swing in sandy land, *(three times)*
   <u>La</u>dies, fare you <u>well</u>.

4. <u>Right</u> and left in sandy land, *(three times)*
   <u>La</u>dies, fare you <u>well</u>.

5. <u>Promenade</u> in sandy land, *(three times)*
   <u>La</u>dies, fare you <u>well</u>.

Formation
Players choose a partner, and form a single circle. Girls are on the right so that players alternate boy, girl, boy, girl, and so forth. All join hands.

Dance
Verse 1: All walk to the left.
Verse 2: All walk to the right.
Verse 3: Partners swing, linking right arms, and skip in a small clockwise circle.
Verse 4: Partners face each other and begin grand right and left. (In grand right and left, players clasp right hands and quickly pass their partner on the right. Then they clasp left hands with the next dancer and pass on the left, alternating right and left hands throughout.)
Repeat verse 4 until original partners meet again.
Verse 5: The boy promenades around the circle with the girl on this left.

SARASPONDA

School Song

Piano, accompaniment pattern XI

223

SATURDAY NIGHT

Song from South Africa

Autoharp, one strum for each measure
Piano, accompaniment pattern V

224

SCARBOROUGH FAIR

English Ballad

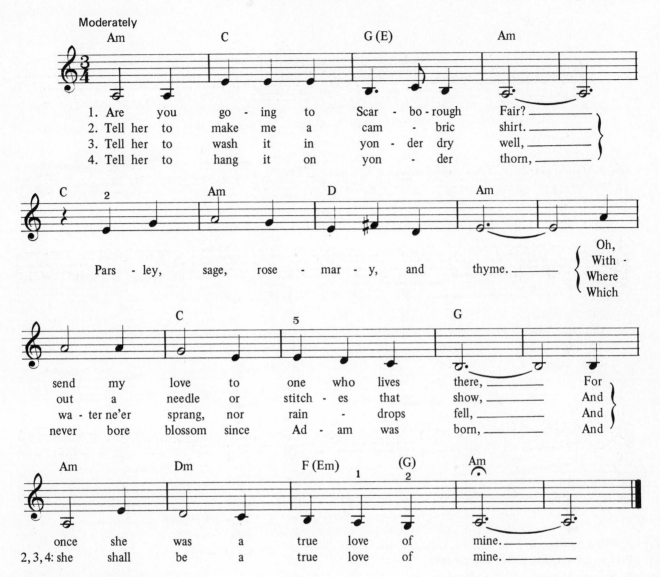

1. Are you go - ing to Scar - bo - rough Fair?
2. Tell her to make me a cam - bric shirt.
3. Tell her to wash it in yon - der dry well,
4. Tell her to hang it on yon - der thorn,

Pars - ley, sage, rose - mar - y, and thyme.

Oh,
With -
Where
Which

send my love to one who lives there, For
out a needle or stitch - es that show, And
wa - ter ne'er sprang, nor rain - drops fell, And
never bore blossom since Ad - am was born, And

once she was a true love of mine.
2, 3, 4: she shall be a true love of mine.

Autoharp (15-bar), strum J
Guitar, strum 15
Piano, accompany using chord roots

"Scarborough Fair" was popularized by contemporary American minstrels—professional singers and instrumentalists. In its purest form, however, the ballad is a story sung by an unaccompanied amateur. The soloist stretches out syllables in the melody or leaves irregular spaces to think of what comes next. Early American balladeers often sang "out of tune" or in archaic scales; instruments were unavailable or inappropriate. Later, when singers played instruments, they chose unfretted banjos, fiddles, or dulcimers. They were of variable pitch, and the singer was still free to "bend" the melody or rhythm, as in old-style balladry. The use of the fretted guitar—popular in this country only since the late 1920s—usually restricts the freedom of the ballad singer. The minstrel of today, however, is often an accomplished instrumentalist.

THE SEA SERPENT
(La Víbora)

Autoharp, strum C
Piano, accompany using chord roots

Translation Sea serpent, pass through here. The ones in front run, the others follow behind. Little golden bell, let us all go through—except the last one!

Game

This game is similar to the "London Bridge" game. Two players form a bridge. One player represents an angel and the devil. As they sing, players in line walk under the bridge. On the words "tras, tras, tras" the bridge is lowered over the player underneath. They sway gently three times from side to side, arms encircling their captive. On "campanita," the captive is released and the song continues. On the words "sin ya tras" the bridge is lowered over the player underneath. After is a whispered conference the captive chooses angel or devil and then goes to stand behind the player representing this choice. A tug-of-war traditionally concludes the game.

SHOES FOR BABY JESUS
(Zapatos para el Niño Jesús)

Collected by Patricia Hackett

Hispanic Christmas Song

Smoothly (♩ = 63-66)

Em   B7

1. El   ni - ño   Dios   es   tan   po -   bre,
   ehl   nee - nyoh   deeohs   ess   tahn   poh -   bray
2. El   rey   Mel - chor   ha ofre - ci -   do,
   ehl   ray   mel - chore   ah ohfray - cee -   doh
3. Can - tan   pas - to - res   y   re -   yes,
   cahn - tahn   pahs - toh - rays   ee   ray -   jehs

Em

Que   no   tie - ne   ni   cu - ni -   ta;   Tres   an - gel -
kay   noh   tie-eh - nay   nee   coo - nee -   tah   trayss   ahng - hel -
Za - pa - tos   de o - ro al In - fan -   te;   Gas - par   se
zah - pah - tohs   day oh-roh ahl Ihn - fahn -   tay   gahs - pahr   say
Glo - ria al ni - ño   que ha na - ci -   do;   La   Vir - gen
glow - ree ahl nee - nyoh   kay ah nah - cee -   doh   lah   bihr-hhehn

B7

li - tos   del   cie -   lo,   La   van a ha - cer   de pa -
lee - tohs   dehl   cee-aye -   loh   lah   vahn ah - sair   day pah -
los   da   de   se -   da,   Y   Bal - ta - sar   de di-a -
loes   dah   day   say -   dah   ee   bahl - tah - sahr   day dee-ah -
lo es - ta   me - si en -   do,   Y   va ha que - dar - se   dor -
loe ehs - tah   mee - see ehn -   doh   ee   bah ah kay - dahr - say   dohr -

Em   Faster (♩ = 88-92)   ⑰

ji -   ta.   El   mo - re - no   po - ne   u - na____   y el
hee -   tah   ehl moh - ray - noh   poh - nay   oo - nah   ee ehl
man -   tes.   Pe - ro   mi - ra   co - mo   ri - e____   tra -
mahn -   tays   pay - roh   mee - rah   coh - moh   ree - aye   trah -
mi -   do.   De pun - ti - llas   se   co - lo - ca____   un
mee -   doh   day poon - tee - yass   say   coh - loh - cah   oon

227

Autoharp (21-bar), strum D

Guitar, strum 6 ⌣ **at beginning of song. At measure 17, change to the strum shown under the last line of humming.**

The English version presents one verse in place of the three Spanish verses. Adjust the songs rhythm (near the ends of phrases) to fit the English version.

God's tiny child is so <u>poor</u>, but fair,
See how He lies in a <u>stable</u> bare.
Three little angels have <u>come</u> to care;
Now they will build Him a <u>cradle</u> fair.
Many kings arrive to praise Him,
Bearing shoes so rich and <u>new</u>,
But the chosen gift for Jesus,
Is a humble wooden <u>shoe</u>.
Sleep, tiny king, rest your head and dream some <u>more</u>,
Now the moon is in the heav'n, and the sun is at the <u>door</u>.
<u>Mm</u>.   __   __   __
<u>Mm</u>.   __   __   __

English version by Patricia Hackett

SHOO, FLY

American Dance Tune

With a strong beat

Refrain:

Shoo, fly, don't both - er me, Shoo, fly, don't both - er me.

Shoo, fly, don't both - er me, For I be - long to some - bod - y.

1. I feel, I feel, I feel, I feel like a morn - in' star; I
2. I hear, I hear, I hear, I hear all the an - gels sing; I

feel, I feel, I feel, I feel, I feel like a morn - in' star. Oh,
hear, I hear, I hear, I hear, I hear all the an - gels sing. Oh,

Autoharp (15-bar), strum C (refrain) and E (verse)
Guitar, strum 12
Piano, accompaniment pattern IV

THE SIDEWALKS OF NEW YORK

James W. Blake
(United States, 1862—1935)

Charles B. Lawlor
(United States, 1852—1925)

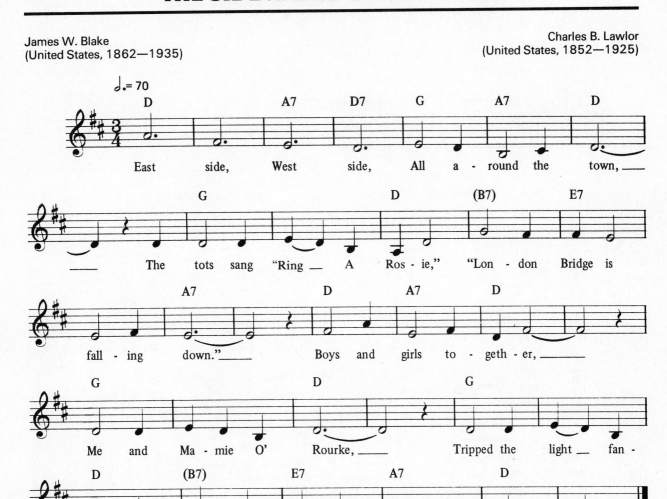

East side, West side, All a - round the town, ____ ____ The tots sang "Ring ___ A Ros - ie," "Lon - don Bridge is fall - ing down." ____ Boys and girls to - geth - er, ____ Me and Ma - mie O' Rourke, ____ Tripped the light ___ fan - tas - tic On the side - walks of New York. ____

Autoharp (15-bar), strum H
Chromatic bells
Guitar, strum 16 or 18
Piano, accompaniment pattern IX

SILENT NIGHT

Josef Mohr
(Austria, 1792—1848)

Franz Grüber
(Germany, 1787—1863)

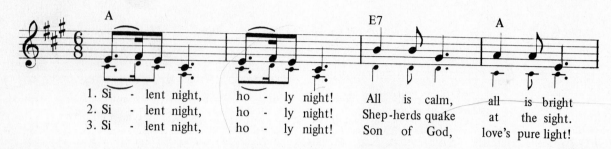

1. Si - lent night, ho - ly night! All is calm, all is bright
2. Si - lent night, ho - ly night! Shep-herds quake at the sight.
3. Si - lent night, ho - ly night! Son of God, love's pure light!

'Round yon vir - gin Moth - er and Child. Ho - ly In - fant, so ten - der and mild,
Glo - ries stream from heav - en a - far, Heaven-ly hosts — sing "Al - le - lu - ia!"
Ra - diant beams from Thy ho - ly face With the dawn of re - deem - ing grace,

Sleep in heav - en - ly peace,___ Sleep — in heav - en - ly peace.
Christ, the Sav - ior, is born,___ Christ, — the Sav - ior, is born.
Je - sus, Lord, at Thy birth,___ Je - sus, Lord, at Thy birth.

Autoharp (21-bar), strum Q
Guitar, strum 32

1. Stille nacht, Heilige nacht!
   shtee-leh nockt Hie-lih-geh nockt
   Alles schläft, einsam wacht
   ah-lehs shlayft ine-sahm vahkt
   Nur das traute hochheilige Paar,
   noor dahs trou-tuh hake-hie-lih-guh pahr
   Holder Knabe im lockigen Haar,
   hohld-ehr knah-bay eem lock-ih-gehn hahr
   Schlaf in himmlischer Ruh!
   schlahf een heem-lih-sher roo
   Schlaf in himmlischer Ruh.
   schlahf een heem-lih-sher roo

"Silent Night" was composed on the day before Christmas, 1818, at Oberndorf, Austria. The organ at St. Nicholas Church had broken down, and could not be repaired prior to the Christmas Eve services. So Franz Grüber, the church organist, composed "Silent Night" and presented it on Christmas Eve, with guitar accompaniment. The poem was provided by Josef Mohr, the church pastor and local schoolmaster. "Silent Night" was soon popularized by a touring troupe of singers from the Tyrol.

SIMPLE GIFTS

American Shaker Song

Autoharp, strum A (high to low, using only eleven bass strings)
Guitar, strum 27
Soprano recorder

SING HALLELU

Black American Spiritual

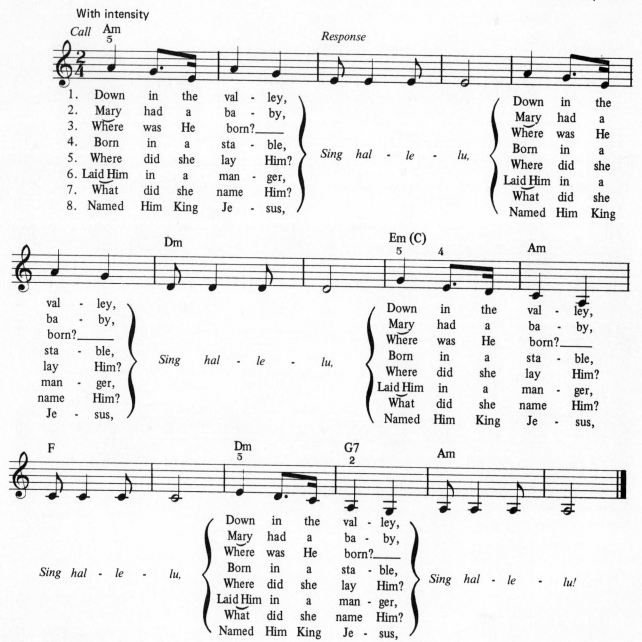

Autoharp, free rhythm
Guitar, strum 3
Piano, accompany using chord roots

SING NOEL

Round from Africa
(West Africa: Liberia)

Sing No - el, sing No - el, no - el, no - el.

Sing no - el, sing no - el, no - el, no - el.

Sing, sing no - el! Sing, sing no - el!

SING WE NOEL
(Noël Nouvelet)

French Carol

No - ël nou - ve - let, No - ël chan - tons i - ci,
noh - el noo - veh - lay noh - el shahn - tohn ee - cee

De - vo - tés gens, cri - ons a _____ Dieu mer - ci!
day - voh - tay jahn kree - ohns ah dyou mare - cee

Refrain:

Chan - tons No - ël pour le Roi nou - ve - let No - ël!
shahn - tohn noh - el poor lay rwahn noo - vay - lay noh - el

Chan - tons No - ël pour le Roi nou - ve - let!
shahn - tohn noh - el poor lay rwah noo - vay - lay

No - ël nou - ve - let, No - ël chan - tons i - ci!
noh - el noo - vay - lay noh - el shahn - tohn ee - cee

Autoharp, strum C
Piano, accompany using chord roots

"Sing We Noel" can be performed as a round during phrases 1, 2, and 5. (Sing in unison
during phrases 3 and 4.)

English version
Christmas comes anew, O let us sing Noel!
Glory to God! Now let your praises swell!
Refrain
Sing we Noel for Christ, the newborn King. Noel!
Sing we Noel for Christ, the newborn King!
Christmas comes anew, O let us sing Noel!

SINKIANG FOLK DANCE

Chinese Folk Melody

With spirit (♩ = 96)

Chromatic bells

Music has permeated Chinese life and thought for more than three thousand years. Instruments and voices were long used in folk, ceremonial, and court music, but ancient treatises tell us little about performance practices. We do know instruments were categorized according to their material: metal, stone, earth (pottery), skin, silk (for strings), wood, gourds, and bamboo. Possibly those instruments played in the same rough unison (heterophony) heard today, using considerable melodic and rhythmic ornamentation. The solo vocal style thought to be traditional uses thin, high, sometimes "squeezed" voices, with careful enunciation of wordy, elaborate melodies.

SIX LITTLE DUCKS

American School Song

1. Six lit - tle ducks that I once knew,
2. Down to the riv - er they once would go,

Fat ones, skin - ny ones, fair ones, too. But the one lit - tle duck with the
Wibble wobble, wib - ble wobble, to and fro.

feath - er in his back: He ruled the oth - ers with a quack, quack, quack,

quack, quack, quack. He ruled the oth - ers with a quack, quack, quack.

Autoharp, strum O
Guitar, strum 29
Piano, accompaniment pattern XVI

Create a pantomime that depicts the song's words.

SKIP TO MY LOU

American Play-Party Song

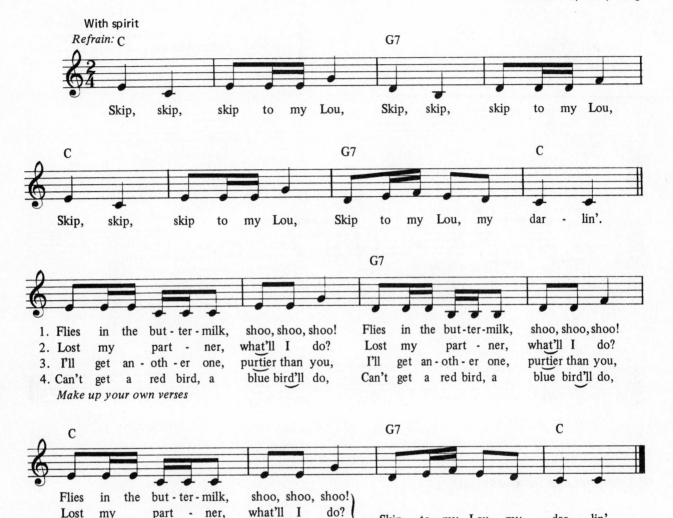

With spirit

Refrain:

Skip, skip, skip to my Lou, Skip, skip, skip to my Lou,

Skip, skip, skip to my Lou, Skip to my Lou, my dar - lin'.

1. Flies in the but - ter - milk, shoo, shoo, shoo! Flies in the but - ter - milk, shoo, shoo, shoo!
2. Lost my part - ner, what'll I do? Lost my part - ner, what'll I do?
3. I'll get an - oth - er one, purtier than you, I'll get an - oth - er one, purtier than you,
4. Can't get a red bird, a blue bird'll do, Can't get a red bird, a blue bird'll do,

Make up your own verses

Flies in the but - ter - milk, shoo, shoo, shoo!
Lost my part - ner, what'll I do?
I'll get an - oth - er one, purtier than you,
Can't get a red bird, a blue bird'll do,

Skip to my Lou, my dar - lin'.

Autoharp, strum E (banjo)
Guitar, strum 5
Piano, accompaniment pattern IV

Nineteenth-century Protestant communities in the south, particularly in Texas and Oklahoma, disapproved of social dancing. Even in square dancing, arms could encircle the waist of a partner. And of course, square dancers were accompanied by "the devil's own instrument," the fiddle. Therefore, the play-party, a sung dance, accompanied by the singing and hand clapping of the dancers themselves, was developed. Line, circle, and partner formations were permitted, as long as there was no embracing. The play-party gave teenagers and young marrieds a chance for fun and frolic but still satisfied parents and grandparents—who sometimes joined in. This homemade entertainment was popular on the frontier, and it spread westward wherever people made their own amusements.

SLEEP, MY BABE
(Dors, Dors, 'Tit Bébé)

Cajun Lullaby
(Recorded from the singing of
Barry Ancelot, Abbeville, LA. 1978)

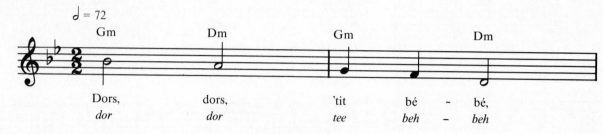

Autoharp, strum A (harp or drone)

English version
Sleep, sleep, tiny babe,
Listen to the river, listen to the river;
Sleep, sleep tiny babe,
Listen to the river____and dream.

SOMETIMES I FEEL LIKE A MOTHERLESS CHILD

Black American Spiritual

1. Some-times I feel like a moth-er-less child, ____ Some-times I feel like a moth-er-less child; ____ Some-times I feel like a moth-er-less child, ____ A long way ____ from home, ____ A long way ____ from home.

2. Some-times I feel like I'm al-most gone, ____ Some-times I feel like I'm al-most gone; ____ Some-times I feel like I'm al-most gone, ____ A long way ____ from

Autoharp, one strum each measure
Piano, accompany using chord roots

SONG FOR THE SABBATH
(Shabat, Shalom)

Hebrew Song

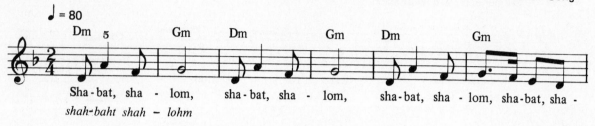

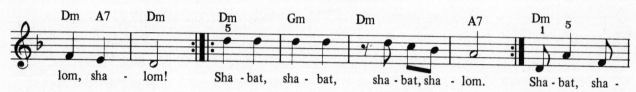

Sha-bat, sha — lom, sha-bat, sha — lom, sha-bat, sha — lom, sha-bat, sha-
shah-baht shah — lohm

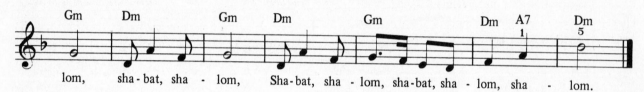

lom, sha — lom! Sha-bat, sha-bat, sha-bat, sha — lom. Sha-bat, sha-

lom, sha-bat, sha — lom, Sha-bat, sha — lom, sha-bat, sha — lom, sha — lom.

Autoharp, strum C

Piano, accompaniment pattern II

THE SONG OF ALI MOUNTAINS
(A Li Shan Jr Ge)

Deng Yu Pying

Song from Taiwan
Hwang You Di

chying;   jyan shwei chang _____   lan,   Gu nyang han na A li
chying   *tseeyehn sshway chahng*   *lahn*   *goo neeyahn hahn nah ah lee*

jung bu _____ fen ya,   bi shwei _ chang wei jr   chying shan jwan.
young boo fehn yah   *bee sshway chahng way jr*   *chying shahn joowahn*

Chromatic bells

English version

Green hills soar; blue seas roar,
Pretty girls of Ali, sweet as the waters,
Handsome Ali boys as bold as hills!
Ah!
Ah! _____
Pretty girls of Ali, sweet as the waters,
Handsome Ali boys as bold as hills!
Green, green hills soar, blue, blue seas roar!
Girls and boys of Ali, faithful ever,
Two will stay as one, as one!

English version by Patricia Hackett

SONG OF KURODA
(Kuroda Bushi)

Japanese Folk Song

Soprano recorder

Translation

Drink, drink sake. Drink and be rewarded with the most famous spear in all of Japan. Then you will also be a samurai of the Kuroda clan.

The high cultures of the Far East were already ancient when Marco Polo first glimpsed their wonders in the thirteenth century. A flourishing trade with distant lands had long conveyed new goods and ideas to Asia—along with music, instruments, and dance. China, Korea, and Japan synthesized these foreign introductions, absorbing them into their prevailing arts and culture. Each nation created a distinctive musical style but shared similar traits. All possessed a refined art music to accompany court and ritual functions and a rich and varied folk music for other festivals and ceremonies. Vocal music was most often for solo performers, but string, woodwind, and percussion instruments might play in groups of several hundred at lavish court spectacles in China. Remarkably, this instrumental music survives in Japan, where even today the imperial orchestra performs ancient court music, including a composition based on the folk melody "Kuroda Bushi."

SONG OF THE EAGLE

Wechihit Indians
(Central California)

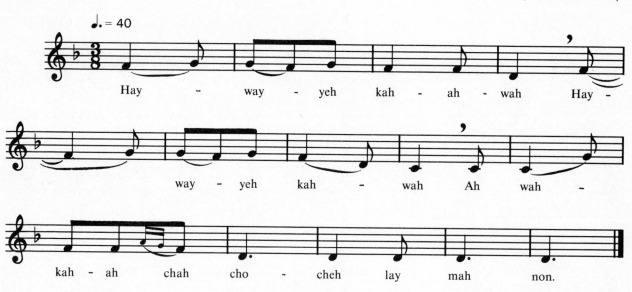

Translation: This song praises the eagle's soaring grace and strength.

"Song of the Eagle" uses a musical style like that of Ishi. Ishi was a Yahi Indian who lived secretly for many years with his small band in the northern California wilderness to escape the white man. In 1911 Ishi wandered into the yard of an Oroville slaughterhouse—the lone survivor of his people. Ishi spent his few remaining years living at the Anthropological Museum in San Francisco, where he patiently demonstrated his skills, told his stories, and sang the songs of his tribe. Ishi's friend Dr. Saxton T. Pope wrote: "He looked upon us as sophisticated children—smart, but not wise. We knew many things, and much that is false. He knew nature, which is always true. His were the qualities of character that last forever. He was kind; he had courage and self-restraint, and though all had been taken from him, there was no bitterness in his heart. His soul was that of a child, his mind that of a philosopher."

THE SOUND OF SILENCE

Paul Simon
(United States, b. 1941)

1. Hel - lo dark-ness, my old friend, I've come to talk with you a - gain,
Be-cause a vi - sion soft - ly creep - ing, Left its seeds while I was sleep - ing
And the vi - sion _____ that was plant - ed in my brain _____ still re - mains _____
_____ With-in the sound of si - lence. _____

2. In rest - less dreams I walked a -
3. And in the nak - ed light I
4. "Fools!" said I "You do not

lone   Nar - row streets of cob - ble - stone   'Neath the ha - lo of a
saw   Ten thou-sand peo - ple may - be more,   Peo - ple talk - ing with - out
know   Si - lence like a can - cer grows,   Hear my words that I might

street lamp, _____   I turned my col - lar to the cold and damp _____   When my eyes were stabbed _____
speak - ing _____   Peo - ple hear-ing with-out lis - ten - ing _____   Peo - ple writ - ing songs _____
teach you, _____   Take my arms that I might reach you." _____   But my words

247

by the flash of a ne - on light that split the night_____ and touched the
that voic - es nev - er share and no-one dare _____ dis - turb the
like silent rain - drops fell,

sound of si - lence.____
sound of si - lence.____

And ech - oed _____ in the

wells of si - lence.____ 5. And the peo - ple bowed and prayed

To the ne - on god they made. And the sign flashed out its warn - ing.__

In the words that it was form - ing, ___ And the signs said "The

words of the proph - ets are writ - ten on the sub - way walls ___ and ten - e - ment

halls" And whis - per'd _____ in the sounds of si - lence.____

Autoharp, strum O (try using pads of fingers)
Guitar, strum 27
Piano, accompaniment pattern XII

SPIN, MY TOP
(S'evivon)

Hebrew Song

S'e - vi - von, sov, sov, sov, Ha - nu - kah _____ hu hag tov,
seh - vee - vawn sove sove sove Hah - nuh - kah huh hahg tove

Ha - nu - kah, hu hag tov, s'e - vi - von, _____ sov, sov, sov.
Hah - nuh - kah huh hahg tove seh - vee - vawn sove sove sove

Autoharp, strum C
Piano, accompany using chord roots

English version
Spin, my top, *sov, sov, sov,*
Hanukah days we love,
Glowing lights, happy sounds,
Dreydl spinning 'round and 'round.

SPINNING WHEEL

David Clayton Thomas
(England)

Guitar, strum 4
Piano, accompaniment pattern V

STANDIN' IN THE NEED OF PRAYER

Black American Spiritual

♩ = 84

Refrain:

It's me, it's me, oh Lord, Stand-in' in the need of prayer; It's me, it's me, oh Lord, Stand-in' in the need of prayer.

Fine

1. Not my fa-ther nor my moth-er, but it's me, oh Lord,
2. Not my broth-er nor my sis-ter, but it's me, oh Lord,

Stand-in' in the need of prayer; Not my fa-ther nor my moth-er, but it's
Stand-in' in the need of prayer; Not my broth-er nor my sis-ter, but it's

D. C. al Fine

me, oh Lord, Stand-in' in the need of prayer.

Guitar, strum 2 (refrain) and 22 (verse)
Piano, accompaniment pattern XII

THE STAR-SPANGLED BANNER

Francis Scott Key
(United States, 1779—1843)

John Stafford Smith
(England, 1750—1836)

1. Oh___ say! Can you see, by the dawn's ear - ly light, What so
2. On the shore dim - ly seen thro' the mists of the deep, Where the
3. Oh___ thus be it e-ver when free men shall stand, Be -

proud - ly we hail'd At the twi - light's last gleam - ing? Whose broad
foe's haugh - ty host in dread si - lence re - pos - es. What is
tween their loved homes and the war's de - so - la - tion! Blest with

stripes and bright stars, thro' the per - il - ous fight, O'er the
that which the breeze, o'er the tow - er - ing steep, As it
vic - t'ry and peace, may the heav'n - res - cued land, Praise the

ram - parts we watch'd, were so gal - lant - ly stream - ing! And the
fit - ful - ly blows, half con - ceals, half dis - clos - es? Now it
Power that hath made and pre - served us a na - tion. Then___

rock - ets' red glare, the bombs burst - ing in air, Gave
catch - es the gleam of the morn - ing's first beam, In full
con - quer we must when our cause it is just, And

252

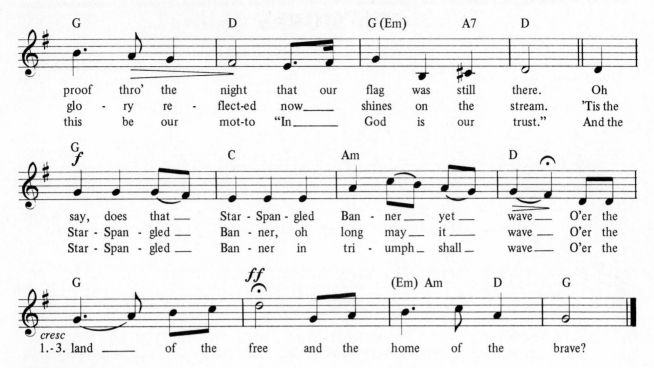

proof thro' the night that our flag was still there. Oh
glo - ry re - flect-ed now____ shines on the stream. 'Tis the
this be our mot-to "In____ God is our trust." And the

say, does that ___ Star - Span - gled Ban - ner ___ yet ___ wave ___ O'er the
Star - Span - gled ___ Ban - ner, oh long may ___ it ___ wave ___ O'er the
Star - Span - gled ___ Ban - ner in tri - umph ___ shall ___ wave ___ O'er the

1.-3. land _____ of the free and the home of the brave?

Autoharp, strum J

An American flag waves both day and night over Ft. McHenry in Baltimore and over a grave at Frederick in northwestern Maryland. These commemorate the attorney Francis Scott Key and the incident in 1814 which inspired him to write " The Defense of Ft. McHenry," later entitled "The Star-Spangled Banner." Key and a friend undertook a mission to secure the release of an American physician held prisoner on a British flagship. The venture was successful, but their boat was detained in Chesapeake Bay by the British, who began a bombardment of nearby Ft. McHenry. The shelling stopped during the night, but only after the morning fog lifted could the Americans see their flag still flying over the fort. On that very day—September 14—Key set down his verses. The text was immediately associated with a well-known hymn tune, already familiar to Key. Since 1931, "The Star-Spangled Banner" has been our official national anthem.

STARLIGHT, STARBRIGHT

Traditional American Song

Star - light, so bright, First star I see to - night.

Wish I may, wish I might Have the wish I wish to - night.

Soprano recorder (play one half step higher)

THE STORKS
(Gólya, Gólya, Gilice)

Hungarian Folk Song

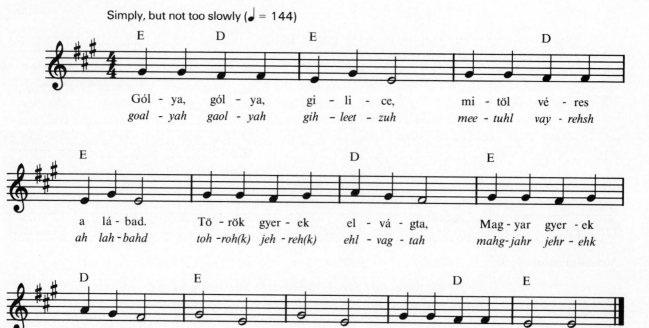

Simply, but not too slowly (♩ = 144)

Gól - ya, gól - ya, gi - li - ce, mi - töl vé - res
goal - yah gaol - yah gih - leet - zuh mee - tuhl vay - rehsh

a lá - bad. Tö - rök gyer - ek el - vá - gta, Mag - yar gyer - ek
ah lah - bahd toh - roh(k) jeh - reh(k) ehl - vag - tah mahg - jahr jehr - ehk

gyó - gyit - ja, Síp - pal, dob - bal, ná - di - he - ge - dü - vel.
joh - jeet - jah shee - pahl doh - bahl nah - dee - heh - geh - doo - val

Piano, use accompaniment pattern XI

This song my describe an ancient shamanistic healing practice.

English version
Lovely storks fly to the nest,
See how one must stop and rest.
Turkish children hurt the bird,
Magyar children want him cured.
Sing, play! Sing, play!
Music will restore you.

English version by Patricia Hackett

SUMMER IS A-COMING IN
(Sumer is icumen in)

English Round attr. to
John of Forsete
Thirteenth-century monk

Sum - er is i - cum - en in, _____ Lhu - de sing, cu - cu. Grow - eth seen and blow - eth med, and springth the woo - de nu; Sing cu - cu. Awe _____ blet - eth af - ter lomb, louth af - ter cal - ve cu; Bul - loc stert - eth, buc - ke vert - eth, mu - rie sing cu - cu. Cu - cu, cu - cu, Wel sing - es thu cuc - cu, Ne swik thu nav - er nu.

Soprano recorder

Translation

Summer is coming, the cuckoo sings loudly. The seeds in the fields and the woods grow. The cuckoo sings merrily. Cuckoo. Ewe bleat after lambs, cow after calf, the bull rises, the buck grazes. The cuckoo sings merrily. Cuckoo. How well sings the cuckoo. Never stop singing!

255

SYMPHONY NO. 1 IN C MINOR
Opus 68
Theme from fourth movement

Johannes Brahms
(Germany, 1833—1897)

Soprano recorder

Since the early nineteenth century, the symphony has been the large-scale, serious composition it remains today. Haydn, Mozart, Beethoven, and Brahms developed symphonic masterpieces, weaving and reweaving their musical ideas within the orchestral texture. Symphonic form typically includes three or four sections (movements) of varying character, tempo, and length. The first and fourth movements are often dramatic and move in a fast tempo. The second is usually slower and more pensive, while the third movement may be a quick, playful dance. Symphonies are usually designated by number, but in the fervor of nineteenth-century romanticism, a few have acquired programmatic subtitles.

SYMPHONY NO. 4 IN A MAJOR
Opus 90 *(Italian)*
Theme from second movement

Felix Mendelssohn
(Germany, 1809—1847)

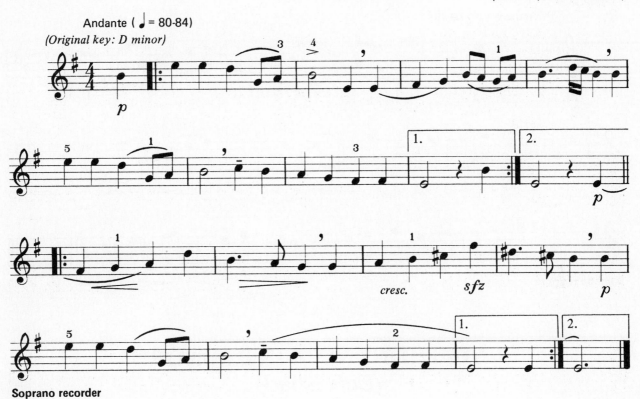

Soprano recorder

SYMPHONY NO. 6 IN B MINOR
Opus 74 *(Pathetique)*
First Movement, second theme

Pete Ilyich Tchaikovsky
(Russia, 1840—1893)

Soprano recorder

SYMPHONY NO. 8 IN B MINOR
(Unfinished)
First movement, third theme

Franz Schubert
(Austria, 1797—1828)

Soprano recorder

The ideals of nineteenth-century Romanticism infused music with a subjective, emotional lyricism. Some of the Romantic composers who sought greater freedom of form and expression were Beethoven, Schubert, Mendelssohn, Chopin, Wagner, Brahms, and Tchaikovsky. No longer subsidized by royal patrons, music began to serve a rising middle class audience. For the typical nineteenth-century artist, music transcended both time and place; it was the perfect expression of the soul.

SYMPHONY NO. 104 IN D MAJOR
(London)
Theme from first movement

Franz Joseph Haydn
(Austria, 1732—1809)

Allegro (♩ = 126)

Soprano recorder

TAILS

Traditional American Song

Lightly

Rac - coon's got a ring - ed tail, Pos - sum's tail is bare,

Rab - bit's got no tail at all, Just a lit - tle bit - ty bunch of hair. __

Chromatic bells

TAKE ME OUT TO THE BALL GAME

Jack Norworth

Albert von Tilzer

Take me out to the ball game, Take me out with the crowd. Buy me some pea-nuts and crack-er-jack, I don't care if we nev-er get back, Let me root, root, root for the home team, If they don't win it's a shame, For it's one, two, three strikes you're out at the old ball game

Autoharp (15-bar), strum J
Chromatic bells

TAKE THE "A" TRAIN

Billy Strayhorn
(United States, 1915—1967)

Piano, accompaniment pattern XI
Chromatic bells

You must take the "A" train
To go to Sugar Hill 'way up in Harlem.
If you miss the "A" train
You'll find you've missed the quickest way to Harlem.
Hurry, get on now, it's coming,
Listen to those rails a-thrumming.
All 'board! Get on the "A" train:
Soon you will be on Sugar Hill in Harlem. __ __

"Take the "A" Train" was the theme song of America's greatest jazz composer and arranger, Edward "Duke" Ellington (1899—1974). His orchestra, renowned for its precision and coordination, was as much Duke's instrument as was his piano. Working with exceptionally gifted individual performers (on trumpet, clarinet, saxophone, trombone, drums, and bass), Duke molded a group sound that was to become his trademark. Instruments were combined to produce tonal effects not possible with individual instruments. It was a well-rehearsed "big band" sound with a driving rhythm—a sound appreciated by jazz enthusiasts around the world. Throughout his long career Ellington remained an innovator, always searching for new techniques and forms of expression.

TALLIS' CANON

Bishop Thomas Ken
(England, 1637—1711)

Thomas Tallis
(England, c.1505—1585)

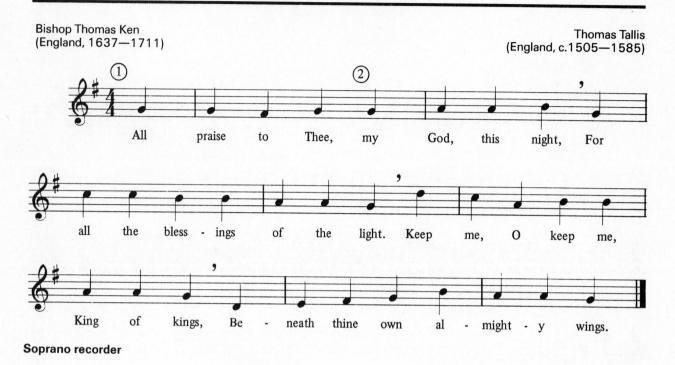

All praise to Thee, my God, this night, For
all the bless - ings of the light. Keep me, O keep me,
King of kings, Be - neath thine own al - might - y wings.

Soprano recorder

TEDDY BEAR

American Play Song

Jump rope tempo

1. Ted - dy bear, Ted - dy bear, turn a - round, ___
2. Ted - dy bear, Ted - dy bear, say your prayers, ___

Ted - dy bear, Ted - dy bear, touch the ground. Ted - dy bear, Ted - dy bear,
Ted - dy bear, Ted - dy bear, go up - stairs.

show your shoe, ___ Ted - dy bear, Ted - dy bear, that will do!

THANKS FOR THE FOOD

Danish Folk Song

Tak for ma-den, tak for ma-den, Bless this food we pray;
tack foor mah-dehn tack foor mah-dehn

Tak for ma-den, tak for ma-den, Thank Thee, Lord, to-day.
tack foor mah-dehn tack foor mah-dehn

Strength-en, love, and guide us, Stay Thou close be-side us;

Tak for ma-den, tak for ma-den, Bless this food we pray.
tack foor mah-dehn tack foor mah-dehn

Autoharp (15-bar), strum L
Guitar, strum 26
Piano, accompaniment pattern XI

THANK YOU FOR THE CHRIS'MUS

Jamaican Folk Song

Collected and transcribed by Olive Lewin. Reprinted by permission of the Organization of American States.

Autoharp, strum L
Piano, accompaniment pattern XI

THIS BEAUTIFUL WORLD
(Nani Ke Ao Nei)

Mary K. Puku'i
(Honolulu, Hawaii)

♩ = 44

1. I - lu - nă, la i - lu - nă,   Na mă - nu o ka lĕ - wa.
A - bove, up a - bove,   The birds fly so high.

2. I lă - lo, la i lă - lo,   Nā pu - a o ka ho - nu - a.
Be - low, down be - low,   The earth's flow - ers grow.

3. I u - kă, la i u - kă,   Ka u - lu lā____ 'au.
The up - lands, in the up - lands,   The green flow - ers grow.

4. I kai, la i kai,   Nā i - a o ka - mo a - na
The sea, in the sea,   The fish swim so free.

5. Ha - 'i - na mai Ka - pu - ȧ - na,   A he hȧ - ni - ke ao nei.
Now this ends my song,   Of a beau - ti - ful world.

Pronunciation Guide

Unstressed vowels
ā as in father
ē as in they
ī as in see
ō as in hoe
ū as in too

Stressed vowels
à as in above
è as in set
ì as in sit
ò as in obey
ù as in book

Consonants
k as in kodiak
w sounds w after *o* and *u*

w sounds soft "v" after a, e, and i

Other
' indicates a glottal stop

When no stress is indicated, use a pronunciation between the stressed and unstressed vowel.

"Nani Ke Ao Nei" is a mele hula *(literally "chant dance") composed in the style of the ancient chants heard by Captain James Cook and his men in 1778. It has two phrases (a couplet) using just two pitches a minor third apart (sol-mi). (Chants can use up to six pitches.) Like all mele hulas, "Nani Ke Ao Nei" has a regular meter and is accompanied by gestures and by one of several instruments made of gourd, bamboo, coconut, pebbles, skin, or wood. In a mele hula, singers use husky, deep-chested voices along with a dance that interprets the text. (There is also a type of chant without dance.) Mele hulas are usually sung in groups, somtimes sitting, sometimes standing. Depending on body position, hands, hips, and sometimes feet keep the rhythm of the dance. Three different rhythms go on simultaneously, that of the chant, that of the dance, and that of the instrument. Hawaiian music is still orally transmitted and performed by experienced musicians, many of whom express the same cosmic energy (mana) that inspired traditional creativity.*

Dancers sit in a row. One dancer gives the calls.

KAHEA   (Call):   "Ho'omakaukau!"   (Get ready! Dancers pick up sticks, which they have
                    "Pa!" (Begin. Literally, "strike.")   placed on the floor in front of themselves.)

(The drawings show the dancer's position from either the front or side, depending on which angle is clearer. The dancer's legs do not move from side to side during the dance. The letter R or L next to the drawings indicates which stick should be on top during striking.)

KI'I PA: These gestures are the introduction, the interludes between verses and the closing movements. On the last four beats if the Ki'i pa, the caller calls the first two or three words of each couplet.

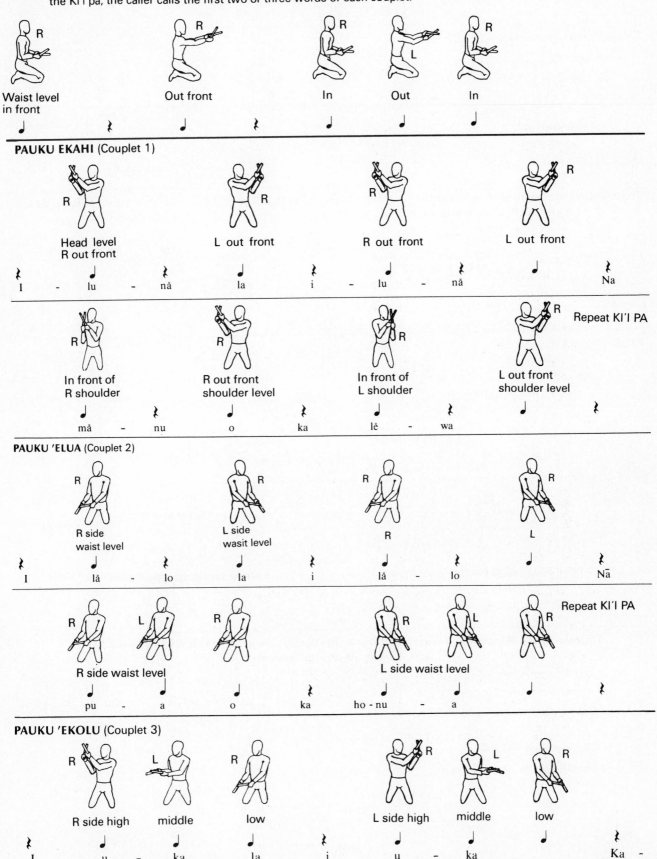

Waist level
in front   Out front   In   Out   In

PAUKU EKAHI (Couplet 1)

Head level   L out front   R out front   L out front
R out front

I - lu - nå   la   i - lu - nå   Na

In front of   R out front   In front of   L out front   Repeat KI'I PA
R shoulder   shoulder level   L shoulder   shoulder level

må - nu   o   ka   lě - wa

PAUKU 'ELUA (Couplet 2)

R side   L side   R   L
waist level   wasit level

I   lå - lo   la   i   lå - lo   Nā

R side waist level   L side waist level   Repeat KI'I PA

pu - a   o   ka   ho - nu - a

PAUKU 'EKOLU (Couplet 3)

R side high   middle   low   L side high   middle   low

I   u - ka   la   i   u - ka   Ka -

267

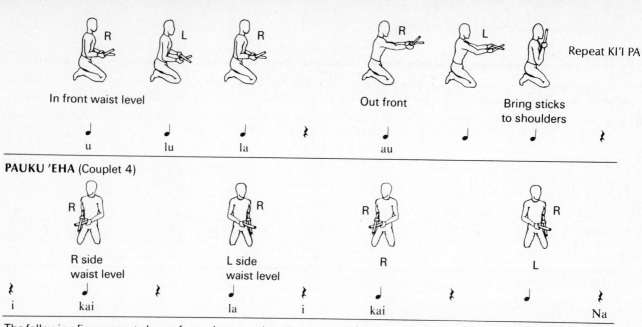

In front waist level | Out front | Bring sticks to shoulders | Repeat KI'I PA

u   lu   la   au

PAUKU 'EHA (Couplet 4)

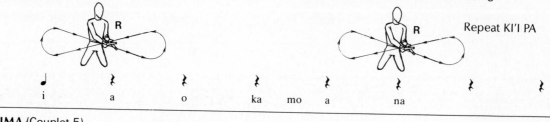

R side waist level | L side waist level | R | L

i   kai   la   i   kai   Na

The following figures are to be performed as a continuous series of swings, L to R; R to L; L to R—R to L—L to R. Sticks are not struck but held in crossed position throughout. The movement represents fish swimming.

Repeat KI'I PA

i   a   o   ka   mo   a   na

PAUKU 'ELIMA (Couplet 5)

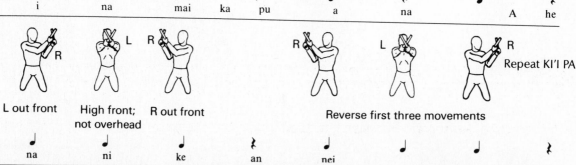

Mouth | R out front | Mouth | L out front

Ha   i   na   mai   ka   pu   a   na   A   he

L out front | High front; not overhead | R out front | Reverse first three movements | Repeat KI'I PA

na   ni   ke   an   nei

The closing KI'I PA requires one extra tap forward. The dancers drop their heads slightly on the last tap and all recite the closing dedication:

"HE INOA NO NA KAMALI'I

Translation: This is a name song for children

Choreography by Mary K. Puku'i

THIS LAND IS YOUR LAND

Words and music by Woodie Guthrie
(United States, 1912—1967)

Verse:

1. As I was walk - ing _____ that rib - bon of high - way. _____

_____ I saw a - bove me _____ that end - less sky - way, _____

_____ I saw be - low me _____ that gold en val - ley, _____

_____ This land was made for you and me. _____

Refrain:

This land is your land. _____ this land is my land, _____

_____ From Cal - i - for - nia _____ to the New York is - land, _____

_____ From the red - wood for - est to the Gulf Steam wa - ters; _____

This land was made for you and me._____

Guitar, strum 24

2. I've roamed and rambled and I followed my footsteps,
   To the sparkling sands of her diamond deserts,
   And all around me a voice came sounding,
   This land was made for you and me. *(Refrain)*

3. When the sun came shining, and I was strolling,
   And the wheat fields waving and the dust clouds rolling,
   As the fog was lifting a voice was chanting:
   This land was made for you and me. *(Refrain)*

4. In the square of the city in the shadow of the steeple,
   By the Relief Office I seen my people;
   As they stood there hungry, I stood there wondering if,
   This land was made for you and me. *(Refrain)*

5. As I went walking, That dirty old highway,
   I saw a sign that read private property,
   But on the other side it didn't say nothing,
   That side was made for you and me. *(Refrain)*

6. Nobody living can ever stop me,
   As I go walking that freedom highway;
   Nobody living can ever make me turn back,
   This land was made for you and me. (Refrain)

Woodrow Wilson Guthrie, American folk singer and ballad composer, was born on July 14, 1912, in Okemah, Oklahoma, and by 13 he was earning his own living. He became a wandering singer and writer of ballads in saloons, migrant labor camps, and hobo jungles. Depression memories of the 1930s mark his work on radio, in concerts, in newspaper columns, and in his autobiography, Bound for Glory. *"This Land Is Your Land" is among his nearly one thousand songs. Woodie's son Arlo Guthrie (born 1947) is also a folk song writer, composing "Alice's Restaurant" and starring in the 1969 film version.*

THIS OLD HAMMER

Black American Work Song

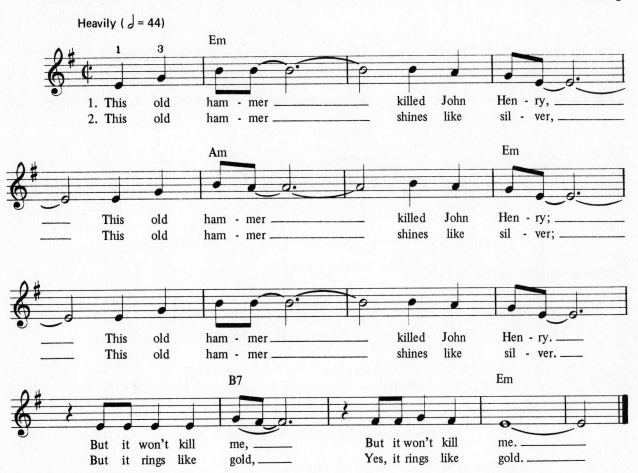

1. This old ham - mer _____ killed John Hen - ry, _____
2. This old ham - mer _____ shines like sil - ver, _____

_____ This old ham - mer _____ killed John Hen - ry; _____
_____ This old ham - mer _____ shines like sil - ver; _____

_____ This old ham - mer _____ killed John Hen - ry. _____
_____ This old ham - mer _____ shines like sil - ver. _____

But it won't kill me, _____ But it won't kill me. _____
But it rings like gold, _____ Yes, it rings like gold. _____

Autoharp (21-bar), strum A
Guitar, strum 6
Piano, accompaniment patttern XI

THIS OLD MAN

Traditional Song

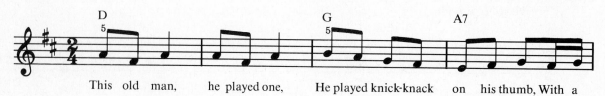

This old man, he played one, He played knick-knack on his thumb, With a

knick-knack pad-dy-whack, Give a dog a bone, This old man came roll-ing home.

Autoharp (15-bar), one strum each measure, use any (or all) of these: strum C, D, and E
Guitar, strum 4
Piano, accompaniment pattern III

2. This old man, he played two, He played knick-knack on my shoe,
   With a knick-knack paddy-whack, give a dog a bone, This old man came rolling home.

3. This old man, he played three, He played knick-knack on my knee,
   With a knick-knack paddy-whack, give a dog a bone, This old man came rolling home.

4. This old man, he played four, He played knick-knack on my door,
   With a knick-knack paddy-whack, give a dog a bone, This old man came rolling home.

5. This old man, he played five, He played knick-knack on my hive,
   With a knick-knack paddy-whack, give a dog a bone, This old man came rolling home.

6. This old man, he played six, He played knick-knack on my sticks,
   With a knick-knack paddy-whack, give a dog a bone, This old man came rolling home.

7. This old man, he played seven, He played knick-knack going to heaven,
   With a knick-knack paddy-whack, give a dog a bone, This old man came rolling home.

8. This old man, he played eight, He played knick-knack on my gate,
   With a knick-knack paddy-whack, give a dog a bone, This old man came rolling home.

9. This old man, he played nine, He played knick-knack all the time,
   With a knick-knack paddy-whack, give a dog a bone, This old man came rolling home.

10. This old man, he played ten, He played knick-knack over again,
    With a knick-knack paddy-whack, give a dog a bone, This old man came rolling home.

THIS TRAIN

Black American Spiritual

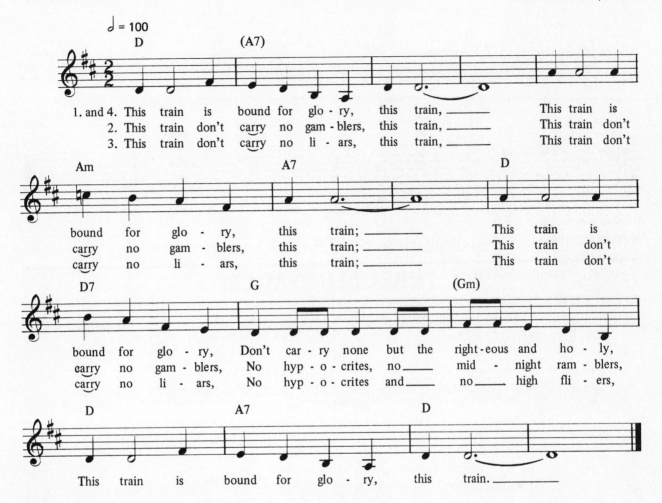

♩ = 100

1. and 4. This train is bound for glo - ry, this train, _____ This train is
2. This train don't carry no gam - blers, this train, _____ This train don't
3. This train don't carry no li - ars, this train, _____ This train don't

bound for glo - ry, this train; _____ This train is
carry no gam - blers, this train; _____ This train don't
carry no li - ars, this train; _____ This train don't

bound for glo - ry, Don't car - ry none but the right - eous and ho - ly,
carry no gam - blers, No hyp - o - crites, no_____ mid - night ram - blers,
carry no li - ars, No hyp - o - crites and_____ no_____ high fli - ers,

This train is bound for glo - ry, this train. _____

Guitar, strum 2
Piano, accompaniment pattern XVI

Black Americans created spirituals as music for worship during the era of slavery. They were collective expressions of a cohesive group, communicating with their God through music. Vividly pictorial, spirituals often told a story in which concepts were depicted in earthly terms. Heaven became a place where the poor might enjoy material abundance and where the streets might be paved with gold. Spirituals described a straightforward ethical code, with salvation the reward for those who spurned drinking, lying, and the like. Trains appear frequently in texts, along with rocks and rivers. Double meanings were common in spirituals: the train was probably a symbol of redemption as well as a means of escape from slavery.

273

THOU, POOR BIRD

Traditional Round

Thou, poor bird, Mourn'st the tree, Where sweet - ly thou didst war - ble In thy wan - d'rings free.

Autoharp, strum A
Soprano recorder

THREE BLIND MICE

Traditional Round

Three blind mice, ___ Three blind mice, ___ See how they run! ___

See how they run! ___ They all ran af - ter the farm - er's wife, She

cut off their tails with a carv - ing knife, Did you

ev - er see such a sight in your life as three blind mice?

Autoharp, strum B

274

THREE ROGUES

Traditional American Song

275

THROW IT OUT THE WINDOW

American Nonsense Song

Quickly

1. Make up a rhyme and sing it in time, And throw it out the
2. Lit - tle Jack Horn - er sat in a cor - ner Eating his Christ - mas

win - dow!_____ Make up a rhyme and sing it in time, And
pie,_____ Stuck in his thumb and pulled out a plum, And

Refrain

throw it out the win - dow!___ The win - dow,___ the win - dow,___ the
threw it out the win - dow!___

sec - ond sto - ry win - dow._____ Make up a rhyme and

sing it in time and throw it out the win - dow!_____

Autoharp, strum B

Patschen: Clap partner's hand(s):
Clap own hands:
Patschen (Pat own knees):

RH   LH   Both hands

*Each following verse is begun by a soloist. All singers join at * in measure 6.

3. Humpty Dumpty sat on a wall, Humpty Dumpty had a great fall,
   All the king's horses and all the king's men,
All: Threw him out the window!

Refrain (all singers):
The window, the window, the second story window,
Make up a rhyme and sing it in time
And throw it out the window!

4. Little Miss Muffet sat on a tuffet, Eating her curds and whey,
   Along came a spider and sat down beside her,
All: And threw her out the window! *(Refrain)*

5. Jack and Jill went up the hill to fetch a pail of water,
   Jack fell down and broke his crown,
All: And threw it out the window! *(Refrain)*

6. Little Tom Tinker, got burned with a clinker, And he began to cry,
   "Ma! Ma!"
All: And throw him out the window! *(Refrain)*

7. Seesaw, Margery Daw, Jack shall have a new master;
   He shall have but a penny a day,
All: And throw him out the window! *(Refrain)*

8. Oliver Twist can't do this, Touch his knees and touch his toes,
   Clap his hands and over he goes!
All: And throw him out the window! *(Refrain)*

TIDEO

American Game Song

Autoharp, strum D
Piano, accompaniment pattern III

Formation
Players stand in a circle with hands joined and arms raised to form arches (windows). One player (it) stands outside the circle.

Game
Measures 1–8: It walks into the circle under one window and out under another continuing until the word "Tideo." It then stops in front of a player in the circle.
Measures 9–12: The two players link elbows and swing. On the song's repeat, the player from the circle becomes it.

A TISKET, A TASKET

American Song

Soprano recorder

TODAY CHRIST IS BORN
(Hodie Christus Natus Est)

Gregorian Chant

Soprano recorder

Translation

Today Christ is born. Today the Savior hath appeared. Today Angels sing on earth, and Archangels rejoice. Today the just exult, saying Glory to God in the highest, alleluia.

Gregorian chant is Western civilization's most ancient music still in use. For centuries the liturgical chant of the Roman Catholic church, these subtle and free-flowing melodies probably originated in the synagogues of Jerusalem. The chant is named in honor of Pope Gregory I, who systematically reorganized the music of the church during his papacy from 590 to 604. Conveying a transcendent peace, the pure melody of Gregorian chant endures as a magnificent expression of humankind's religious faith.

TOEMBAI

Israeli Round

♩ = 100

① Am / Em / B7 / Em

Toem - bai, toem - bai, toem - bai, toem - bai, toem - bai, toem - bai, toem - bai.
toom - buy toom - buy toom - buy toom - buy toom - buy toom - buy toom - buy

② Am / Em / B7 / Em

Tra la la, la la la la la, La la la la la la.

③ Am / Em / B7 / Em

Tra la la la la, La la la la la, La la la la la, la.

Autoharp (21-bar), strum N
Guitar, strum 2

281

TOM DOOLEY

American Folk Song

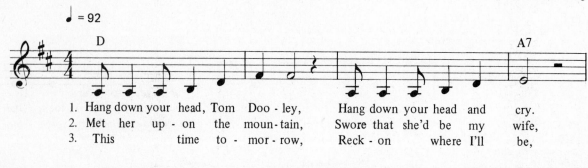

1. Hang down your head, Tom Doo-ley, Hang down your head and cry.
2. Met her up-on the moun-tain, Swore that she'd be my wife,
3. This time to-mor-row, Reck-on where I'll be,

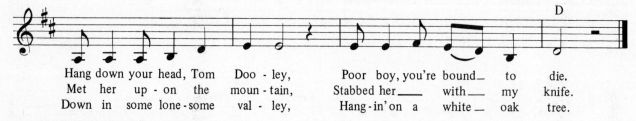

Hang down your head, Tom Doo-ley, Poor boy, you're bound to die.
Met her up-on the moun-tain, Stabbed her with my knife.
Down in some lone-some val-ley, Hang-in' on a white oak tree.

Autoharp, strum A
Guitar, strum 6 or play melody

"Tom Dooley" is one of many songs written about Tom Dula, a native of Wilkes Country, North Carolina. Tom rode hard and drank hard and had a way with the ladies. He served with the Confederates during the Civil War and was taken prisoner. After the war he renewed his relationship with Laura Foster, a former sweetheart. But at the same time he became involved with Ann Melton, though she had a husband and children. Tom lured Laura into riding off with him, and on a hillside, stabbed her and buried her in a shallow grave. Both Tom and Ann were arrested because many believed she instigated the crime. (Ann was later freed because Tom refused to implicate her.) The two year trial was covered by correspondents from as far away as New York City. Tom was convicted and hanged in 1868.

THE TORTILLAS VENDOR

Chilean Folk Song

No-che-os - cu - ra, nada ve - o, Pe - ro
noh-chay-ohs - coo - rah nah - dah bay - oh pay - roh

lle - vo mi fa - rol, Por tus puer - tas, voy pa -
yay - voh mee fah - rohl pour toos pwehr - tahs boy pah -

san - do, Y can - tan - do con a - mor.
sahn - doh ee cahn - tahn - doh cohn ah - more

Refrain:

Mas voy can - tan - do Con
mahs boy cahn - tahn - doh cohn

har - ta pe - na, Quien com - pra mis tos ta
hahr - tah pay - nah k'yehn cohm - prah mees tohs tah

di - tas, Tor - ti - llas bue - nas.
dee - tahs tohr - tee - yahs bway - nahs

Autoharp, strum H
Guitar, strum 16
Piano, accompaniment pattern VII

English version
Night is falling, comes the darkness,
But a lantern is my light.
I walk slowly past your window,
And I sing a sweet goodnight.

(Refrain:)
Please hear my singing, for you it's ringing:
"Who'll buy my fine *tostaditas?* Tasty tortillas!

THE TREE FROG
(El Coquí)

Puerto Rican Folk Song

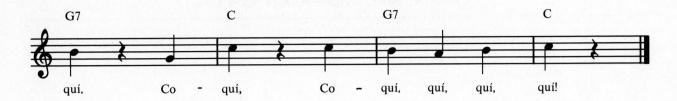

qui,   Co - quí,   Co - quí, quí, quí,   quí!

Autoharp, strum H
Piano, accompaniment pattern VIII

English version
El coquí sings his songs oh so sweetly,
I can hear *el coquí* all night long;
Though I fall fast asleep when it's bedtime
In my dream comes his nice little song;
Coquí! Coquí! Coquí-quí-quí-quí!
Coquí! Coquí! Coquí-quí-quí-quí!

TURN THE GLASSES OVER

Anglo-American
Folk Song

Walking tempo

I've been to Haar - lem, I've been to Do - ver, I've trav - eled all this

wide world o - ver, O - ver, o - ver, three times o - ver,

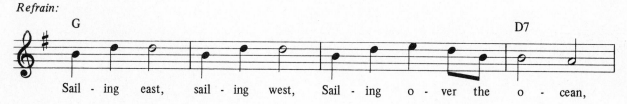

Drink all you want to drink and turn the glass - es o - ver.

Refrain:

Sail - ing east, sail - ing west, Sail - ing o - ver the o - cean,

Bet - ter watch out when the boat be - gins to rock, Or you'll

lose your girl in the o - cean.

Autoharp, strum A
Guitar, strum 2 or 5
Piano, accompaniment pattern XVI
Soprano recorder

286

TURN! TURN! TURN!
(To Everything There Is a Season)

Words from Ecclesiastes
Adaptation and Music by Pete Seeger
(United States, b.1919)

Autoharp (21-bar), strum A; at measure 9, one strum for each measure
Guitar, strum 27; at measure 9, one strum for each measure
Piano, accompaniment pattern XVII

A member of a well-known musical family, Pete Seeger has been active on the folk-music scene since his student days at Harvard University. Seeger is a composer, performer, political activist, and a leader in the environmental effort to save New York's Hudson River from pollution.

TURN YE TO ME

John Wilson
(Scotland, 1785—1854)

Scottish Folk Song

♩ = 84

| Am | (G) | C | | Am | C |

1. The stars are shin - ing cheer - i - ly, cheer - i - ly, } Ho - ro,
2. The waves are danc - ing mer - ri - ly, mer - ri - ly, }

| Am | C G7 | C | Am | (G) | C |

Mhai - ri dhu, Turn ye ___ to me. { The sea mew is moan - ing
mah - ree doo { The sea birds are wail - ing

| Am | C | Am | C G7 |

drea - ri - ly, drea - ri - ly, } Ho - ro, Mhai - ri dhu, Turn ye ___ to
wea - ri - ly, wea - ri - ly, } *mah - ree - doo*

| C | Am | F | C |

me. { Cold is the storm wind that ruf - fles his breast, But warm are the
{ Hushed be thy moan - ing, lone bird of the sea, Thy home on the

| Am | C | G | C | Am |

down - y plumes lin - ing his nest, Cold blows the storm ___ there,
rock is a shel - ter to thee; Thy home is the an - gry wave,

| F | G7 | C | Am | C G7 | C |

soft falls the snow ___ there, } Ho - ro, Mhai - ri dhu, Turn ye ___ to me.
mine but the lone - ly grave, } *mah - ree doo*

Autoharp, strum J

288

THE TWELVE DAYS OF CHRISTMAS

English Folk Song

1. On the first day of Christ-mas my true love sent to me A par-tridge in a pear tree.

2. On the sec-ond day of Christ-mas my true love sent to me
3. On the third day of Christ-mas my true love sent to me
4. On the fourth day of Christ-mas my true love sent to me

Two tur-tle doves, And a par-tridge in a pear tree.
Three French hens,
Four call-ing birds,

5. On the fifth day of Christ-mas my true love sent to me

Five gold-en rings; Four call-ing birds; Three French hens;

Two tur-tle doves and a par-tridge in a pear tree.

6. On the sixth day of Christ-mas my true love sent to me
7. On the seventh day of Christ-mas my true love sent to me
8.-12.

Six geese a lay-ing; Five gold-en rings; Four call-ing birds;
Seven swans a-swim-ming;

Three French hens; Two tur-tle doves and a par-tridge in a pear tree.

Autoharp, try a different strum for each verse, such as/or strum D C use strum per measure for measures 14, 15, 21, 24, and 25

Piano, accompaniment pattern XVII use X for measures 14, 15, 21, 24, and 25

8. On the eighth day...
   Eight maids a-milking;...

9. On the ninth day...
   Nine ladies dancing...

10. On the tenth day...
    Ten lords a-leaping...

11. On the eleventh day...
    Eleven pipers piping...

12. On the twelfth day of Christmas
    My true love sent to me,
    Twelve drummers drumming;
    Eleven pipers piping;
    Ten lords a-leaping;
    Nine ladies dancing;
    Eight maids a-milking;
    Seven swans a-swimming;
    Six geese a-laying; Five golden rings;
    Four calling birds; Three French hens;
    Two turtle doves and a partridge in a
        pear tree.

TWINKLE, TWINKLE LITTLE STAR

French Song

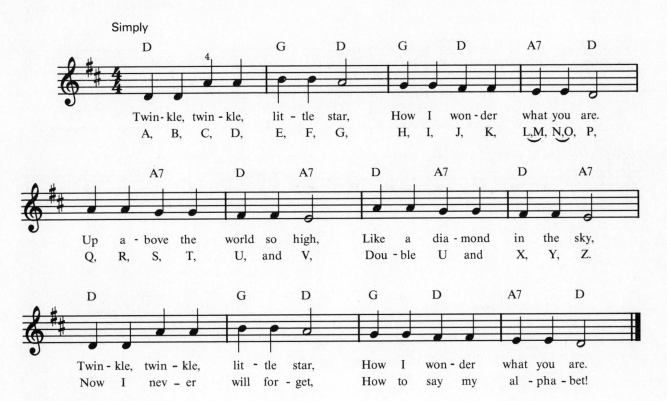

Simply

Twin-kle, twin-kle, lit-tle star, How I won-der what you are.
A, B, C, D, E, F, G, H, I, J, K, L, M, N, O, P,

Up a-bove the world so high, Like a dia-mond in the sky,
Q, R, S, T, U, and V, Dou-ble U and X, Y, Z.

Twin-kle, twin-kle, lit-tle star, How I won-der what you are.
Now I nev-er will for-get, How to say my al-pha-bet!

Autoharp (15-bar), strum A
Guitar, strum 28 or play melody
Piano, accompaniment pattern XIV
Soprano recorder

Adjust the rhythm of this nursery rhyme to fit the "Twinkle, Twinkle Little Star" melody:

Baa, baa, black sheep, have you any wool?
"Yes sir, yes sir, three bags full.
One for my master and one for my dame,
And one for the little boy who lives in the lane."
Baa, baa, black sheep, have you any wool?
"Yes sir, yes sir, three bags full."

UP ON THE HOUSETOP

Benjamin R. Hanby
(United States, 1833—1867)

1. Up on the house-top the rein-deer pause, Out jumps good old Santa Claus; Down through the chim-ney with lots of toys, All for the lit-tle ones' Christ-mas joys.
2. First comes the stock-ing of lit-tle Nell, Oh dear San-ta fill it well; Give her a dol-ly that laughs and cries, One that can o-pen and shut its eyes.
3. Next comes the stock-ing of lit-tle Will, Oh, just see what a glori-ous fill; Here is a ham-mer and lots of tacks, Al-so a ball and a whip that cracks.

Ho, ho, ho! Who would-n't go! Ho, ho, ho! Who would-n't go, _____ Up on the house-top, click, click, click, Down through the chim-ney with good Saint Nick!

Autoharp (15-bar), strum O
Guitar, strum 24

Create a pantomime or dramatization for this song.

UP THE HICKORY

American Folk Song

Lively (♩ = 112)

Let us chase the squir - rel, Up the hick - o - ry, down the hick - o - ry,

Let us chase the squir - rel, Up the hick - o - ry tree.

Autoharp (15-bar), strum C
Guitar, strum 5
Piano, accompaniment pattern II

ÜSKÜDAR

Popular Turkish Song

♩ = 96

Üs - kü - dar' a gi - der _ i ken al - li - da bir yağ mur,
uhs - kuh-dahr ah gih - dehr ih kehn ahl - lih - dah bihr yahj muhr

Ka - ti - bi - min se - tre - si u - zun e - te - ği ça -
kah - tih - bih - mihn seh - treh - sih uh - zuhn eh - teh - jih - sah -

mur. e te - ği ça - mur.
muhr eh - teh - jih - sah - muhr

Autoharp (21-bar), strum C (middle eastern)
Guitar, strum 3
Piano, accompany using chord roots

English version
Ushkada'a, Ushkadar' a.
See how it rains out here! *(repeat lines 1 and 2)*
Come, my darling, do not worry:
Love will keep us warm! *(repeat lines 3 and 4)*

293

A WAND'RING MINSTREL
(From The Mikado)

William S. Gilbert
(England, 1836—1911)

Arthur S. Sullivan
(England, 1842—1900)

A wan-d'ring min-strel I, A thing of shreds ___ and patch-es, Of bal-lads, songs and snatch-es, And dream-y lul-la-by! ___ My cat-a-logue is long, Thro' ev-'ry pas-sion rang-ing, And to your hu-mours chang-ing I tune my sup-ple song! ___ I tune ___ my sup - - - ple song!

dream - y lul - la - by, ___ And dream - y lul - - la-lul - la - by, ___ lul - la - by! ___

Autoharp (15-bar), strum B

The plot of The Mikado, or The Town of Titipu (1885), is as follows: Learning that his former rival has been beheaded, the wand'ring minstrel appears, to renew his courtship of the delectable Yum Yum. In truth, his rival has survived, and also returns to wed Yum Yum. The minstrel nevertheless declares his love to Yum Yum—and reveals that he is the Mikado's son in disguise! After an incredible series of events in which the minstrel succeeds in escaping betrothel to an elderly courtesan and avoids execution by his own father (the Mikado), he finally succeeds in marrying Yum Yum.

WAR DANCE

Collected by Patricia Hackett

Native American Dance Song

Soloist initially; all singers join on repetition

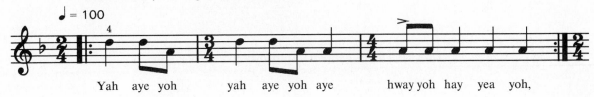

Yah   aye   yoh   yah   aye   yoh   aye   hway   yoh   hay   yea   yoh,

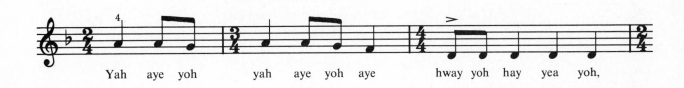

Yah   aye   yoh   yah   aye   yoh   aye   hway   yoh   hay   yea   yoh,

Yah   aye   yoh   yah   aye   yoh   aye   hway   yoh   hay   yea   yoh,

Yah   hay   yah   ho   yah   aye   hah hway yoh   hay   yea   yoh,

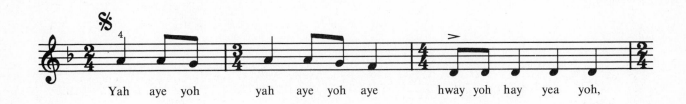

Yah   aye   yoh   yah   aye   yoh   aye   hway   yoh   hay   yea   yoh,

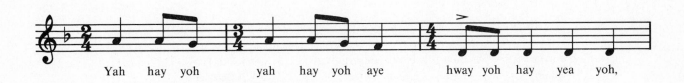

Yah   hay   yoh   yah   hay   yoh   aye   hway   yoh   hay   yea   yoh,

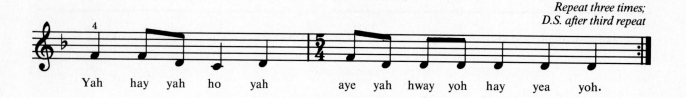

Repeat three times;
D.S. after third repeat

Yah   hay   yah   ho   yah   aye   yah   hway   yoh   hay   yea   yoh.

On a large drum, perform this rhythm during "War Dance":

Dance
Dancers move in a large circle, each inde-
pendently dancing the traditional toe-heel
step. A large drum in the center is played
by a group of about six male singers.
The dancers do not sing.

One might as well attempt to catch the wind in a bottle as to transcribe Native American song into music notation. It is impossible to suggest the pulsating, throaty, accented style of singers from the Plains. A noisy, individualized unison is heard in war dance songs, when four to eight drummers sing and accompany themselves on a drum nearly as booming as their big-chested, wide-voiced singing. Vocal slides and glottal strokes add to the slurred enunciation and make the vocables difficult to understand. This "War Dance" is typical of the terraced melodies of the Plains, descending from a high pitch to the lowest sung note, where the song ends. Sing this dance three times at a fast tempo, but with a controlled sound. Strive for intensity, but within tranquility.

THE WASHINGTON POST
March

John Philip Sousa
(United States, 1854—1932)

297

Chromatic bells

John Philip Sousa, the "March King," is best remembered as the composer of 140 military marches. He was also a dynamic and successful bandmaster, who directed the U.S. Marine Band from 1880 to 1892 and, later, his own world-famous group.

WASSAIL SONG

English Carol

1. Here we come a - was-sail-ing, A - mong the leaves so green, __ Here we come a - wan - d'ring, So fair __ to be seen;

2. Our was-sail cup is made __ Of the rose - mar - y tree, __ And so is your beer Of the best __ bar - ley:

3. We are not dai - ly beg - gars That beg from door to door, __ But we are neigh-bors' chil - dren Whom you have seen be - fore;

Refrain:

Love and joy come to you, And to you your was - sail too, And God bless you, and send __ you a hap - py New Year, And God send you a hap - py New __ Year.

Autoharp (15-bar), strum B and A

299

4. Call up the butler of this house
   Put on his gold ring;
   Let him bring us up a glass of beer,
   And better we shall sing: *(Refrain)*

5. We have got a little purse
   Of stretching leather skin;
   We want a little money
   To line it well within: *(Refrain)*

6. Bring us out a table
   And spread it with a cloth;
   Bring us out a mouldy cheese,
   And some of your Christmas loaf: *(Refrain)*

7. God bless the master of this house
   And the mistress too,
   And all the little children
   That 'round the table go: *(Refrain)*

8. Good master and good mistress
   While you're sitting by the fire,
   Pray think of us poor children
   Who are wand'ring in the mire: *(Refrain)*

THE WATER IS WIDE
(Waly, Waly)

Elizabethan Folk Song
(England)

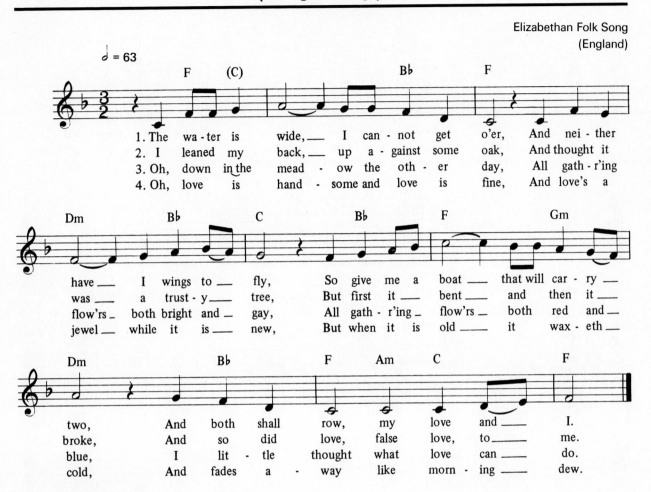

1. The wa-ter is wide,___ I can-not get o'er, And nei-ther
2. I leaned my back,___ up a-gainst some oak, And thought it
3. Oh, down in the mead-ow the oth-er day, All gath-r'ing
4. Oh, love is hand-some and love is fine, And love's a

have___ I wings to___ fly, So give me a boat___ that will car-ry ___
was___ a trust-y___ tree, But first it___ bent___ and then it___
flow'rs_ both bright and _ gay, All gath-r'ing_ flow'rs _ both red and ___
jewel___ while it is___ new, But when it is old ___ it wax-eth ___

two, And both shall row, my love and ___ I.
broke, And so did love, false love, to___ me.
blue, I lit-tle thought what love can ___ do.
cold, And fades a-way like morn-ing ___ dew.

Autoharp, free strum
Piano, accompaniment pattern X

301

WEEVILY WHEAT

American Dance Song

1. Char - lie's neat and Char - lie's sweet, Char - lie is a dan - dy,
2. Your weevi - ly wheat's not fit to eat, nei - ther is your bar - ley,
3. Char - lie is a brave young man, Char - lie is a sol - dier,
4. Char - lie is a nice young man, Char - lie is a dan - dy,

Char - lie is a nice young man, he feeds the girls on can - dy.
What I want is the best of rye to bake a cake for Char - lie.
Sword and pis - tol by his side, his mus - ket on his shoul - der.
Char - lie likes to swing the girls, and he can do it han - dy.

Refrain:
Rise you up in the morn - ing, all to - geth - er ear - ly; You
need not feel at all a - fraid be - cause I love you dear - ly.

Autoharp, strum A
Piano, accompaniment pattern XVI

Formation
Two lines of five or six couples face each other.

Action
Verse 1: First couple take both hands, straight across, and "sashay" down the middle (eight counts) and back again (eight counts).
Verse 1, Refrain: Begin the reel; first couple turns clockwise once and a half, hooking right elbows. The the first boy turns the second girl, hooking left elbows, counterclockwise once around, while the first girl turns the second boy the same way. Then the first couple turn each other once around again with right elbows, and so forth, continuing to the last couple.

Verse 2 and 3: Continue the reel and finish the reeling just before the refrain of verse 3.

Verse 3, Refrain: The last couple join raised hands forming an arch. Dancers cast off by moving in line to the top and then down the outside. The boys' line casts off to the left, the girls' line casts off to the right; partners meet below the arch and come back up the middle to places. Use a skipping step throughout.

302   Repeat until each couple has done all figures.

WE GATHER TOGETHER

English version by Theodore Baker

Netherlands Melody

♩ = 76

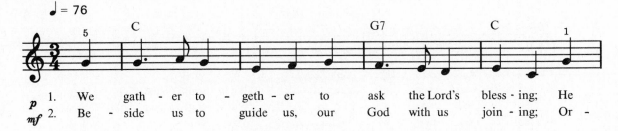

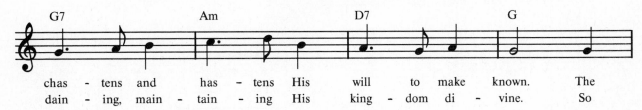

1. We gath-er to-geth-er to ask the Lord's bless-ing; He
2. Be-side us to guide us, our God with us join-ing; Or-

chas-tens and has-tens His will to make known. The
dain-ing, main-tain-ing His king-dom di-vine. So

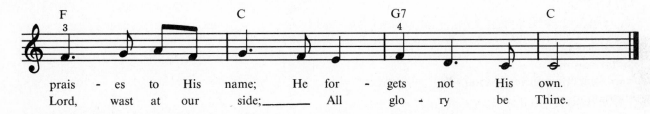

wick-ed op-press-ing, now cease____ from dis-tress-ing. Sing
from the be-gin-ining, the fight____ we were win-ning. Thou,

prais-es to His name; He for-gets not His own.
Lord, wast at our side;____ All glo-ry be Thine.

Autoharp, strum J (harp)
Piano, accompaniment pattern VI

3. We all do extol Thee, Thou leader triumphant.
   And pray that Thou still our defender wilt be.
   Let Thy congregation escape tribulation.
   Thy name be ever praised!
   O Lord make us free!

WE SHALL OVERCOME

Civil Rights Song

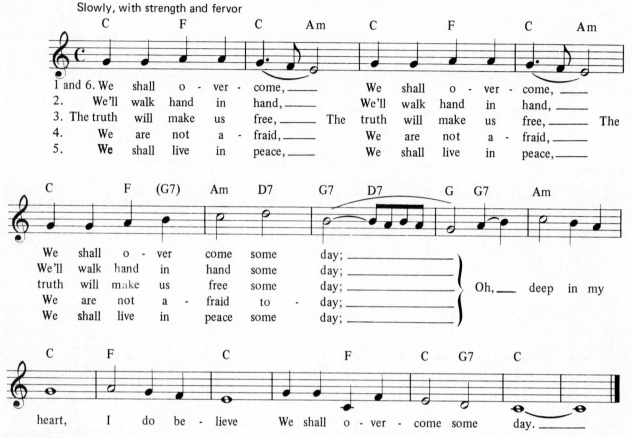

Slowly, with strength and fervor

1 and 6. We shall o - ver - come, _____ We shall o - ver - come, _____
2. We'll walk hand in hand, _____ We'll walk hand in hand, _____
3. The truth will make us free, _____ The truth will make us free, _____ The
4. We are not a - fraid, _____ We are not a - fraid, _____
5. We shall live in peace, _____ We shall live in peace, _____

We shall o - ver come some day; _____
We'll walk hand in hand some day; _____
truth will make us free some day; _____ } Oh, _____ deep in my
We are not a - fraid to - day; _____
We shall live in peace some day; _____

heart, I do be - lieve We shall o - ver - come some day. _____

Autoharp, strum A
Guitar, strum 2
Piano, accompaniment pattern XI
Soprano recorder

Other verses sung during the movement for integration included:
  We shall brothers be...
  We shall end Jim Crow...
  Black and white together...
  We shall all be free...

A Spanish text was sung during the drive to unionize farm workers:
  Nostros venceremos, nostros venceremos,
  Nostros venceremos ahora;
  En mi corazón yo creo.
  Nostros venceremos.

WEST VIRGINIA

American Ballad

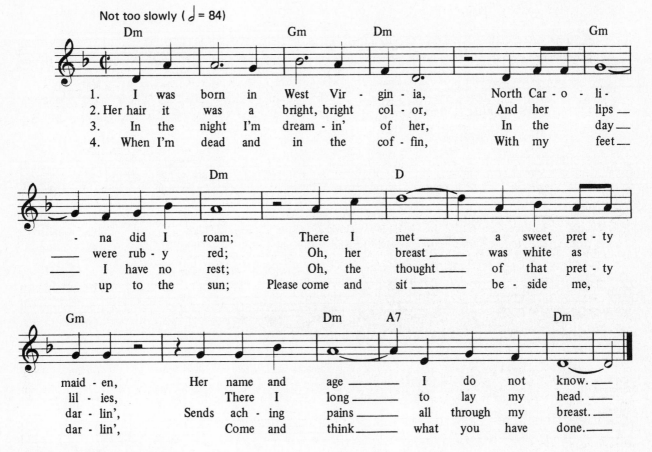

Not too slowly (♩ = 84)

1. I was born in West Vir - gin - ia, North Car - o - li -
2. Her hair it was a bright, bright col - or, And her lips __
3. In the night I'm dream - in' of her, In the day __
4. When I'm dead and in the cof - fin, With my feet __

__ na did I roam; There I met __ a sweet pret - ty
__ were rub - y red; Oh, her breast __ was white as
__ I have no rest; Oh, the thought __ of that pret - ty
__ up to the sun; Please come and sit __ be - side me,

maid - en, Her name and age __ I do not know. __
lil - ies, There I long __ to lay my head. __
dar - lin', Sends ach - ing pains __ all through my breast. __
dar - lin', Come and think __ what you have done. __

Autoharp (15-bar), strum O

WHAT CHILD IS THIS?

William Chatterton Dix (England, 1837—1898)

English Folk Song

1. What Child is this, ___ who laid to rest ___ On Mar - y's
2. Why lies He in ___ such mean es - tate ___ Where ox and
3. So bring Him in - cense, gold and myrrh, ___ Come peas - ant,

lap ___ is sleep - ing? Whom an - gels greet ___ with an - thems
ass ___ are feed - ing? Good Chris - tian, fear, ___ for sin - ners
king ___ to own Him; The King of Kings, ___ sal - va - tion

sweet, ___ While shep - herds watch ___ are keep - ing?
here, ___ The si - lent word ___ is plead - ing.
brings, ___ Let lov - ing hearts ___ en - throne Him.

Refrain:

This, this ___ is Christ the King, ___ whom shep - herds
Nails, nails ___ shall pierce Him through, ___ the cross He
Raise, raise ___ the song on high, ___ the Vir - gin

guard ___ and an - gels sing; Haste, haste, to
bore ___ for me, for you; Hail, hail, the
sings ___ her lul - la - by; Joy, joy, for

| C | | | Dm | | A(7) | | Dm | |

bring   Him   laud, ——
word   made   flesh, —— } The   Babe,   the   Son —— of   Mar - y!
Christ   is   born ——

Autoharp, strum once each measure, harp strum
Guitar, strum 21
Piano, accompaniment pattern VIII

New Year's version (1642)
    The old year now away is fled, The new year it is enteréd,
    And let us now our sins down tread, And joyfully all appear.
      Let's merry be this day
      And let us now both sport and play;
      Hang grief, cast care away!
    God send us a happy New Year!"

Greensleeves

1. Alas, my love, you do me wrong To cast me off discourteously,
   When I have loved you so long, Delighting in your company.
Refrain:
Greensleeves was all my joy, Greensleeves was my delight,
Greensleeves was my heart of gold, And who but my lady Greensleeves.

2. I have been ready at your hand, To grant whatever you would crave;
   I have both wagered life and land, Your love and goodwill for to have. *(Refrain)*

3. Thou couldst desire no earthly thing, But still thou hadst it readily;
   My music still to play and sing, And yet thou wouldst not love me. *(Refrain)*

4. I bought thee kerchers to thy head, That were wrought fine and gallantly;
   I kept thee both at board and bed, Which cost my purse well favouredly. *(Refrain)*

5. Thy gown was of the grassy green, Thy sleeves of satin hanging by,
   Which made thee be our harvest queen, And yet thou wouldst not love me. *(Refrain)*

6. Well, I will pray to God on high, That thou my constancy mayst see;
   And that yet once before I die, Thou will vouchsafe to love me. *(Refrain)*

7. Oh, Greensleeves, now farewell, adieu, God I pray to prosper thee;
   For I am still thy lover true, Come once again and love me. *(Refrain)*

The tune "Greensleeves" is a love song from the Elizabethan period and was so well known that Shakespeare used it in several of his plays. The melody is sometimes varied, perhaps with the fifth note of the tune sung a half step higher or the third note of the refrain sung a half step lower.

WHAT'LL I DO WITH THE BABY-O?

American Fiddle Melody

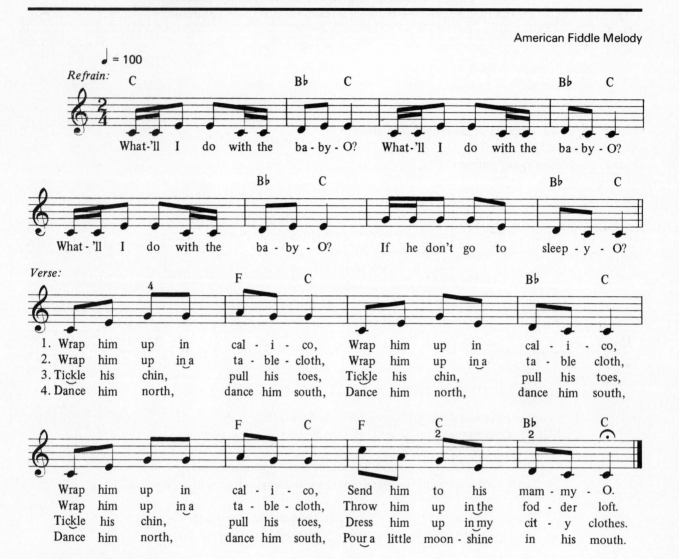

Refrain:

What-'ll I do with the ba-by-O? What-'ll I do with the ba-by-O?

What-'ll I do with the ba-by-O? If he don't go to sleep-y-O?

Verse:

1. Wrap him up in cal-i-co, Wrap him up in cal-i-co,
2. Wrap him up in a ta-ble-cloth, Wrap him up in a ta-ble cloth,
3. Tickle his chin, pull his toes, Tickle his chin, pull his toes,
4. Dance him north, dance him south, Dance him north, dance him south,

Wrap him up in cal-i-co, Send him to his mam-my-O.
Wrap him up in a ta-ble-cloth, Throw him up in the fod-der loft.
Tickle his chin, pull his toes, Dress him up in my cit-y clothes.
Dance him north, dance him south, Pour a little moon-shine in his mouth.

Autoharp, strum E (banjo)
Piano, accompany using chord roots

308

WHEN JESUS WEPT

William Billings
(United States, 1746—1800)

When Je - sus wept, ___ the fall - ing tear In
mer - cy flowed ___ be - yond all bound; When Je - sus groaned ___ a
trem - bling fear Seized all ___ the guilt - y world ___ a - round.

WHEN THE SAINTS GO MARCHIN' IN

Black American Spiritual

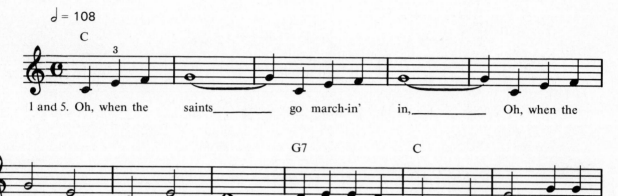

Autoharp, strum M
Guitar, strum 25
Piano, accompaniment pattern XI

2. <u>Oh</u>, when the sun refuse to shine, Oh, when the sun refuse to <u>shine</u>,
   Oh Lord, I <u>want</u> to be in that <u>number</u>, When the <u>sun</u> refuse <u>to</u> <u>shine</u>.

3. <u>Oh</u>, when the stars have disappeared, Oh, when the stars have disappeared,
   Oh Lord, I <u>want</u> to be in that <u>number</u>, When the <u>stars</u> have dis<u>appeared</u>.

4. <u>Oh</u>, when the day of judgement comes, Oh when the day of judgement <u>comes</u>,
   Oh Lord, I w<u>ant</u> to be in that <u>number</u>, When the <u>day</u> of judg<u>ement</u> <u>comes</u>.

WHILE STROLLING THROUGH THE PARK

Words and music by Ed Haley

Chromatic bells

Create a medley of turn-of-the-century songs: "While Strolling Through the Park," "Give My Regards to Broadway," and "Hello! Ma' Baby." For page numbers, see the Alphabetical Index of Melodies.

WILDWOOD FLOWER

Words and music by Maud Irving
and J. D. Webster

1. I will tie up my ring-lets of ra-ven black hair With the
2. I will sing, I will dance, and my life will be gay, I will
3. Oh, he taught me to love and he called me his flow'r, And I
4. Oh, he prom-ised to love me, he prom-ised to care, Through our
5. Now I dance, now I sing and my life, it is gay; I will

ros - es of red and white lil - ies so fair. And the
charm ev - 'ry heart, ev - 'ry man will I sway. I woke
told him I'd cheer him thro' life's drear - y hour. I still
days and our nights all our tri - als we'd share. Now my
cry now no more, turn my nights in - to day. I'm a -

myr - tle so green with its em - erald hue, ___ Lac - ing
up from my dream, and my i - dol was clay, ___ Now the
long for to see him in this lonely hour, ___ But he's
poor heart is bro - ken no mis - ery can tell, ___ How he
wake from my dream, for my i - dol's a - way, ___ And my

li - lacs so pale 'round my sad eyes so blue.
pas - sion of lov - in' has all flown a - way.
gone and for - got - ten this frail wild - wood flow'r.
left with no warn - ing, no word of fare - well.
vi - sions of love have all fad - ed a - way.

Autoharp, strum M
Guitar, strum 24
Piano, accompaniment pattern XVI

WILL THE CIRCLE BE UNBROKEN?

American Folk Song

Guitar, strum 29
Piano, accompaniment pattern XVI

313

WINDS OF MORNING

Words and music by Tommy Makem
(Ireland)

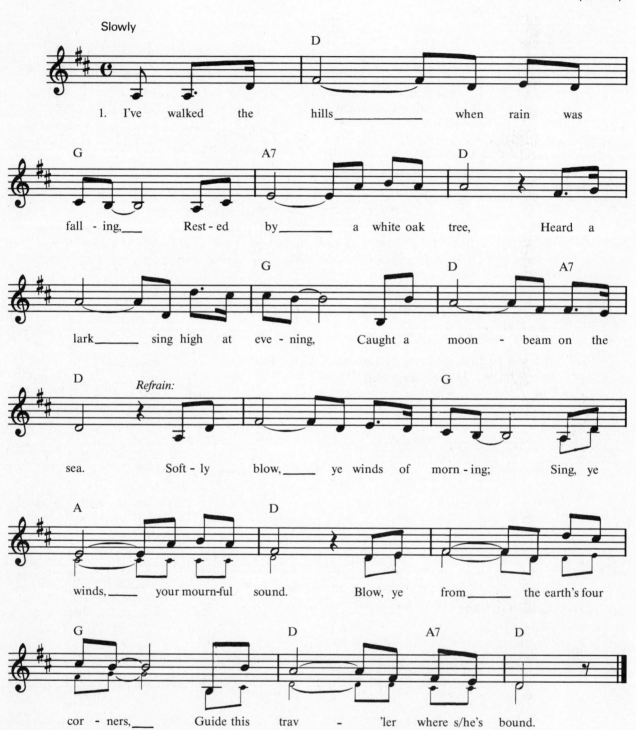

Slowly

1. I've walked the hills _____ when rain was fall - ing, _____ Rest - ed by _____ a white oak tree, Heard a lark _____ sing high at eve - ning, Caught a moon - beam on the sea.

Refrain: Soft - ly blow, _____ ye winds of morn - ing; Sing, ye winds, _____ your mourn-ful sound. Blow, ye from _____ the earth's four cor - ners, _____ Guide this trav - 'ler where s/he's bound.

Autoharp (15-bar), strum L (harp)
Guitar, strum 27

2. I've helped a ploughman tend his horses,
   Heard a rippling river sing,
   Talked to stars when night was falling,
   Seen a primrose welcome spring. *(Refrain)*

3. By foreign shores my feet have wandered,
   Heard a stranger call me friend;
   Every time my mind was troubled,
   Found a smile around the bend. *(Refrain)*

4. There's a ship stands in the harbor,
   All prepared to cross the foam;
   Far off hills were fair and friendly,
   Still there's fairer hills at home. *(Refrain)*

WIND THROUGH THE OLIVE TREES

American Christmas Song

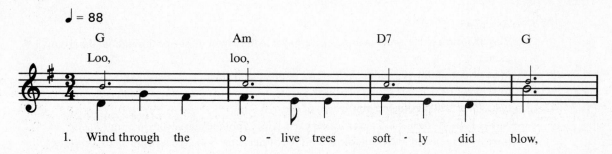

Autoharp, strum I
Guitar, strum 15 or melody
Soprano recorder

2. Sheep on the hillside, lay whiter than snow,
   Shepherds were watching them, Long, long ago.

3. Then from the happy skies angels bent low,
   Singing their songs of joy, Long, long ago.

4. For in a manger bed, cradled, we know,
   Christ came to Bethlehem, Long, long ago.

315

WINDY WEATHER

American Folk Song

Guitar, strum 2

Formation

Players form a circle and join hands; one player in the center is the tree throughout the entire game.

Measures 1–2: Players in the circle stand in place and sing.

Measures 3–4: The tree selects two players from the circle to come into the center, close to the tree. These two players are now leaves of the tree.

As the song is repeated, the two leaves each select another player to come into the center (measures 1–2); four leaves huddle near the tree (measures 3–4). Repeat until all players have been chosen as leaves, and all huddle close to the tree at the conclusion.

WISHY WASHY WEE

American Folk Song

Oh, we are two sail - ors come from o'er the sea, If you want to go a - way a - gain, come a - long with me. Oh,

wish - y wash - y, wish - y wash - y, wish - y wash - y wee, If you want to go a - way a - gain, come a - long with me.

Autoharp (15-bar), strums G or L
Guitar, strums 10 and 22
Piano, accompaniment pattern XI

Formation
Players stand in a large circle with two sailors in the center.

Dance
During the verse, all stand in place while the two sailors link elbows and swing in the center. At the end of the verse on "come along with me" each of the two sailors stops in front of a person standing in the circle. During the refrain, these two join hands. They dance by hopping on the left foot, at the same time sliding the right heel forward, and then hopping on the right foot while sliding the left heel forward. This alternating footwork continues. At the same time, the right hand pushes straight ahead along with the right heel, and then the left hand pushes straight ahead with the left heel, and so forth.

On "come along with me," at the end of the refrain, the four dancers change places. The two players from the circle move to the center and become the new sailors for a repetition of the song. The dance continues until every player in the circle has an opportunity to dance as a sailor.

WORRIED MAN BLUES

American Song

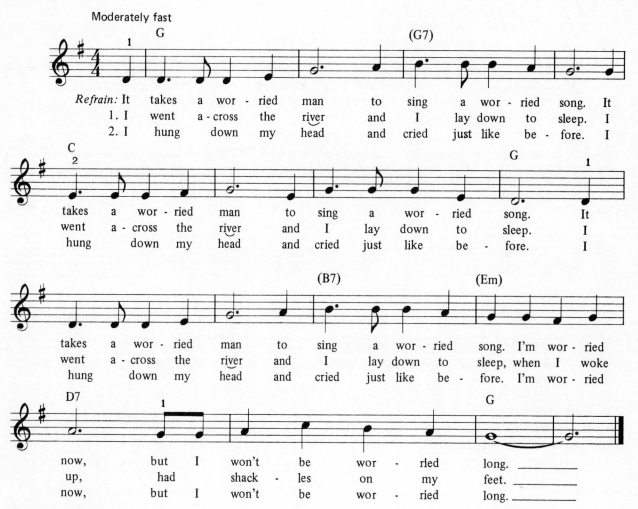

Moderately fast

Refrain: It takes a wor-ried man to sing a wor-ried song. It
1. I went a-cross the river and I lay down to sleep. I
2. I hung down my head and cried just like be-fore. I

takes a wor-ried man to sing a wor-ried song. It
went a-cross the river and I lay down to sleep. I
hung down my head and cried just like be-fore. I

takes a wor-ried man to sing a wor-ried song. I'm wor-ried
went a-cross the river and I lay down to sleep, when I woke
hung down my head and cried just like be-fore. I'm wor-ried

now, but I won't be wor-ried long. _____
up, had shack-les on my feet. _____
now, but I won't be wor-ried long. _____

Autoharp, strum N
Guitar, strum 25
Piano, accompaniment pattern XV

YANKEE DOODLE

Revolutionary War Song

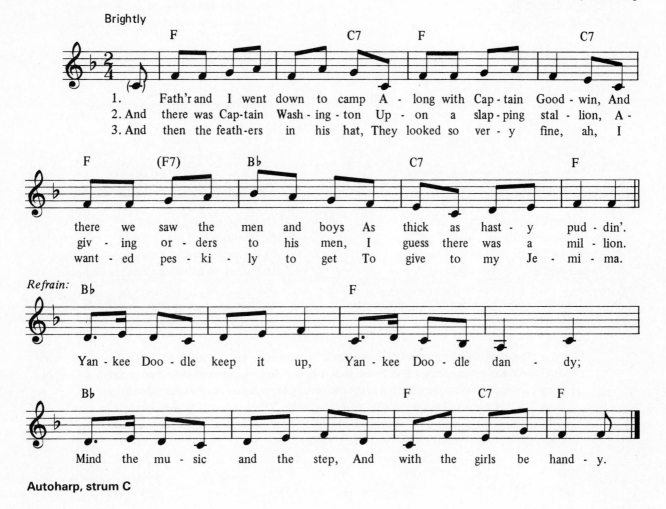

Brightly

1. Fath'r and I went down to camp A - long with Cap - tain Good - win, And
2. And there was Cap-tain Wash - ing - ton Up - on a slap - ping stal - lion, A -
3. And then the feath-ers in his hat, They looked so ver - y fine, ah, I

there we saw the men and boys As thick as hast - y pud - din'.
giv - ing or - ders to his men, I guess there was a mil - lion.
want - ed pes - ki - ly to get To give to my Je - mi - ma.

Refrain:

Yan - kee Doo - dle keep it up, Yan - kee Doo - dle dan - dy;

Mind the mu - sic and the step, And with the girls be hand - y.

Autoharp, strum C

319

4. And there I see a swamping gun,
   As large as log of maple,
   Upon a deucéd little cart;
   A load for father's cattle. *(Refrain)*

5. And every time they fired it off
   It took a horn of powder;
   It made a noise like father's gun,
   Only a nation louder. *(Refrain)*

6. And Captain Davis had a gun,
   He kinda clapt his hand on't,
   And stuck a crooked stabbing iron
   Upon the little end on't. *(Refrain)*

7. And there I see a little keg,
   Its heads were made of leather.
   They knocked upon't with little sticks
   To call the folks together. *(Refrain)*

8. And there they'd fife away like fun,
   And play on cornstalk fiddles;
   And some had ribbands, red as blood,
   All wound about their middles. *(Refrain)*

9. The troopers, too, would gallop up
   And fire right in our faces;
   It scared me almost half to death
   To see them run such races. *(Refrain)*

10. I see another snarl of men,
    A-diggin' graves, they told me;
    So tarnal long, so tarnal deep,
    They 'tended they should hold me. *(Refrain)*

11. It scared me so, I hooked it off,
    Nor stopped, as I remember,
    Nor turned about till I got home,
    Locked up in mother's chamber. *(Refrain)*

The amiable mockery of "Yankee Doodle" has been with Americans for more than 200 years. During the French and Indian War, a British army doctor was the first to create verses poking fun at the ragtag attire of the Colonial fighters. No one knows the origin of the tune or of the epithet "yankee doodle." But the scruffy "Yankees" were as amused by the satire as were the British, and the song was adopted by the Colonials—to become virtually their battle march during the Revolutionary War.

THE YELLOW ROSE OF TEXAS

Traditional American Song

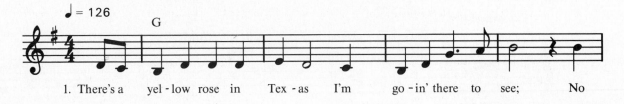

1. There's a yel-low rose in Tex-as I'm go-in' there to see; No

oth - er sol - dier knows her, no sol - dier, on - ly me. She

cried so when I left her, it like to broke my heart, And

if I ev - er find her, we nev - er more will part.

Autoharp, banjo strum
Piano, accompaniment pattern XVI

2. She's the sweetest rose of color this soldier ever knew,
   Her eyes are bright as diamonds, they sparkle like the dew.
   You may talk about your dearest May and sing of Rosa Lee,
   But the yellow rose of Texas beats the belles of Tennessee.

3. Where the Rio Grande is flowing and the starry skies are bright,
   She walks along the river in the quiet summer night.
   She thinks if I remember where we parted long ago:
   I promised to come back again and not to leave her so.

4. Oh, now I'm going to find her for my heart is full of woe,
   And we'll sing the song together that we sang so long ago.
   We'll play the banjo gaily and we'll sing the songs of yore,
   And the yellow rose of Texas shall be mine forever more.

YESTERDAY

Paul McCartney
(England, b.1942)

Yes-ter-day, all my trou-bles seemed so far a-way Now it looks as tho' they're
Sud-den-ly, I'm not half the man I used to be There's a shad-ow hang-ing

here to stay __ Oh I be-lieve __ in yes-ter-day. __
o - ver me __ Oh yes-ter-day __ came sud-den-ly. __

Why she had to go I don't know, she would-n't say.

I said some-thing wrong now I long for yes-ter-day. __

Yes-ter-day, love was such an eas-y game to play. Now I need a place to hide a-way, __ Oh

I be-lieve __ in yes-ter-day. __ Mm _____

Autoharp, strum each chord change (substitute E7 for each Bm7)
Guitar, strum 27
Piano, accompany using chord roots

322

ZUM GALI GALI

Israeli Round

Autoharp, strum A (drone)
Guitar, strum 2
Piano, accompaniment pattern XI

Translation

The pioneer is meant for work. Work is meant for the pioneer.

THE AUTOHARP

Autoharp and *ChromAharp* are trademark names for zitherlike instruments invented about one hundred years ago. They are designed for playing simple harmonies to accompany melodies. Chords are played by pressing a chord button with the left hand and strumming across the strings with the right hand.

15-bar Autoharp

Playing Positions

Two playing positions are frequently used: the lap (or table) position and the folk-singer's position. In both positions, the left hand presses a chord button and the right hand strums the strings. Strumming is usually to the left of the chord bars.

For the lap or table position, place the Autoharp with its longest side near you. Your left hand will press a chord button, and your right hand will cross over to strum.

For the folk-singer's position, place the longest side of the Autoharp diagonally across your chest. Your left hand approaches the chord bars from the left and from behind the instrument. Your right hand strums up high, near the shoulder.

Lap Position

Folk-Singer's Position

Keyboard

The letter name on each chord bar identifies the chord root (the strongest tone of each chord). Autoharps have three types of chords: major (Maj.), minor (Min.), and seventh (Sev.) chords. The G major and G minor chords may appear to be similar, but the quality of each chord is different. Compare the sound of the two G chords to demonstrate this subtle but important difference.

Autoharps can have from 5 to 21 chord bars, but the most frequently used are the 12-bar, 15-bar, and 21-bar Autoharps. A diagram of the bar arrangements of the 12-chord and 15-chord Autoharps is shown here:

12 Chord-Bar Model

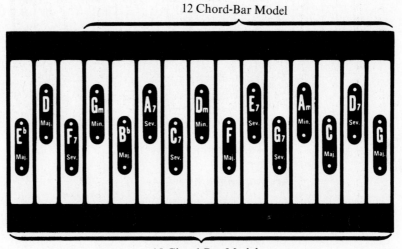

15 Chord-Bar Model

The bar arrangement of the 21-chord ChromAharp is as follows:

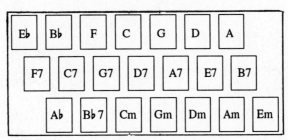

21-chord ChromAharp

Strums

You can strum with your thumb or the fingernail of your index finger, or you can use a soft or hard pick. A plastic pick produces a brilliant, "twangy" sound, while a felt pick gives a mellow effect. The pick you select should fit the mood and style of the song.

The basic stroke is an upstroke, and it is produced by placing your hand near your body and swinging it outward across the strings (low strings to high strings). An arrow pointing upward indicates an upstroke.

high

The upstroke is often shortened and played in different octaves, for example, in the bass/lower octave, middle octave, or (less frequently) the higher octave. These three octaves are shown on the following chart:

Pitch and Octave Locations on the Autoharp

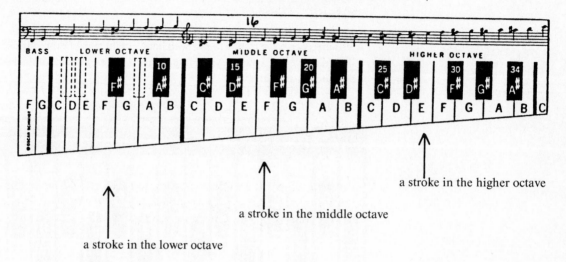

a stroke in the higher octave

a stroke in the middle octave

a stroke in the lower octave

Accompaniments

Autoharp strokes are used in different ways to create song accompaniments. The accompaniment needs to match the song's rhythm and enhance its character and mood.

An accent is created by playing an upstroke on the lower strings. Various patterns with accents can be used in songs with the following meter signatures:

A downstroke toward the body can also be used. An arrow pointing downward indicates a downstroke.

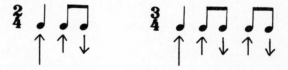

Other accompaniment patterns are possible, many of which are shown at the end of this chapter, in the section entitled, Strums for Autoharp. Also described there are special strums such as the harp, banjo, drone (bagpipe), and Middle Eastern strums.

Fingering the Chord Bars

Many songs can be accompanied with just three different chords. The chords are indicated by letter names above the song's notation. These three primary (principal) chords are often referred to by their numerical position in a key: I (tonic), IV (subdominant), V7 (dominant seventh).

When playing the chord bars, use a pattern of fingering that remains constant throughout the song. The chord bars of some Autoharps can be repositioned so that you can finger them with greater consistency and ease.

Songs for which autoharp accompaniment is appropriate are indicated in the Classified Index of Songs under the heading Autoharp.

Beginning a Song

To begin a song, you need to sing the first pitch, and then strum a short introduction in the tempo of the song.

To find the first pitch so that you can sing it, pluck the string that corresponds to the song's first note. For example, if the song begins on bottom-line E, pluck string number 16, in the middle octave of the Autoharp (this is for women's and childrens' voices). String 16 is shown in the chart Pitch and Octave Locations on the Autoharp, which appeared earlier in this chapter.

To establish the key and tempo of the song, strum a one-measure introduction using the I chord or one of these chord progressions: I–V7–I; or I–IV–V7–I. This introduction can also serve as an interlude between the verses of the song.

Autoharp Tuning

Autoharps must be kept in tune. To do so, it might be advisable to enlist the help of a trained musician. Electronic tuners are also useful and are available from companies that sell Autoharps.

To tune an Autoharp you will need access to an in-tune piano (or an electronic tuner) and an Autoharp tuning key. To raise the pitch of any string, place the tuning key over the peg, press down, and turn the key clockwise (this tightens the string). To lower the pitch of any string, turn the key counterclockwise (this loosens the string).

Tuning by chords is the way to tune an Autoharp. Begin with the F major chord. Pressing down the F major chord button, check all Fs, then all As, and finally all Cs with the corresponding pitch at the piano (or on the electronic tuner). Finally, strum the chord to see if it is in tune. Continue tuning chords in the following order. Note the strings that need to be tuned in each.

The following procedures will tune all the chords on a 12-bar, 15-bar, or 21-bar Autoharp.

Chords	Strings to tune
F Major	F, A, C
C Major	E, G
G Major	B, D
G7	————
D7	F♯
B♭	B♭ (same as A♯)
E7	G♯
A7	C♯
E♭	E♭ (same as D♯)

Remaining chords do not need to be tuned, because the pitches in those chords are common to those of the chords already tuned.

AUTOHARP ACCOMPANIMENTS

Specific Autoharp accompaniments are suggested for many songs in this book. To locate these songs, refer to the Classified Index of Songs under Autoharp (12-bar, 15-bar, or 21-bar). Songs are listed by key and according to the number of chords needed (one-chord songs, two-chord songs, and so on).

The Autoharp Accompaniments chart that follows presents patterns of strums with a circled letter to the left. A letter corresponding to a letter in this chart appears when "Autoharp" is specified for a particular song in the Anthology of Melodies. Thus, "Autoharp (15-bar), strum L" below a song means that strum L is suggested as a song accompaniment.

Special effects accompaniments such as the harp, banjo, bagpipe, and Middle Eastern strums conclude this chapter.

Special Effects

1. *Harp.* Use either a slow upstroke or downstroke, and vary the length of the strum. Use a felt pick.

2. *Banjo.* Strum to the right of the chord bars in a rhythm that is faster than the beat, Use a flat plastic pick.

3. *Drone or Bagpipe.* Press two chord buttons with the same letter names simultaneously, such as G major and G minor. This produces an   open fifth.

4. *Middle Eastern.* Press and hold a chord button down while scrubbing or bouncing lightly two or more mallets (rubber or wood) on the strings. This works best with two players.

STRUMS FOR AUTOHARP

↑ = upstroke outward across all strings

⬆ = upstroke from middle strings outward

↓ = downstroke on middle strings

329

Autoharp Keyboard (15 chord-bar model)

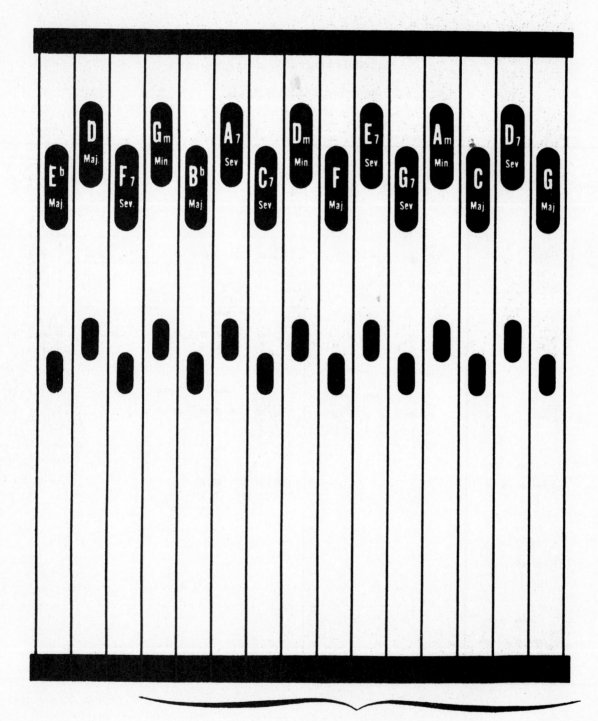

12 chord-bar model

THE GUITAR

The modern guitar is the most widely used musical instrument in the world. Both acoustic and electronically amplified models are available.

The classical guitar and the flat-top guitar are popular acoustic models. The flat-top guitar has a bright tone, steel strings, and a narrow neck. The classical guitar has a mellow tone. It is a good choice for beginners because it has a wide neck and nylon strings. (Nylon strings are easier on the fingers than are steel strings.)

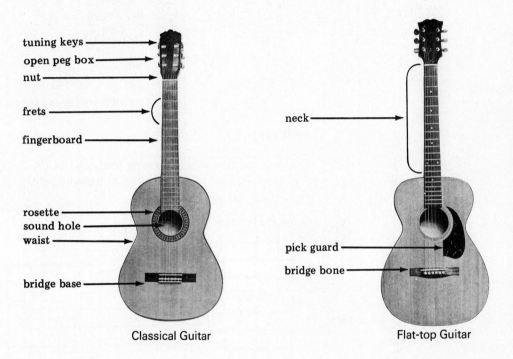

tuning keys
open peg box
nut
frets
fingerboard
rosette
sound hole
waist
bridge base

neck

pick guard
bridge bone

Classical Guitar

Flat-top Guitar

Body and Hand Position

Hold the guitar with its neck at an upward angle, keeping the face of the instrument almost vertical. When sitting, rest the guitar's waist on the right leg. A neck strap on the guitar makes playing while standing easier.

The left-hand fingers press down individual strings on the neck of the guitar, while the right hand strums the strings near the sound hole. The right forearm rests on the top edge of the guitar, above the bridge. The fingers of the left hand should approach the strings from an arched, nearly vertical position. (Left-handers can finger chords in this same way, or they can restring their guitars, reversing the order of the strings, then use the right hand to finger the chords and the left hand to strum.)

Folk Style Playing Position

Tuning

The six guitar strings are tuned to the pitches E (low), A, D, G, B, and E (high). When tuning, you can use a special pitch pipe available at a music store. Match the pitch of each string to the pitch of the corresponding pipe.

Guitar Pitch Pipe with Tuning

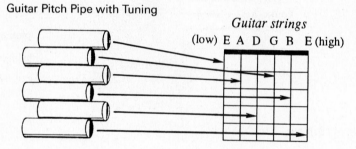

Guitar strings

(low) E A D G B E (high)

Or if you are familiar with the piano keyboard, you can tune the guitar strings to these pitches:

Tuning to the Piano

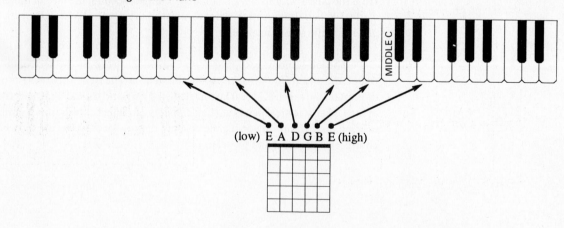

MIDDLE C

(low) E A D G B E (high)

The relative tuning method is the one most commonly used by guitarists. Twist the tuning key while continuously plucking the string to check its pitch. If a string is difficult to tune, lower it well below the desired pitch, and gradually bring it up. (Never raise a string too high, because excessive tension will damage the neck of the guitar.)

Strings

E Tune the bass E string to a piano or to your pitch pipe.

A Place your finger just behind the fifth fret of the E string, as shown in the diagram. You will be fingering the correct pitch for the next string, the A string. Pluck the A string and match it to the sound of the note on the E string.

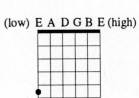

(low) E A D G B E (high)

D Press down the A string at the fifth fret. Pluck the next string, D, and match it to the sound of the note on the A string.

G Press down the D string at the fifth fret. Pluck the next string, G, and match it to the sound of the note on the D string.

B Press down the G string at the *fourth* fret. Pluck the next string, B, and match it to the sound of the note on the G string.

E Press down the B string at the fifth fret. Pluck the top E string and match it to the sound of the note on the B string.

Strum an E minor or E major chord to check your tuning.

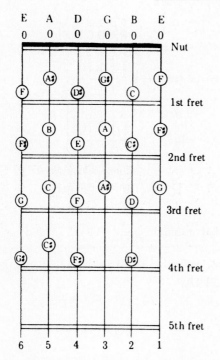

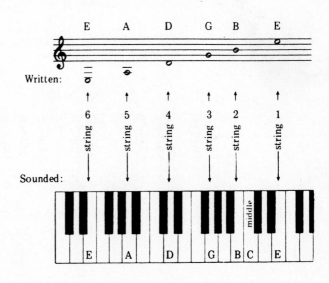

Guitar Pitches

Fingering

Finger designations are shown here. Left-hand fingerings are indicated in chord diagrams; right-hand finger numbers will be used in the chart on various strums for guitar at the end of the chapter.

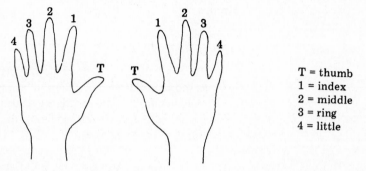

T = thumb
1 = index
2 = middle
3 = ring
4 = little

Guitar Chords

Chord diagrams for guitar look like the fingerboard of the guitar; showing the strings and the frets. Numbers (sometimes circled) show where to place the fingers of the left hand to play the chords.

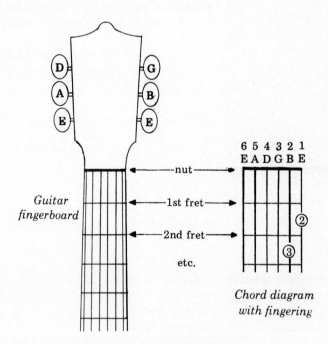

Guitar fingerboard

Chord diagram with fingering

A complete chord chart is presented at the end of this chapter.

For songs to accompany with guitar, see the Classified Index of Songs under Guitar, One-Chord; Guitar, Two-Chord; Guitar, Melody playing.

The Capo

The capo is a strap or clamp that can be fixed to the guitar neck at any fret to shorten all six strings at once. It allows guitarists to play in a higher key without learning new chord fingerings. The use of the capo and a photograph are presented in the section on transposition in Appendix G.

Strums

Six strokes and strums are illustrated and described in this section. They include the brush stroke, the thumb stroke, the thumb-brush stroke, the arpeggio strum, the thumb-pluck strum, and the syncopated strum, and they are discussed in order of difficulty. (A chart of strums for guitar and ukulele is presented at the end of this chapter.

Brush stroke

↓

The right hand thumb sweeps downward across all strings.

Thumb ("rest") stroke

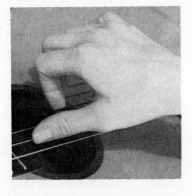

The right-hand thumb plucks and then rests on the next string—for just a moment. The thumb usually plucks the root of each chord (labelled *R* in chord diagrams). The player can also alternate between plucking the root and the fifth of the chord (labelled *5* in chord diagrams).

Thumb-brush stroke

T ↓
thumb brush

This strum is a combination of the brush and the thumb strokes. The thumb of the right hand plucks the string, rests momentarily, then sweeps downward across the remaining strings.

Arpeggio strum

3

2

1

T

Plucking strings one at a time (arpeggio) adds expression to an accompaniment. While holding a chord with the left hand, place the right-hand fingers as follows:
1. Index finger just under the G string
2. Middle finger just under the B string
3. Ring finger just under the high E string

One at a time, snap each finger into the palm of the hand: index (1), middle (2), and ring (3). (Do this without moving your arm.) Keep each finger on its string until time to play.

The thumb starts the arpeggio strum by plucking the chord root (labeled *R* on the chord diagram).

Thumb-pluck strum

3

2

T   1

thumb pluck

Place fingers as described for the arpeggio strum. The thumb plucks the string and rests, and the remaining fingers (index, middle, ring) *simultaneously* pluck the G, B, and high E strings.

Syncopated strum

♪ ♩ ♪ ♩ ♩

syn-co – pa-ta – ta
↓ ↓   ↑ ↓   ↓

In the syncopated strum, all movements are downward, except for the strum on *-pa*. The index finger should lead each movement.

The Baritone Ukulele

The ukulele is a Hawaiian instrument that probably developed from a small Portuguese guitar. The modern ukulele in built in two sizes: the small, higher pitched soprano and the larger, lower pitched baritone. Portable, inexpensive, and relatively easy to play, a four-string ukulele can be used for song accompaniments instead of the six-string guitar.

The baritone ukulele is tuned D–G–B–E. This is the same as the four highest guitar strings. Therefore, chord diagrams have four lines. Diagrams for baritone ukulele are presented on a chart at the end of this section, Chords for Guitar and Baritone Ukulele.

Because the two instruments are similar, almost any song for guitar can be played on baritone ukulele. See the Classified Index of Songs, Guitar.

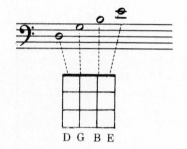

D G B E

Baritone ukulele tuning.

STRUMS FOR GUITAR AND UKULELE

Specific strums are suggested for many songs in this book. To locate these songs, refer to the Classified Index of Songs under Guitar, where songs are listed by key and by the number of chords needed (one-chord songs, two-chord songs, and so on).

The strums shown in the chart have a circled number to the left. This letter appears in the list of accompaniment instruments following each appropriate song throughout the anthology.

Strums shown in the chart apply to the E major chord for guitar. With different chords, you will need to choose bass notes other than T6 and T5. Chord diagrams for different chords show which strings to use for those bass notes (labeled R and 5).

Use the following key for abbreviations within the chart:

B = brush thumb downward across all strings
T = thumb (rest stroke)
1 = index finger (on G string)
2 = middle finger (on B string)
3 = ring finger (on E string)
↓ = scratch down with index finger
↑ = scratch up with index finger

Strums in 2s
Duple meter

Strums in 3s
Triple meter

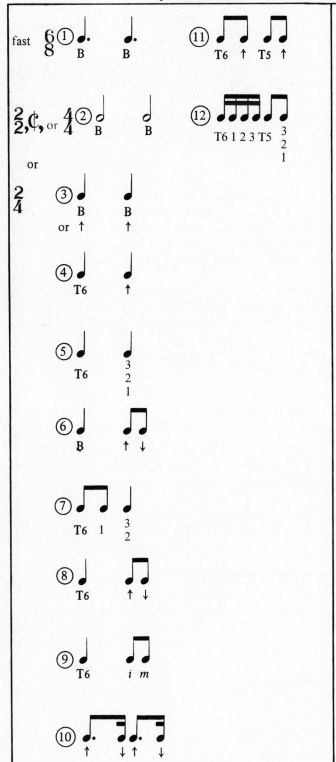

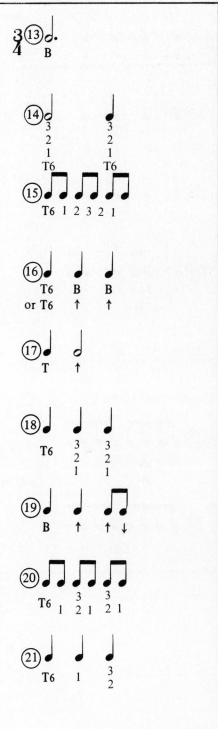

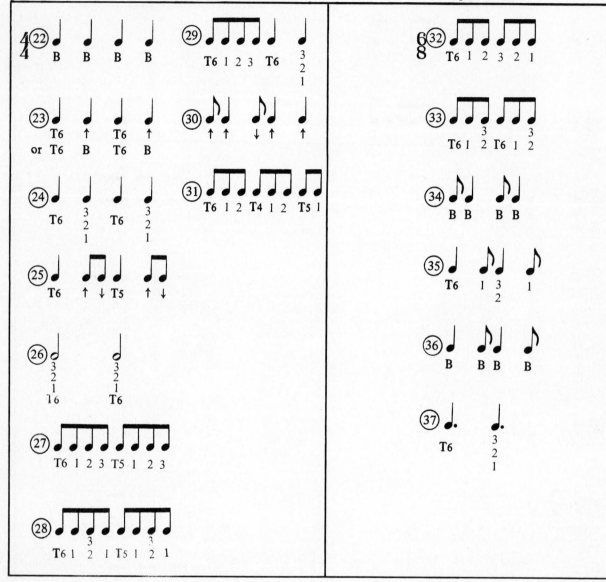

338

CHORDS FOR GUITAR AND BARITONE UKULELE

For guitar, use the six-string chord diagram; for baritone ukulele, use the four-string chord diagram.

When strumming the thumb stroke, play the string labeled *R* (chord root), or alternate between playing *R* and *5* (chord fifth). The third finger of the left hand sometimes changes strings to play the chord fifth; this is indicated by a circled *3* on the chord diagram.

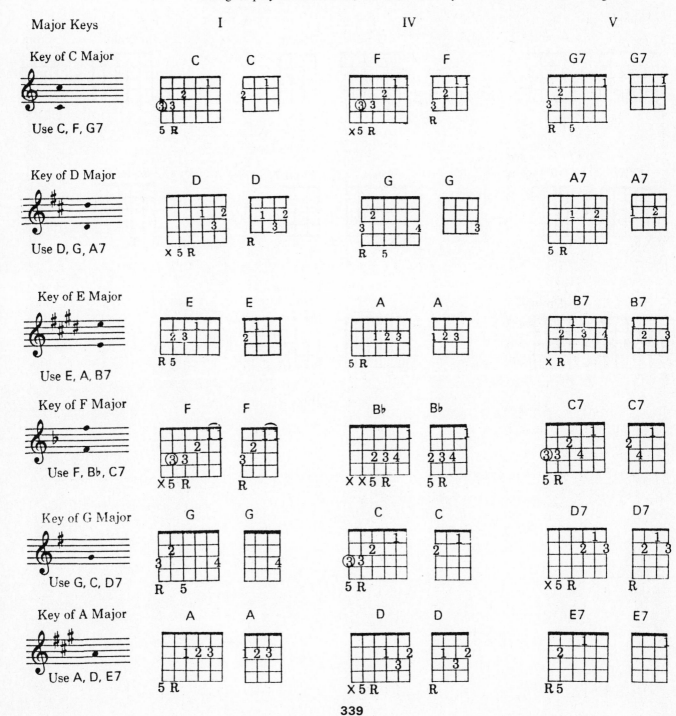

Selected additional chords:

Amin.   Amin.

5 R

Dmin.   Dmin.

5 R   R

Emin.   Emin.
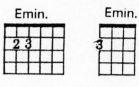

Amin.7   Amin.7

5 R

Bmin.   Bmin.

X X

Cmin.   Cmin.
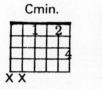
X X

Gmin.   Gmin.

X X 5   5

Emin.7   Emin.7

R 5

easier G

R   5

Dmin.7   Dmin.7
 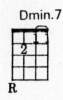
X 5 R   R

F7   F7

X X

340

THE PIANO

The piano was the first keyboard instrument on which soft and loud dynamics could be produced by the touch of the fingers. Since the late eighteenth century, pianos have been in wide use, particularly in the home. Piano study and performance is rewarding to individuals of all ages because keyboard skills can be applied to several styles of music and to many different musical situations.

Body and Hand Position

Sit directly in front of the middle of the keyboard. You can lean slightly forward, but keep your torso straight. Sit far enough back from the keys so that your arms and elbows can move freely.

Your hands, wrists, and forearms should be level with the keyboard. Fingers should remain close to the keys at all times, and the fingers should strike the keys, not press them, with the pad of each finger.

Fingering

The fingers of each hand are numbered 1 through 5, from the thumbs outward: the thumbs are 1; the index fingers, 2; the middle fingers, 3; the ring fingers, 4; and the little fingers, 5.

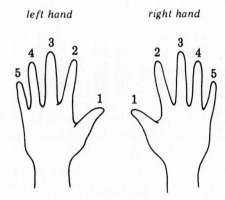

Small arabic numbers appear above, below, or beside the notes in piano music to show the recommended fingering.

Fingerings are chosen according to the shape and scope of the melody. Use a fingering without excess motion and one that is consistent. Avoid placing the same finger on two consecutive keys, and try not to use the thumb on a black key. Release each key as the next key is struck (legato or connected style), unless there are other directions.

Names of the Keys

The keys of the piano are named using the first seven letters of the alphabet: A, B, C, D, E, F, G. The black keys use the same letter names as the white keys, but with the addition of a sharp (♯) or flat (♭). Each sharp/flat key has two names.

341

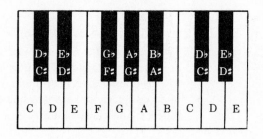

The Staff and the Keyboard

Notes in the *treble* (upper) staff are usually played by the right hand, and notes in the *bass* (lower) staff with the left hand. Each note on the staff has an exact location on the piano keyboard.

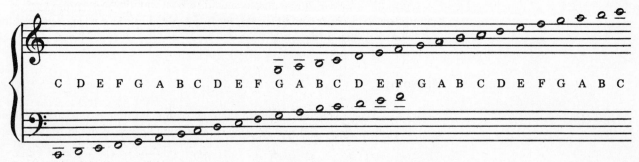

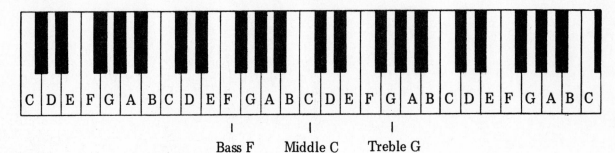

Bass F   Middle C   Treble G

Right Hand

The right hand usually plays the melody. Many simple melodies use only the first five pitches of a scale, allowing the thumb and fingers of the right hand to touch five consecutive notes, such as C, D, E, F, and G, without changing position. This is referred to as the *five-finger position (pattern)*. The first pitch of each five-finger pattern that follows is called the *tonic*.

Major five-finger pattern

The major five-finger pattern includes five pitches with the following arrangement of whole and half steps: whole, whole, half, whole.

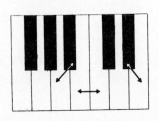

half steps

342

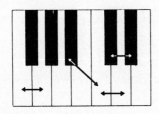

whole steps

A whole step equals 2 half steps.

The following major five-finger patterns are sometimes used in simple melodies:

C Major Five-Finger Pattern

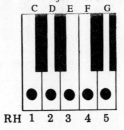

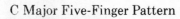

G Major Five-Finger Pattern

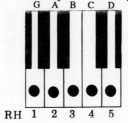

D Major Five-Finger Pattern

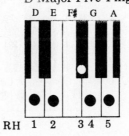

F Major Five-Finger Pattern

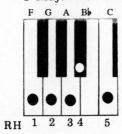

343

Minor five-finger pattern   The minor five-finger pattern includes five pitches with this following arrangement of whole and half steps: whole, half, whole, whole.

The following minor five-finger patterns may be used in simple melodies:

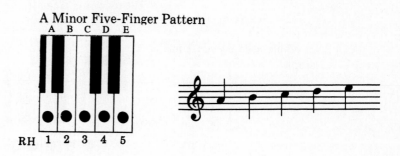

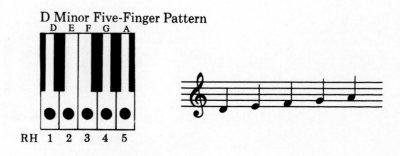

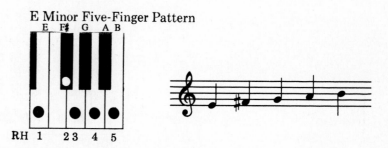

Songs in Major and Minor Five-Finger Patterns

For melodies that can be performed using the five-finger pattern, see the Classified Index of Songs under Piano: Five-Finger Patterns.

Left Hand

The left hand often plays several notes simultaneously (chords). A few melodies use just one chord, but most use two or more chords. The movement between chords should be as smooth as possible. The following diagram and bass staff notation show a relatively easy way to move between the three primary (or principal) chords in the key of C major—I (tonic), IV (subdominant) and V7 (dominant seventh).

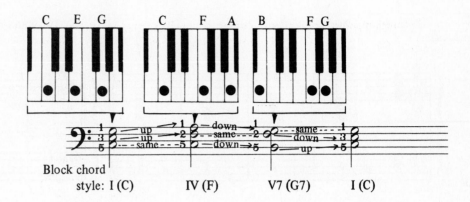

Block chord
style: I (C)   IV (F)   V7 (G7)   I (C)

At the end of this chapter, chords in several major and minor keys are shown in the chart of primary chords in selected major and minor keys.

Chord Accompaniments

Chords are played in different ways for different songs, adding interest to the music. The chosen accompaniment pattern should match the song's rhythm and meter, and also enhance the character and mood of the song.

In the block chord style shown in the previous section, all tones are sounded at the same time. In other accompaniments, chord tones are sounded successively. Usually, the lowest chord tone is played first, falling on the first beat (downbeat) of each measure. For example, Arpeggio style uses pitches played one at a time, beginning with the lowest pitch.

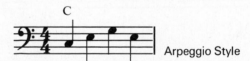

Arpeggio Style

Several additional accompaniment styles follow in the chart entitled Piano Accompaniment Patterns. Melodies for practice can be found in the Classified Index under Piano.

PIANO ACCOMPANIMENT PATTERNS

Duple meter patterns for $\frac{2}{4}$

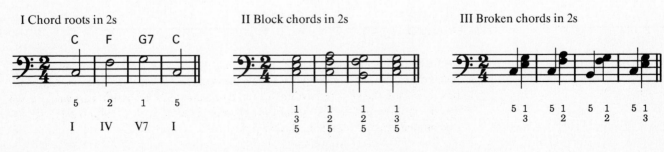

I Chord roots in 2s

II Block chords in 2s

III Broken chords in 2s

345

IV Two-hand alternating style in 2s

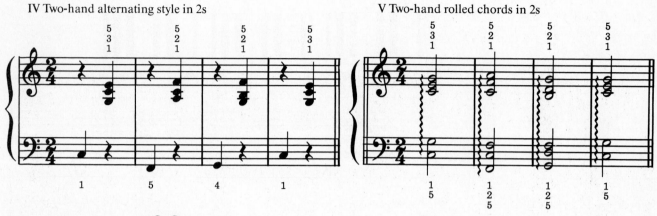

V Two-hand rolled chords in 2s

Triple meter patterns for 3/4 3/2

VI Block chords in 3s

VII Broken chords in 3s

VIII Arpeggios in 3s

IX Jump bass in 3s

X Two-hand rolled chords in 3s

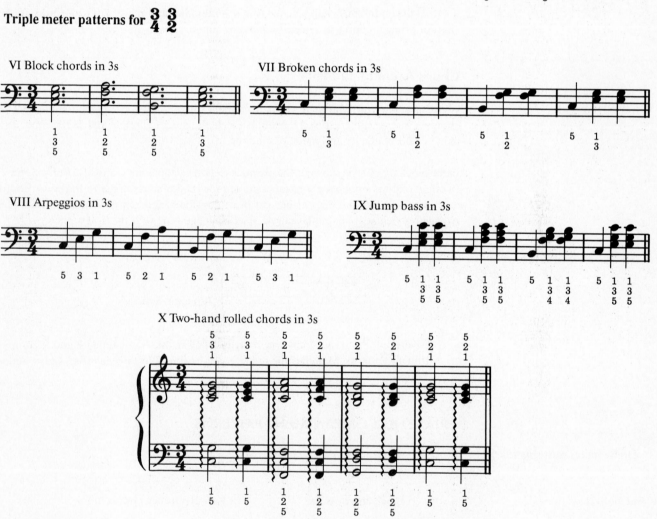

Quadruple meter patterns for $\frac{4}{4}$ C $\frac{2}{4}$ ¢

XI Block chords in 4s

XII Broken chords in 4s

XIII Arpeggios in 4s

XIV Alberti bass style in 4s

XV Jump style in 4s

XVI Two hand alternating style in 4s

XVII Two hand rolled chords in 4s

PRIMARY CHORDS IN SELECTED MAJOR AND MINOR KEYS

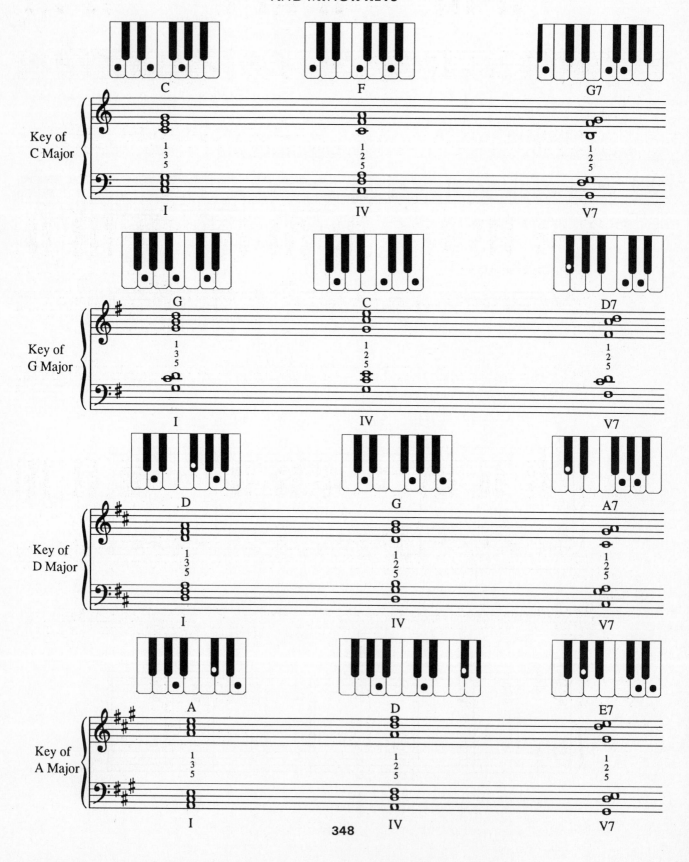

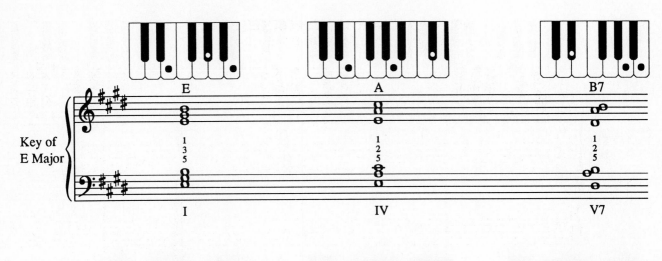

Key of E Major

E   A   B7

I   IV   V7

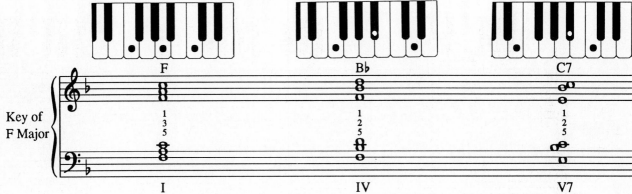

Key of F Major

F   B♭   C7

I   IV   V7

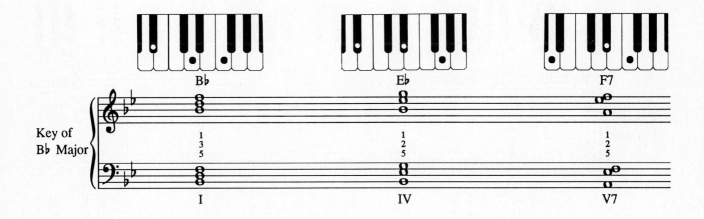

Key of B♭ Major

B♭   E♭   F7

I   IV   V7

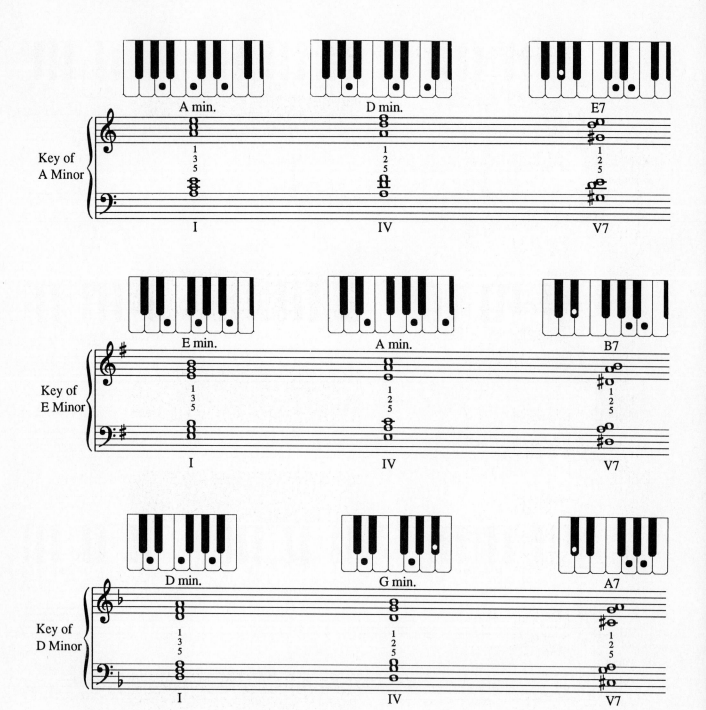

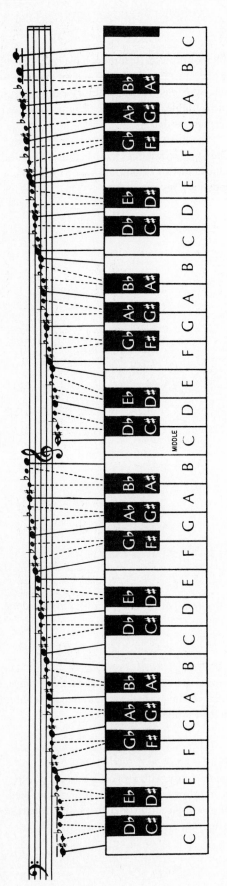

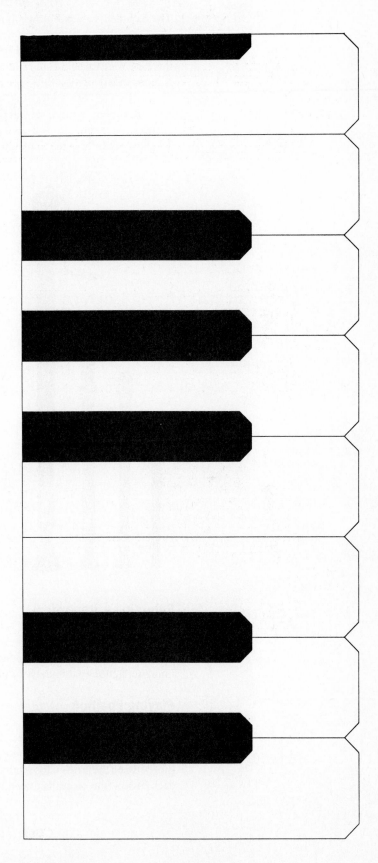

THE RECORDER

The recorder is an end-blown flute with a whistle mouthpiece. Recorders have been played since the fifteenth century and were especially popular in Elizabethan England. Interest in the recorder has been renewed because it is a relatively easy instrument for beginners and there is a wide variety of solo and ensemble music available. The Baroque (English) recorder is more widely used in this country than the German model.

Recorders come in several pitch ranges. The soprano recorder has a brilliant tone and is high in pitch. The alto and tenor recorders produce a mellower tone and have a lower range. The bass recorder is the lowest in pitch and produces a resonant tone.

From left to right: Soprano, Alto, Tenor, and Bass Recorders.

Selecting a Recorder

Inexpensive plastic and wooden recorders are available in music stores. The serious player will want to consider a more expensive model, which will have a better tone and more reliable tone production (particularly of the highest and lowest pitches).

Playing Position

Hold the recorder at a 45-degree angle away from the body, with arms in a relaxed position close to the body. Place the mouthpiece between your lips and slightly in front of your teeth (not between the teeth). Close your lips around the mouthpiece and open them slightly to take each breath (the breath is drawn in through the mouth, not the nose).

Correct Playing Position

Breathing

Try to produce a light, steady stream of air, because control of the breath is important for playing in tune. The correct body position for recorder playing is the same as for singing, and is described in "The Voice," the chapter following this one.

Blow more gently on low pitches and increase breath pressure for high pitches. Ration each breath to last through all the notes in a phrase, unless other directions are given.

Use a gentle attack for each note. An explosive attack will produce a penetrating sound and will exhaust your supply of air.

Tonguing

The tongue articulates each note struck by the fingers unless the notes are marked with a slur. The tongue should form the syllable *doo* (or *too*) against the back of the upper front teeth (or the gum just above the teeth). When two or more notes are slurred together, play the notes on a single *doo*.

For short notes (staccato or detached), end the syllable *doo* with the first half of the consonant *t,* as in *doot*.

Fingering

Left-hand fingers cover the top three holes, and the left thumb covers the hole on the back. The left-hand little finger is not used. The four right-hand fingers cover the lower holes. (The little finger covers a pair of holes at the bottom.) The right thumb supports the instrument, as do the lips.

The pads of the fingers (not the tips) cover each hole. Use the fingers as though they were small "hammers" covering each hole. Be sure fingers lift quickly.

Exactly coordinate your fingers with your tonguing.

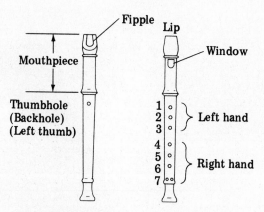

Soprano Recorder (Back and Front Views)

Melodies to Play

For music to play, see the Classified Index of Songs under Recorder, Harmony: Rounds, Harmony: Two-Part, Themes from Western Music, and Non-Western Melodies.

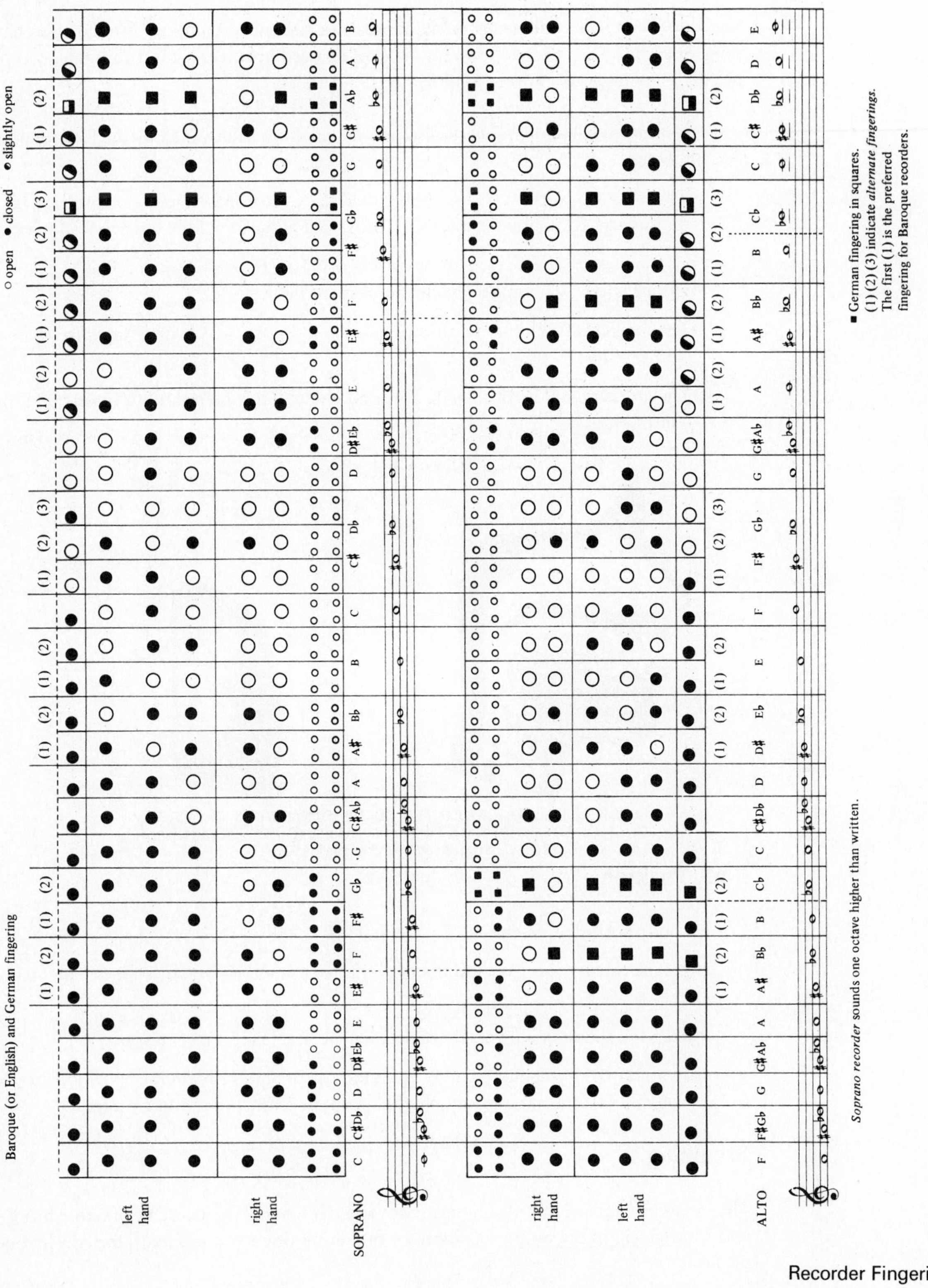

Recorder Fingering Chart

355

THE VOICE

The voice is an incredible instrument, because it can express emotion through speech and song. Speech is a familiar activity, but most of us need practice in controlling the complex physical functions that govern singing.

Volume, pitch, and quality (timbre) of the voice are determined by the functioning of the following:

- The *vibrators*: Narrow, elastic folds called the vocal cords. The vocal cords are inside the larynx ("LARE-inks"), located in the throat at the top of the trachea (windpipe).

- The *activator*: The breath pressure from the respiratory system. The vocal cords vibrate when a column of air pushes against them.

- The *resonators*: The larynx, throat, mouth, and nose, which give the voice intensity and timbre.

- The *articulators*: The lips, teeth, jaw, and palate. They help modify vowels and form consonants.

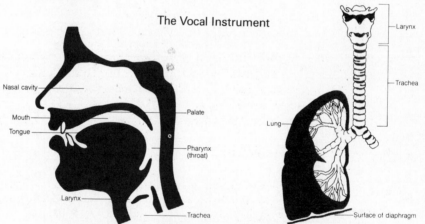

The Vocal Instrument

From MUSICLAB: AN INTRODUCTION TO THE FUNDAMENTALS OF MUSIC by Carolynn A. Lindeman and Patricia Hackett © 1989 by Wadsworth, Inc. Reprinted by permission of the publisher.

Body Position

Correct body posture is essential for good singing.

- Posture lineup: ears over shoulders over hips over ankles. Balance the weight on both feet.

- Keep the shoulders down, chest elevated, neck relaxed, and jaw loose.

If while singing you play a guitar, or Autoharp, or piano, or conduct, position yourself so that you can maintain the recommended position of the lungs and rib cage.

Breathing

The steadiness and volume of singing are governed by controlled use of the breath. The lungs and rib cage are in the proper position for breathing when you maintain the correct body posture.

First, breathe deeply, trying not to make any sound as you inhale. As the lungs fill with air and

356

expand, the rib cage will expand in the front, back, and sides. The diaphram, located just below the rib cage, will descend. To feel this deep breathing, place your hands on your waist, just below the rib cage.

Release the breath gradually and economically by consciously controlling the muscles of the abdominal walls. As the air is released, the vocal cords begin vibrating and creating pitch.

Resonance

The vocal resonators (the larynx, throat, mouth, and nose) give intensity and timbre to the pitch coming from the vocal cords. The singer must direct or focus the tone forward into the resonating cavities.

Each voice has a distinctive timbre, based on the size or the shape of the larynx and other resonators. An experienced singer can learn to vary the voice's timbre so that it becomes more appropriate for the style of a particular song (gospel, country/western, Chinese opera, and so on).

Articulation

The lips, teeth, tongue, jaw, and palate all contribute to enunciation, which in singing is exaggerated beyond that of normal speech. (This is particularly true of Western European art song and choral music.) Short, precisely articulated consonants punctuate sustained vowels. Open the mouth at least one inch on vowels. The tongue will lie forward in the mouth with its tip touching the bottom front gum (on the back of the bottom front teeth).

Adult Voice Ranges

Range refers to the highest and lowest pitches that can be sung by an individual. The range, pitch, and timbre of each voice depend on the sex, age, and physical maturity of the singer. Typical adult vocal ranges are illustrated here.

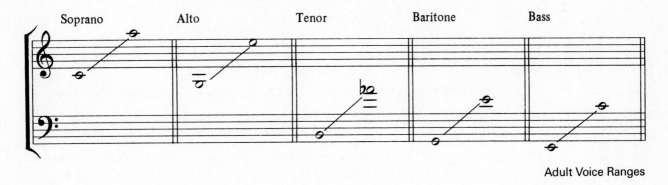

Adult Voice Ranges

To find your own voice range, sing the scale on p. 000 using a syllable such as "loo." Mark the highest and the lowest pitches you can produce comfortably. With practice you can expand your range, particularly into the higher pitches. The singer makes use of the body, which can be trained and conditioned for activities beyond the ordinary, as in singing.

Voice Ranges of Young Singers

If you choose songs and lead singing at schools and camps, you need to be knowledgeable about the child's voice range. At five or six years of age, a youngster accurately sings five or six pitches from about middle C to A above. The range of an older singer will expand, with experience, to an octave or more.

To select a song for childrens' voices, study the song's range to locate the highest and lowest pitches in the melody. *The song's range must correspond to the voice range of the young singers.*

When leading songs, maintain the body position described previously, and use a vocal style that is free from mannerisms.

Songs for special vocal needs are listed in the Classified Index of Melodies under Limited-Range: 2 to 4 pitches, 5 pitches (range of a 5th), and 5 pitches (range of a 6th). The Classified Index also lists selections with harmony under Harmony: Rounds, Harmony: Counter-melodies.

APPENDIX A
MUSIC NOTATION

Notes

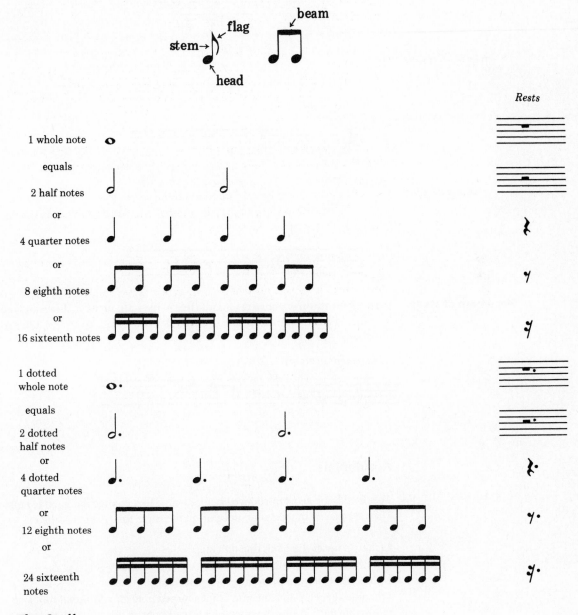

The Staff

The staff (plural *staves*) is a series of five horizontal lines on or between which musical notes are written. The lines and spaces of the staff are numbered from the bottom up.

The staff

Leger lines   Short lines called leger lines can be added above or below the staff to extend the range of pitches.

Ledger lines

Treble or G clef   This clef sign establishes G above middle C on the Second line.

Treble of G clef

Bass or F clef   This clef establishes F below middle C on the fourth line.

Bass or F clef

Placement of stems   When notes are on or above the middle line of the staff, stems go down and are placed on the left side. When notes are below the middle line, stems go up on the right side of the notehead.

Placement of stems

Accidentals

Accidentals are signs introduced before a note that change the pitch for one measure only. They are placed in the same space or on the same line as the notehead:

♯ (sharp): raises the pitch one half step
♭ (flat): lowers the pitch one half step
♮ (natural): cancels a preceding sharp or flat
✕ (double sharp): raises the pitch of a sharped note an additional half step
♭♭ (double flat): lowers the pitch of a flatted note an additional half step

The Grand Staff

The grand staff is two staves joined together.

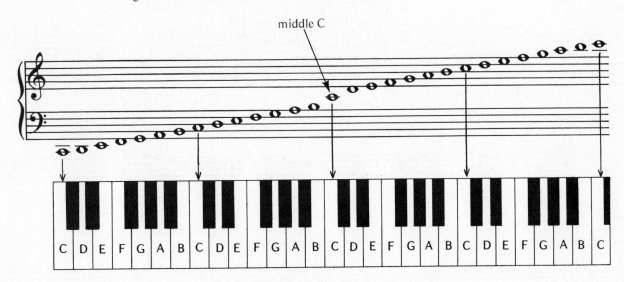

middle C

APPENDIX B
SCALES

Chromatic Scale

The chromatic scale is a twelve-tone scale consisting entirely of half steps.

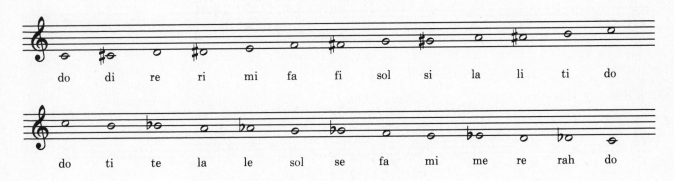

do   di   re   ri   mi   fa   fi   sol   si   la   li   ti   do

do   ti   te   la   le   sol   se   fa   mi   me   re   rah   do

Frequently Used Major Scales (With Piano Fingerings)

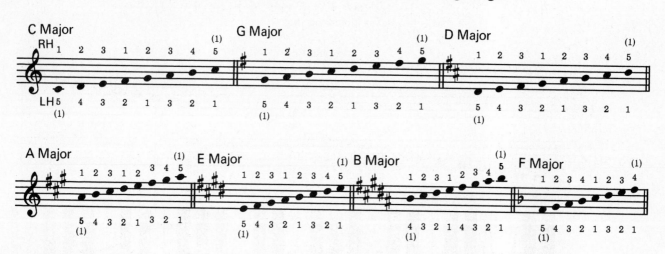

Frequently Used Minor Scales (With Piano Fingerings)

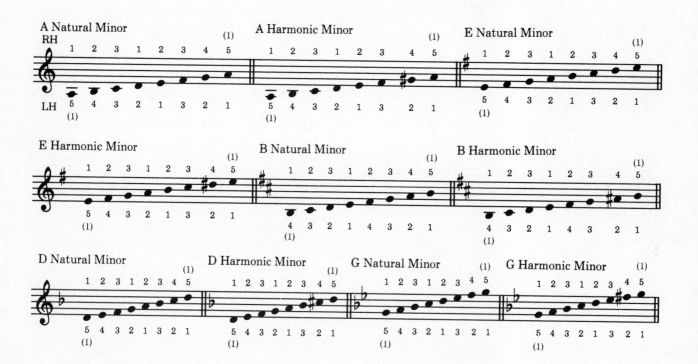

APPENDIX C
SOL-FA SYLLABLES AND CURWEN HAND SIGNS

SYLLABLES AND HAND SIGNS

Tonic *sol-fa* syllables

Curwen hand signs

Major scale:

do re mi fa sol la ti do

Minor scale:

la ti do re mi fa sol la

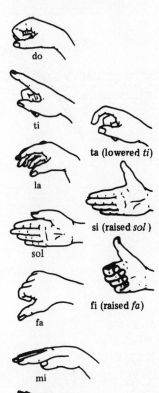

APPENDIX D
KEY SIGNATURES

Key Signatures for Major and Minor Scales

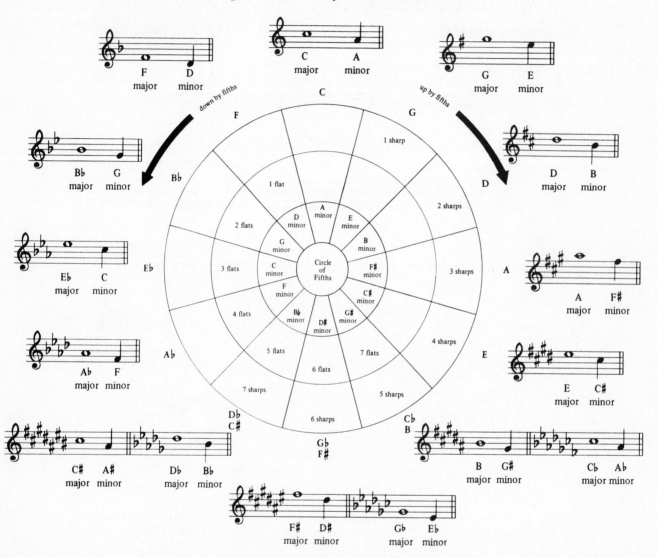

The major and minor keys paired in each pie-shaped wedge share the same key signature, so they are *relative* keys.

Identifying Major and Minor from Key Signatures

• In a key signature of sharps, the sharp farthest right is scale degree 7 or *ti*. The next line or space above is scale degree 1 or 8 or *do*, the tonic or *major*. Scale degree 6 or *la* is the tonic for *minor*.

• In a key signature of flats, the next to the last flat is scale degree 1 or 8 or *do*, the tonic for *major*. (You have to *memorize* that the key of F has one flat.) Scale degree 6 or *la* is the tonic for *minor*.

APPENDIX E
METER SIGNATURES AND CONDUCTOR'S PATTERNS

Meter signatures are the two numbers, one above the other, that appear at the beginning of a piece of music. The top number specifies the beat grouping or meter, and the bottom number indicates the note that receives the beat.

2 = two beats in a measure = **2**
2 = the half note receives the beat = ♩

4 = four beats in a measure = **4**
4 = the quarter note receives the beat = ♩

3 = three beats in a measure = **3**
8 = the eighth note receives the beat = ♪

Meter Signatures   Conductor's Pattern

$\frac{2}{2}$ ¢ $\frac{2}{4}$ $\frac{2}{8}$ (also $\frac{6}{8}$ in fast tempi)

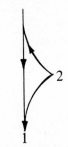

$\frac{4}{2}$ $\frac{4}{4}$ C $\frac{4}{8}$

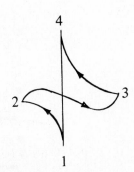

365

$\frac{3}{2}$ $\frac{3}{4}$ ($\frac{3}{8}$ in slow tempi)

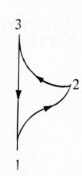

$\frac{6}{2}$ $\frac{6}{4}$ ($\frac{6}{8}$ in slow tempi)

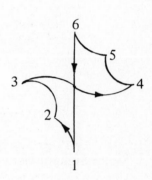

APPENDIX F
RHYTHM SYLLABLES

APPENDIX G
MUSICAL TERMS, SIGNS, AND SYMBOLS

Dynamic terms and signs

pp *Pianissimo,* very soft

p *Piano,* soft

mp *Mezzo piano,* medium soft

mf *Mezzo forte,* medium loud

f *Forte,* loud

ff *Fortissimo,* very loud

sfz *Sforzando,* a sudden strong accent

Crescendo (cresc.), gradually louder

Decrescendo (decresc.), gradually softer

Diminuendo (dim., dimin.), gradually softer

Common tempo terms

*mm 40-60   *Largo,* very slow

mm 60-66   *Lento,* slow

mm 66-76   *Adagio,* slowly, leisurely

mm 76-108   *Andante,* moderately slow

mm 108-120   *Moderato,* moderately

mm 120-138   *Allegretto,* moderately fast

mm 138-168   *Allegro,* fast, lively

mm 168-200   *Presto,* very rapidly

mm 200-208   *Vivace,* animated, lively

Accelerando (accel.), gradually increasing tempo

a tempo, return to original tempo

Ritardando (rit.), gradually slower and slower

*mm = Maelzel metronome (an apparatus that sounds regular beats at an adjustable speed)

Additional Signs and Symbols

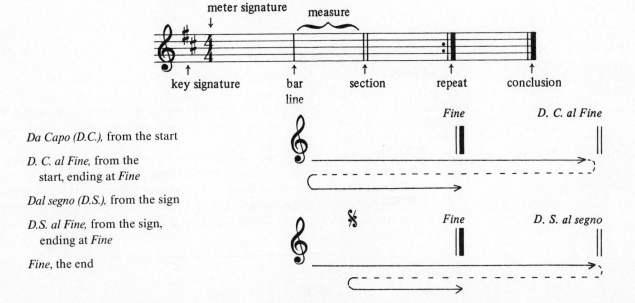

Da Capo (D.C.), from the start

D. C. al Fine, from the start, ending at *Fine*

Dal segno (D.S.), from the sign

D.S. al Fine, from the sign, ending at *Fine*

Fine, the end

Accents: (≥) slight (≥) strong (≥) very strong

Arpeggio: { play "harp style" from the bottom up

Breath mark: ,

Cantabile: in a singing style

Dolce: sweetly

Fermata: (⌒) hold

Grace note: ♫ ♪ (small notes played quickly; not counted in the rhythm of the measure)

Metronome: ♩ = 76 (set at 76 and play the composition's quarter notes at this tempo)

Ottava alta (8va): play an octave higher than written

Ottava bassa (8va): play an octave lower than written

Portamento: slide the pitch up ⌒ or down ⌒

Slur:  (play on a single breath, or sing on one syllable)

Staccato: (♩): short, detached

Tie:

Trill (tr): rapid alternation with the note above

♪ = ♫♫♫ ♫♫♫ (rapid strokes, as on a drum)

Lead Sheet

Melodies are often notated on lead sheets, a kind of musical shorthand in which only the melody, harmony, and lyrics are indicated. The performer uses this musical shorthand to create accompaniment.

Lead sheets show harmony by chord symbols (uppercase letters) notated above the melody. The name of the chord is identified by the chord root. Following are some common chord symbols and abbreviations (using C chords). These chords may look similar because they all have the same chord root, but each has a special quality created by the combination of other chord tones.

C	= C major	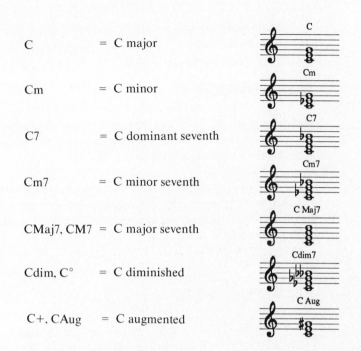
Cm	= C minor	
C7	= C dominant seventh	
Cm7	= C minor seventh	
CMaj7, CM7	= C major seventh	
Cdim, C°	= C diminished	
C+, CAug	= C augmented	

Accompaniments   Each time a chord symbol is shown, the player changes to a different chord. If no chord appears over a measure, the chord from the previous chord is continued.

Perform chords in a rhythm that corresponds to the meter of the melody. The following example shows a steady beat chord rhythm in quadruple meter. Different meter signatures would need a different chord rhythm. You can use rhythms other than a steady beat rhythm, as long as the meter of the song is retained.

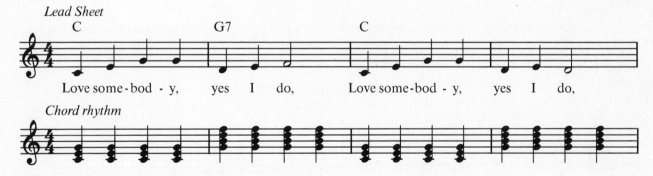

A chord can be broken and inverted (rearranged) in an accompaniment. Play the lowest pitch of the inverted chord on the downbeat of each measure.

369

Additional accompaniments are presented in the Accompaniment Patterns chart in the chapter on the piano.

TRANSPOSITION

Transposition changes a melody from one key (scale) to another. Performers often find music that is too high or too low for their voice or instrument. It is helpful to transpose such music, to move it from a higher to a lower key, or vice versa.

Transposition is accomplished in several ways. One way is to label each pitch in the original melody by scale number or by *sol-fa* syllable. Then change each scale number or syllable to the letter name of the new scale. For example, "Twinkle, Twinkle, Little Star" is in the key of C major, whose scale numbers and syllables are as follows:

C D E F G A B C
1 2 3 4 5 6 7 1(8)
do re mi fa sol la ti do

To transpose "Twinkle, Twinkle, Little Star" to D major, these changes are necessary:

D E F♯ G A B C♯ D
1 2 3 4 5 6 7 1(8)
do re mi fa sol la ti do

In the transposed version, a new key signature identifies the new tonic. The melodic contour (the upward and downward movement of pitch) of the original and of the transposed version are identical.

Twinkle, Twinkle, Little Star
(C Major)

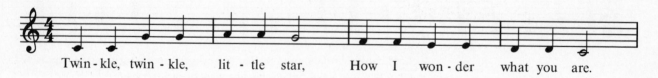

Twin-kle, twin-kle, lit-tle star, How I won-der what you are.

Twinkle, Twinkle, Little Star
(D Major)

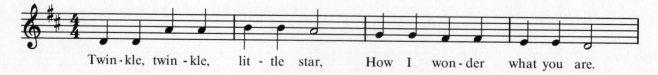

Twin-kle, twin-kle, lit-tle star, How I won-der what you are.

Transposition by Interval Distance

Another way to transpose a melody is to use interval distances. First, calculate the interval (up or down) between the original key and the new one. For example, in "Twinkle, Twinkle, Little Star," the interval distance between the key of C major and the key of D major is one whole step (major 2nd) higher.

It is relatively easy to transpose a melody up or down by one half step. In transposing "Rain, Rain" up one half step, G♭ becomes G, E♭ becomes E, and A♭ becomes A. (Here is a short cut: In a key of seven flats or seven sharps, disregard the key signature and play the notes without flats or sharps.)

Rain, Rain
(C♭ Major)

Rain, rain, go a - way, Come a - gain some oth - er day.

Rain, Rain
(C Major)

Rain, rain, go a - way, Come a - gain some oth - er day.

Transposition with the Guitar Capo

By placing a capo across a chosen fret of the guitar, the music sounds higher, but the performer plays the same chords as in the original. The capo may be use to transpose music without learning new chord fingerings.

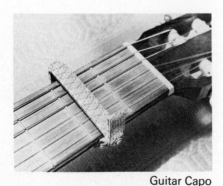

Guitar Capo

The capo raises all the strings at the same time when clamped around the guitar neck. Each fret on the guitar neck equals one half step. When the capo is placed on the first fret, all strings are one half step higher; on the second fret, one step higher; on the third fret, one and one half steps higher; and so on.

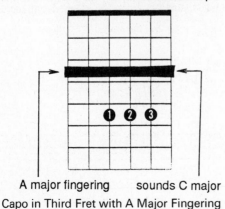

A major fingering   sounds C major
Capo in Third Fret with A Major Fingering

"America, the Beautiful" is notated in the key of A major in this book. To raise the pitch to C major, put the capo on the third fret. The capo now becomes the upper end (nut) of the fingerboard. Retain the fingering for the A major chord. The strings sound three half steps (a minor 3rd) higher, resulting in the C major chord. All the chords in the song will sound three half steps higher. Similarly, the melody should be sung three pitches higher (in C Major).

PIANO ACCOMPANIMENTS (SELECTED)

Piano, one chord

Piano, two chords

PIANO, MELODY ONLY (5-FINGER PATTERNS)

RECORDER MELODIES (SELECTED)

Also see Western Music by Style Period

Recorder, two to four pitches

Recorder, five or more pitches (one sharp or flat)

Recorders, two-part harmony

VOICES, SELECTED SONGS

Many songs listed are suitable for young choirs

Songs, quodlibets

Sing these songs at the same time to create harmony. The two songs need to be in the same key.

Songs, responsorial

Songs, rounds

Songs, two-part

MODAL AND PENTATONIC SONGS

Modal songs

Pentatonic songs with sol-fa syllables

ALPHABETICAL INDEX OF SONGS AND MELODIES

The key is shown in parentheses after the title or source: an upper case letter designates major keys, and *min* designates minor keys. An asterisk (*) indicates a foreign language text.

Abiyoyo (*see* *Lullaby), 144
Acorn Song (*see* *Grinding Song), 85
Adeste Fideles (*see* *O Come, All Ye Faithful), 171
Ain't Gonna Study War (Black American spiritual) (E), 2
Alegria (*see* *Happily Singing), 90
A Li Shan Jr (*see* *The Song of Ali Mountains), 144
All Around the Kitchen (Black American play song) (g min), 4
Alleluia (F), 5
All My Trials (Black American spiritual), (C), 6
Amazing Grace (early American) (E), 8
America, arr. Henry Carey (C), 9
America (From *West Side Story*) (C), 10
America, the Beautiful (A), 12
Angels We Have Heard on High (French carol) (G), 13
*Are You Sleeping? (French round) (D), 14
Arirang (*see* *Hills of Arirang), 101
Artsa Alina (*see* *Our Land), 183
Ash Grove, The (Welsh folk song) (G), 15
At the Foot of Yonder Mountain (American folk song) (D), 16

Baa, Baa, Black Sheep (*see* Twinkle, Twinkle, Little Star), 291
B-A-Bay (American folk song) (F), 17
Bahay Kubo (*see* *My Nipa Home), 164
Balari Women (*see* *Recreation of the Balari Women), 205
Banks of the Ohio (American ballad) (D), 18
Barb'ra Allen (Anglo-American ballad) (A), 19

Battle Hymn of the Republic, The, (G), 20
Bicycle Built for Two by Harry Dacre (G), 22
Bill Bailey (F), 23
Bingo (American school song) (E), 24
*Bird in the Cage (Kagome) (Japanese game song) (a min), 25
Black Is the Color (American folk song) (e min), 26
Blow the Man Down (American halyard shanty) (D), 27
Bluebird (American game song), (D), 28
Bluetail Fly (American minstrel song) (d min), 29
Boysie (Trinidad lullaby) (C), 30
*Buffalo Dance (Native American song) (d min), 31
Bury Me Beneath the Willow (American country song) (E), 32
Bye, Baby Bunting (nursery song) (C-flat), 32

*Cheh Cheh Koolay (African song) (F), 33
Cherry Blossoms (*see* *Sakura), 217
Chicken Chowder (rag) (F) (no words), 34
Children, Go Where I Send Thee (Black American song) (E), 37
*Christmas Is Here! (Swedish folk song) (F), 38
*Cielito Lindo (A), 39
Circle 'Round the Zero (Black American game song) (D), 41
Clapping Land (Danish folk song) (D), 42
Coffee Grows On White Oak Trees (American play-party song) (D), 43
Come, Follow (English round) (A), 44
Concerto for Orchestra (second movement) by Béla Bartók (no words), 45
Concerto for Violin in E minor (second movement) by Felix Mendelssohn (no words) (C), 46
*Condor, The (*El Condor*) (Latin American melody) (a min), 47

*Counting Song (African children's song) (C), 49
Coventry Carol (English melody) (e min), 50
Cowboy's Lament, The (American cowboy song) (D), 51
Crocodile Song, The (Nova Scotia folk song) (F), 52

Danny Boy (*see* A Londondery Air), 139
*De Colores (traditional Mexican song) (D), 53
Don Gato (Mexican folk song) (d min), 55
Doodle Doo Doo (F), 56
Dors, Dors, 'Tit Bébé (*see* *Sleep, My Babe), 240
Down By the Riverside (*see* Ain't Gonna Study War), 2
Down By the Station (American school song) (F), 57
Down in the Valley (American folk song) (E-flat), 58
Drunken Sailor, The (American sea shanty) (d min), 59
Dry Bones (American song) (F), 60
*Duck Dance (Native American song) (d min), 62
*Ducklings, The (*Los Patitos*) (Salvadoran folk song) (G), 63

Eency, Weency Spider (traditional American finger play) (E-flat), 65
El Condor (*see* *The Condor), 47
El Coqui (*see* *The Tree Frog), 284
El Jarabe (*see* Mexican Hat Dance), 151
El Tecolote (*see* The Owl), 186
Entertainer (rag), The, (no words) (F), 66
*Epo I Tai Tai E (Maori Song) (G), 68
Everspring (*see* *Heng Chwun Folk Song)
Ev'ry Night When the Sun Goes Down (American mountain song) (C), 69
Ev'ryone But Me (New England folk song) (F), 71

Farmer in the Dell, The (American game song) (E-flat), 72

*Flower Drum Song (*Feng Yang Hwa Gu*) (Chinese folk song) (C), 73
For Health and Strength (traditional round) (G), 74
Frère Jacques (*see* *Are You Sleeping?), 14

Give My Regards to Broadway (B-flat), 75
Golden Ring Around the Susan Girl (American folk song) (F), 76
Golden Vanity, The (Anglo-American ballad) (G), 78
Gólya, Gólya, Gilice (*see* *The Storks), 254
Good King Wenceslas (English carol) (G), 80
*Good Night (*Gute Nacht*) (German folk song), 81
Go Tell Aunt Rhody (American lullaby) (C), 82
Go Tell It On the Mountain (Black American spiritual) (E), 83
Greensleeves (*see* *What Child is This?), 306
*Greetings of Peace (*Hevenu Shalom A'leychem*) (d min), 84
*Grinding Song (Native American song) (e min), 85
*Guantanamo Lady (*Guantanamera*) (D), 86
Gute Nacht (*see* *Good Night), 81

*Handgame Song (Native American) (D), 88
Hanukah (Hebrew melody) (C), 89
*Happily Singing (*Alegria*) (Puerto Rican carol) (D), 90
*Happy Are They (*Hineh Ma Tov*) (Israeli echo song) (A), 91
*Happy Are They (*Hineh Ma Tov*) (Israeli round) (d min), 92
Hatikvah (*see* *The Hope), 104
*Hava Nagila (Israeli dance song) (e min), 93
Hava Nashira (*see* *Praise Song), 196
Head-Shoulders, Baby (Black American game song) (G), 96
He Is Born (French carol) (F), 97
Hello, Ev'rybody (American folk melody) (C), 98

376